Kimberly Wagner has a life message that... reassuring. As a longtime friend, I've see... and it's so refreshing to watch. Now othe... opportunity to learn from her and to be encouraged that strong women—grounded in the Word and trusting God—are beautiful to behold. This book is good for both the newly engaged and the long-time married woman. Buy it, read it, share it!

    —**CAROLYN MCCULLEY**, author of *Did I Kiss Marriage Goodbye?* and *Radical Womanhood*

Kimberly Wagner's life is a continual pursuit of all that is true, right, and holy. She not only strives for this in her own life but lives a life of sacrifice and investment into the lives of others, such as me, spurring us on in the faith, coming alongside, and speaking truth in love. This book portrays the beauty of strength under control . . . His control.

    —**MELISSA HUDNELL**, wife, mom, and follower of Jesus Christ

If your marriage feels like a battlefield, you need this book! Kim presents the radical idea that fierceness is woven into God's design for womanhood, but softness is the application. She knows what it's like to wrestle with the urge to control, to crave power, and to rush toward battle. In a style that makes you feel like you're having coffee with a close friend, Kim shares her story while opening the Word to reveal God's truth. This book has the tools you need to equip you to move you and your husband from adversaries to allies.

    —**ERIN DAVIS**, author of *Beyond Bath Time: Embracing Motherhood as a Sacred Role*

WOW! Pull out your highlighters, because this inspiring book is full of profound and quote-worthy truths. Dig deep into its pages and discover the power and potential of your own fierce beauty.

    —**MARY A. KASSIAN**, author of *Girls Gone Wise in a World Gone Wild*

As a pastor's wife, this is the book I have needed for decades! I have longed for a tool to put in the hands of struggling, discontented, strong women . . . women who are wrestling with how and why they can restore their love for their husband and marriage. Kim does a masterful job of crafting her own life story into a message that is a handbook for restoration of any marriage. Kim is writing from the perspective of the trenches, about how to win the battle, and it is powerful!

> —**HOLLY ELLIFF**, wife of Bill Elliff, Directional Pastor of The Summit Church

Can there be such a thing as sanctified ferocity? Kimberly Wagner has walked the path of sinful, self-focused boldness to find that there is a meek and humble kind of tenacity that ought to characterize every woman who loves Jesus. Fierce and humble can, and should, describe every woman of God.

> —**BOB LEPINE**, cohost of FamilyLife Today

When I first met Kimberly Wagner, she was a miserable wife whose fierce spirit had intimidated her husband and stripped him of confidence and joy. I have watched as she has become a soft warrior who is a source of strength and encouragement to LeRoy and to others around her. I believe this account of Kim's journey and the truths God used to change her heart and restore her marriage will minister much grace and help to other "fierce women."

> —**NANCY LEIGH DEMOSS**, author, host of Revive Our Hearts radio

Finally, a beautiful treatise on why God made women to be strong and how that can be expressed with a gentle spirit! Kimberly writes with conviction and tells her own story with transparency. Dare to pick this up and become gently fierce!

> —**DANNAH GRESH**, bestselling author of *And the Bride Wore White*

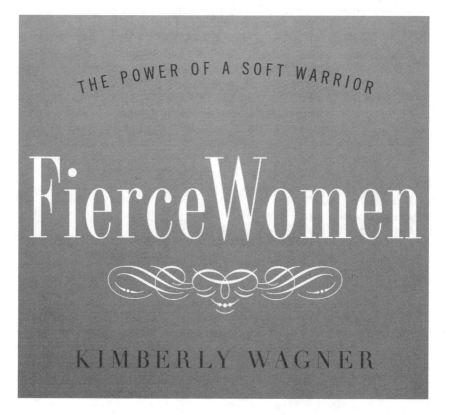

THE POWER OF A SOFT WARRIOR

FierceWomen

KIMBERLY WAGNER

MOODY PUBLISHERS
CHICAGO

All Scripture quotations, unless otherwise indicated, are taken from *The Holy Bible, English Standard Version*. Copyright © 2000, 2001 by Crossway Bibles, a division of Good News Publishers. Used by permission. All rights reserved.

Scripture quotations marked NASB are taken from the *New American Standard Bible*®, Copyright © 1960, 1962, 1963, 1968, 1971, 1972, 1973, 1975, 1977, 1995 by The Lockman Foundation. Used by permission. (www.Lockman.org)

Scripture quotations marked (NIV) are taken from the Holy Bible, New International Version®, NIV®. Copyright © 1973, 1978, 1984 by Biblica, Inc.™ Used by permission of Zondervan. All rights reserved worldwide. www.zondervan.com.

Scripture quotations marked KJV are taken from the King James Version.

Edited by Pam Pugh
Interior Design: Smartt Guys design
Cover Design: Connie Gabbert Design and Illustration LLC
Cover Image: iStockphoto.com / 17668588 and 13809210
Author Photo: Genevieve Townley, Viva Rose Photography

Library of Congress Cataloging-in-Publication Data

Wagner, Kimberly.
    Fierce women : the power of a soft warrior / Kimberly Wagner.
       p. cm.
    Includes bibliographical references.
    ISBN 978-0-8024-0620-0
    1. Marriage—Religious aspects—Christianity. 2. Man-woman relationships —Religious aspects—Christianity. 3. Women—Religious aspects—Christianity. I. Title.
    BV835.K63 2012
    248.8'435—dc23

                                            2012014084

We hope you enjoy this book from Moody Publishers. Our goal is to provide high-quality, thought-provoking books and products that connect truth to your real needs and challenges. For more information on other books and products written and produced from a biblical perspective, go to www.moodypublishers. com or write to:

Moody Publishers
820 N. LaSalle Boulevard
Chicago, IL 60610

3 5 7 9 10 8 6 4 2

Printed in the United States of America

To my comrade in battle, my loyal friend, faithful lover.
Your silly jokes make me laugh and your
deep understanding of Scripture makes me cry.
Thank you, LeRoy, for going the long haul with me
through the years of darkness when we'd lost all hope.
Of all women, I am most blessed to be loved by you.

CONTENTS

Getting Started:
Fierce and Soft

❧❧❧

When I was a little girl, I was captivated by stories of heroism—especially ones where the heroine was still young—like little Lucy in Narnia who bravely followed King Aslan into battle. I related to her willingness to valiantly serve her king. But her fierce courage was even more inspiring to me because she was a good and gentle warrior "with a very merry face."[1] Perhaps every woman holds similar little girl dreams within her heart—of victorious battles for truth, love, and justice—dreams that are really but a dim reflection of the Great Story that lies ahead.

Most young women dream about the man who will one day win her love. She imagines the details of her wedding day with great anticipation. When the day arrives, no bride expects heartache or broken vows, but many soon realize the marriage doesn't measure up to the dreams she had held. Two sinners attempting to meld into one glorious unit will undoubtedly experience conflict, stress, and even spiritual attack. The wise bride recognizes that her vows are an entrance to a spiritual battlefield.

Often marriages are caught in a destructive relationship dynamic that I call the Fierce Woman/Fearful Man cycle. In this cycle, a wife's strengths can intimidate her husband. The Fierce Woman can be a living inspiration but her ferocity can also morph into her husband's worst nightmare.

He may respond to her fierceness by shutting down, running, responding in harsh anger, or passively retreating to his own silent world. Rather than experiencing joy and companionship, the couple caught in this miserable cycle relate to each other more like alienated roommates than passionate lovers and friends.

LeRoy and I have experienced both extremes in our marriage, and I want to share with you some things I've learned over the years. The good news is that this destructive cycle can be reversed. But a strong woman doesn't need to take on a wimpy persona or undergo a personality transplant in order to be the ideal wife. As a Fierce Woman, you can develop a fresh and intimate relationship with your husband. In fact, God desires for your fierceness to play an integral role in His plan for your marriage.

The bride on the cover of this book portrays this kind of woman. She expresses the passion and strength of the Fierce Woman as she enters marriage. Her raised arms communicate determination and praise for her God, while the bowed head conveys her softness and humble submission to His plan. She lingers in holy moments before entering the sanctuary—pausing to pray rather than rushing in. She's standing at the entrance of an old church, preparing her heart before closed doors that will soon open to a new adventure . . . a young woman returning to the ancient paths . . . a soft warrior preparing for what lies ahead.

Whether or not you realize it, you are in a battle, and God has placed strengths within you to be used in powerful ways. When you enter the marriage relationship, you are entering the sacred metaphor God designed to explain Himself to a watching world. Marriage is the great mystery, the glorious platform God created to display His love relationship with His bride. This is why marriage is a flashpoint for Satan's attacks; he seeks to destroy the beauty and effectiveness of God's model. In light of this, we must strive for the Great Story to be lived out in our marriages.

I hope as you read, you will take moments to pause, ponder, and pray. May you encounter the Lord of Battles within these pages and receive insight and instruction for serving Him as a soft warrior— the Fierce Woman who is empowered by the Spirit and softened by His grace.

Let's get started.

Kimberly Wagner

The Beauty of Fierceness

〰〰〰

"These boots are made for walkin'
and that's just what they'll do!
And one of these days these boots are gonna walk all over you!" [1]

— LEE HAZELWOOD

Maybe you're too young to recognize these lyrics, but this was a popular song back in the day. The first grade girls were into knee-high, white, patent leather boots (yes, in first grade!). We'd sport our shiny boots as we strutted around the playground at recess, singing these words at the top of our lungs.

Recalling it now, I'm amused by the comical picture of a group of six-year-old girls and the strident aggression fueled by this silly little song. As we sang, we'd glare at the boys while digging our heels into the ground, giving the impression of grinding them into powder! I doubt we understood what we were singing. Our little game may have been innocent, but we sure liked the feeling of power that surged every time we belted out the words, "Walk all over you!"

By the time I was in junior high, more refined lyrics fueled our intensity as we proudly joined Helen Reddy to "roar" our defiance in songs like "I Am Woman." Each phrase increased our passion: "I am STRONG . . . I am invincible . . . *I am woman!*" We were proud of our gender and ready to tell the world that "If I have to, I can do anything!"[2]

I think one reason these songs had such attraction is that they gave us a sense of power and strength. I never wanted to be a wimpy woman. I've always been drawn to strong women—aren't you? A refined strength has an alluring appeal. I love to see a fierce woman in action. Nothing fazes her. She's indomitable, determined, and she's a passionate force beyond contention. When given a challenging assignment, she boldly goes for it and doesn't let anything or anyone stand in her way.

She's fierce.

But I'm not talking about an ugly fierceness that is really just raw aggression. There is a beauty to the right kind of fierceness. Not the brand of fierceness that recklessly walks over people or is rooted in self-centered goals. Not the fierceness that produces ice queens or conniving shrews but a fierceness that is humble strength and power under control. The fierceness I admire grabs on to the hem of God's will and won't let go. A fierceness that determinedly stands strong in a gale of opposition. This kind of fierceness looks fear in the eye without blinking and confidently forges ahead.

You may not agree. I mean, the word "fierce" carries some negative baggage, but today it's a term many women in our culture embrace. While doing research for this book, I found various definitions for the word, ranging from: "savage; wild; of a violently cruel nature; harsh" to the more desirable: "intensely eager; intense;

ardent." No matter what terminology we use, I think we might all recognize at least traces of fierceness within each of us.

I asked a group of women their thoughts on this topic and their responses varied:

"Fierceness is a good thing! I'm glad my mom fiercely stood for truth while I was growing up. In a world with so many confusing messages, it's good to have women who know God's Word and fiercely stand against the cultural tide."

Another commented:

"When I hear the phrase 'fierce woman,' I think of a woman who's loud, pushy, obnoxious, arrogant, and demanding."

And this one was surprising to me:

"She's a sharp dresser. A woman who's strutting her stuff!"

THERE'S A FIERCE WOMAN IN EACH OF US

I believe a fierce heart resides within every woman, but it manifests itself in varying shades of beauty and ugliness. Oh, I've seen (um, even at times *been*) the fierce woman who is the self-centered shrew, ranting and shrieking to get her way. But in contrast to her, the fierce woman may also be the quiet but courageous martyr who is willing to die for her faith.

Whether you're an extrovert or more introverted—women are a compelling force. You may not see yourself as beautifully fierce or even slightly strong, but what if God has placed a powerful fierceness within you, within every woman? And what if this fierce power was meant to be used in a way that is big . . . I mean really big, like *staggering the imagination big*!

What if woman was designed to be a living inspiration? Like a song that rallies men before battle or a vision that compels them to embark on the most dangerous of conquests. This power and drive enables a woman to persevere through daunting challenges. It gives her the grit and determination to continue pressing onward in the face of tremendous opposition. I love this verse in Daniel that underscores this thought: "The people who know their God will display strength and take action" (Daniel 11:32 NASB).

When you're told the hurdle is higher than you can jump, fierceness is what gets your blood going and takes you flying over the top. It's the passion that motivates you to leave the cozy comfort of safety for the dangerous adventure of the unknown. It's that element of determination that holds you in place when weak soldiers flee. It's loyalty and doing what's right; brilliant intensity and going the long haul. Fierceness is fervent faith and lonely stands; solitary boldness and trying one more time.

I love reading stories of women who have taken courageous stands for righteous causes at the risk of their own lives. And although their fierceness is seen on a much larger scale than what you or I may ever experience, don't discount the power and potential of your own fierce beauty. Demonstrating your fierceness may look a lot different than it does in a courageous martyr or the leader of a movement, but it is no less important. Your fierce beauty may be seen as you stand beside your husband at his point of greatest failure, giving him the courage to get up and keep pressing on. It may be heard in your voice of truth, inspiring your husband's faith, when the enemy tells him he'll never be able to change.

MEN ARE DRAWN TO FIERCE WOMEN

Men seem to be drawn to fierce women. Generally men run from the clingy, whiny, weak-willed types. Perhaps it's the fierce woman's strength of character they admire, or her passion for life. It may be the unwavering loyalty and intense devotion they find appealing. The courageous heroism of a fierce woman has inspired many a great leader.

Rebecca Motte's name may not sound familiar to you, but she holds my respect. Her fierce loyalty to her country served to inspire the Patriot army during the Revolutionary War. She was a wealthy widow with a large estate on the Congaree River in South Carolina. In 1781 the British set up camp there; 175 soldiers took residence in her home and surrounded it with a trench and parapet. Rebecca escaped to the Patriots, who laid siege to the British compound.

After several days of fighting, the Patriots concluded the only way to force the British from their newly occupied "fort" was to set fire to Rebecca's house. When Lee, the leader of the Patriot force, broke the news to Mrs. Motte, she responded that she was "gratified with the opportunity of contributing to the good of her country." The widow produced a bow and set of arrows and told Lee to put them to use. The flaming arrows set fire to the roof and forced the British to surrender. The Patriots quickly climbed to the roof and managed to put out the flames and salvage her home. After the victory, true to the spirit of a beautifully fierce woman, Rebecca Motte served dinner to both the American and British officers in her dining room.

My husband says it was my fierceness that initially grabbed his attention and drew him to approach me. At the time, however, he had no idea how his world was about to be turned upside down by one really fierce woman. That fierceness he found so attractive? Well, he learned real fast it could work both ways, because the fierceness that drew his interest . . . also gave me the spunk to verbally *slam* him in our first conversation!

It was the first day of the fall semester. I wasn't prepared for the shock of entering a large classroom crammed full with young men. Way in the back corner I spied one lone female. She was dressed in military fatigues and sporting a camo cap, so at first she blended in with the all-male landscape. She and I were the only women in

Dr. Stagg's Greek 101. I guess I'd never considered whether this was a popular subject with female students; I just wanted to study the language.

I soon picked up on the fact that this class was filled with what I referred to as "young preacher-boys." And were they ever the cocky lot! Every Monday morning I watched them try to one-up each other by re-preaching their Sunday sermons. Lots of big stories, loud and long alliterations, exaggerated hand gestures. If they were trying to impress the two women in the room, they didn't.

One day at the end of class, most of us headed to the cafeteria for lunch. I was standing in line waiting my turn to pick up a tray and silverware, minding my own business, when one of the cocky preacher-boys just behind me in line startled me with, "Do you mind if I ask you a personal question?"

I'd never spoken to this guy before, didn't even know his name but had a vague notion he was in my class. I was thinking, *This is his impressive opening line? Smooth. We've never spoken and this is how you introduce yourself?*

Now, how is a girl supposed to respond to an opening question like that? I have nothing to hide. I've always been a transparent person and often too blunt for my own good, so I mumbled, "Um . . . no, I guess not." I could feel my eyebrow arching a bit. (It does that sometimes. I'm ashamed to admit, but if you ever meet me and see me do that . . . sorry, it could be indicating I'm a bit irritated.)

"Why are *you* in Greek class?" The question may seem innocent enough, but did you note his emphasis on the word *you*? With that one carefully turned word, he spoke volumes. The grip on my plastic lunch tray tightened as I realized—*This guy thinks Greek class is no place for girls . . . Who does he think he is, asking me why I'm studying Greek?* My eyebrow arched pointedly as I gave him a dead level glare while every ounce of my being flooded with Helen Reddy's theme song, *I am woman, hear me roar*! My response was delivered in cold, even tones.

"I'm taking the class so that I can study the original language of the New Testament for myself in order to prepare to *pastor and shepherd my flock.*" Delivering the slam, I turned to pick up my salad plate. Stunned, he mumbled a subdued, "Oh."

I left him to think as I picked up condiments. But the Holy Spirit wouldn't let me do it. I couldn't lie to this guy with my impromptu fabrication about being a "woman preacher"—even if he did seem to be a male chauvinist. With the last of my items placed on my tray, I took a deep breath and turned to tell him, "*No*, the real reason I'm studying Greek is because I've grown up hearing pastors claim what the original language says and I want to be able to read it myself, for my own personal growth." His "Oh!" this time sounded much different, like he was extremely pleased with my answer. And with that, I concluded my first conversation with the man who would one day be my husband.

> WHY IS FIERCENESS IN WOMEN APPEALING TO MEN? I THINK THEY LIKE A CHALLENGE.

We both laugh about it now and he gets a kick out of telling people how my spirited response triggered his interest in me. I've heard many husbands say they experienced similar feelings of attraction when they met their feisty wives, like being drawn by the beauty and danger of climbing Mount Everest—the climb is filled with breathless anticipation and excitement, but woe to the man who attempts that climb unprepared!

Why is fierceness in women appealing to men? I think they like a challenge. They admire the strength, courage, loyalty, and determination of a fierce woman. They like spunk and passion. Fierce women don't grovel for their attention and aren't desperate for a man to meet their deepest needs. Men admire a woman who doesn't depend solely on them for their identity or happiness.

The truly beautifully fierce woman has an otherworldly strength derived from a source beyond herself. She's plunged in fully to the forgiveness and love of Christ, and He holds her heart so completely that she's reached true contentment. Her identity is forged through abiding in Him, and her courage is displayed by her commitment to Him and His cause. He is her driving motivation and propels her by the wind of His Spirit. Her passion is stoked by His fire. She is no "halfhearted creature" but is drinking deeply of Him and experiencing infinite joy.

She is a warrior at heart—not violent or aggressive—but tempered by humility. She's a soft warrior; fleshing out the beauty of fierceness in her daily life. Loving God and others with sacrificial devotion. This is the kind of fierceness I'm talking about when I said I love to see a fierce woman in action. I strive for this ideal. Check her out in the characteristics below.

Characteristics of a Beautifully Fierce Woman:

* Her identity and value are rooted in her relationship with Christ rather than a relationship with a man.
* She's filled with gratitude for God's good gifts. Her heart is ruled by the peace of contentment.
* She courageously faces her fears rather than running or hiding in shame.
* She's passionate about things that matter rather than living for the trivial.
* She loves God and others. She's more focused on giving love than getting love.
* She's willing to battle for a worthy cause rather than shrinking in defeat.

* She grabs the hem of God's will and doesn't let go.
* She protects and defends the helpless rather than using her strength to bully others. She is known as a sincere encourager.
* She's honest but kind.
* Others feel comfortable in seeking her counsel.
* She embraces God's Word as her ultimate authority rather than being swayed by the voices of the culture.
* She faithfully confronts by speaking truth in love rather than enabling sin by keeping silent.
* She walks in confidence and humility that flow from her recognition of Christ's work of grace in her life.
* She has the power to influence and inspire because she lives under the Spirit's control.
* Her life is lived all out for God's glory rather than the smallness of self.

God wants to use these characteristics to fulfill His calling on your life. I love seeing how the fierce women of Scripture did this. Esther courageously stood ready to perish as she fought for the lives of her people. Deborah led the armies of Israel to victory in spite of fearful Barak. Priscilla, along with her husband, Aquila, once literally "risked her neck" to save Paul's life (see Romans 16:4); she was bold, courageous, and a diligent student of the Word.

SEIZE THE KINGDOM!

The call to follow Christ requires fierceness. In fact, this kind of fierceness is commended by Jesus: "From the days of John the Baptist until now the kingdom of heaven has suffered violence, and the violent take it by force" (Matthew 11:12).

This intriguing verse contains some pretty descriptive words:

"suffered violence" and "the violent take it by force." The Greek word that is translated "suffered violence" is only used twice in the New Testament and both times in a favorable light. It's the idea of positive aggression; commendable fierceness. Think of the phrase "Seize the day!" in the sense of putting all your effort into making the most of the moment. Seize the kingdom life. Take it by force. Don't allow anything to stand in your way or prevent you from living all out for God's glory.

Jesus isn't talking about physical aggression here; this isn't a text that supports using violence to advance a cause.

LIVING AN EXTRAORDINARY LIFE CAN WEAR YOU OUT!

Though a kind of violent action is required, it isn't aggression against others. It's fiercely grabbing hold of my proud and lazy self and putting it to death!

This verse gives us a glimpse of the intensity required to flesh out our Christianity. This kind of living goes against our natural tendency. It's the principle Jesus laid out to the disciples when He clued them in on the seriousness of the call to follow Him: "And whoever does not take his cross and follow me is not worthy of me" (Matthew 10:38).

It's the challenge of living an extraordinary life through the process of self-denial: "If anyone would come after me, let him deny himself and take up his cross and follow me" (Matthew 16:24).

It's easy to read a familiar verse like this and block out its real-life meaning. We like coasting in the comfortable and easy, but this verse flies in the face of that kind of nominal Christianity.

Living an extraordinary life can wear you out! Most people don't want anything that's too hard or asks too much. If it requires self-control or self-denial, the faint of heart heads home quickly. "I can put off studying for that test until later . . . I'll start my diet tomorrow, this dessert is too good to pass up . . . Just let me sleep a few minutes longer . . . I know I shouldn't be getting this angry, but I can't handle this kind of incompetency!" Anything here sound familiar?

The fierce woman picks up Jesus' challenge with the intensity required to follow hard after Him. Her passionate love for Him takes over when her flesh raises a fuss. Her longing to know Him more gives her the motive to press in further when things get hairy. Pushing aside fear of man, turning a deaf ear to self-conscious clambering, stepping out in faith, the fierce woman seizes the kingdom of God, grabs on to Jesus and hangs on for the ride of her life!

JESUS LOVES FIERCE WOMEN

This kind of determination and fiery faith reminds me of a woman who kept pressing on when life's tough challenges hit her in the face. Imagine having the courage to make an urgent request and then being referred to as a *dog*—not by your enemies—but *by Jesus!* This is one of those times in Scripture when Jesus really surprises me. I mean, He didn't respond like the normally tender, holding-a-child-in-His-lap-type of Jesus. No, this time He puts some huge roadblocks in this needy woman's path.

This woman had a real problem on her hands. Her daughter was demon possessed. There's no greater misery for a mother than watching her child suffer. Knowing she has no way to alleviate her daughter's pain, powerless before the torment and destruction, this mother looks beyond herself for help.

I love the fact that I can relate to this woman. She's in extreme need and she's not a member of the religious elite—she's a Gentile. For religious Jews, a Gentile woman was the lowest on the significance scale. But the one thing she has going for her is she recognizes Jesus for who He is and trusts His heart.

We find her story recorded in Matthew 15:22–28:

And behold, a Canaanite woman from that region came out and was crying, "Have mercy on me, O Lord, Son of David; my daughter is severely oppressed by a demon." But he did not answer her a word. And his disciples came and begged him, saying, "Send her away, for she is crying out after us."

He answered, "I was sent only to the lost sheep of the house of Israel."

Jesus seems to ignore her at first, and the disciples try to get rid of her. When He does speak, it isn't the tender words she's heard from His lips when other people came for His help. Instead, it seems as though He puts up a wall of rejection. But none of this stops her. She is desperate in her need and relentless in her pursuit:

But she came and knelt before him, saying, "Lord, help me."

A simple prayer lifted from a heart of worship. This is the cry of the true woman. This is the humble dependence of the woman who delights His heart. This is the faith and persistence of the beautifully fierce woman.

And he answered, "It is not right to take the children's bread and throw it to the dogs."

No matter how rough His words may sound to you, He was not being unkind. Really. He was laying out a challenge for her to rise and meet. He doesn't use the word for dog that would refer to a common mongrel roaming the streets but a dog that is a house pet.[3] Although His response may seem cold or offensive, He was letting her stretch her trust level and plunge in fully to demonstrate her faith by laying out some difficult obstacles:

She said, "Yes, Lord, yet even the dogs eat the crumbs that fall from their masters' table." Then Jesus answered her, "O woman, great is your faith! Be it done for you as you desire." And her daughter was healed instantly."

I love it! Jesus puts up walls of resistance but she passes the test and He loves her reaction. No argument from her. Yes, an undeserving dog. She doesn't deny His humbling assessment, but she also doesn't run away sobbing in self-pity or in a huff. She presses in and appeals to His merciful character. She looks beyond the slight, pushes past the rebuff, and goes for His heart.

This is the beauty of fierceness that I admire in women. This is a woman at her best. She's not using her strengths to take advantage of others. She's not using cruel manipulation tactics to get what she wants. She's not arrogant in her approach and demeanor, nor is she groveling in self-condemnation or self-pity. She's tackling the obstacles in her life with humility and determination. She's resourceful and creative. She's walking by faith, not by sight.

And Jesus honors her for it.

STRONG WOMEN ARE HIS IDEA

I hope you're not under the mistaken impression that God created women as some kind of second-class citizens of the kingdom. He loves strong women. We're His idea.

Before the fall, before the curse, God created a fierce woman. She was formed as a worthy complement to Adam—the first man. Eve was created to rule with him. God placed His divine imprint on her life. She had His likeness and bore His image. She was perfect in every way. Every woman since is inferior to this mother of all living. Before the depleting effects of the fall, her physical strength and energy were unsurpassed. Her intellect and creativity were keen and fresh, unmarred by the effects of sin, and her beauty timeless.

I wish we had more exposure to this pre-fall Eve. We barely meet her before she runs into trouble, but we know she must have been a specimen beyond compare. God entrusted Adam and Eve with His new creation. He gave this first couple the divine mandate to take dominion over His young earth. Together they would fill the earth and subdue it. They held dominion over every living thing.

She was prepared to stand as his counterpart with courage and resolve. Placing her hand with his in a unity of purpose, held by an indissoluble bond, they ruled over creation together and functioned as one. Her fierce strength was like steel in his spine, she was iron sharpening iron, and her role in his life was powerful.

I distinctly remember overhearing a conversation as a young girl that had a lasting impression on me. A gentleman was explaining how women have an enormous power of influence and they can use it to either inspire men or destroy them. (I guess that was a dangerous thing to learn at such a young age, because I admit I enjoyed using that power the wrong way many times!) Not all women necessarily experience this, but most will admit they have an uncanny ability to influence men. And most men agree that women have this gift.

WOMAN'S FIERCE ROLE

In Genesis chapter 2, women are given the unique responsibility to use this power by serving as man's "helper." When I first learned that women were given the "helper" assignment, I thought, "Oh, great. We aren't good enough to actually be doing something really important—we just get to 'help out.'" Even that word—"helper"—on paper always looked lame to me. (It would be nice to inherit a working knowledge of Hebrew and Greek as a package deal with salvation, because knowing the meaning of certain words can change your whole perspective.)

I felt much better when I found out that the Hebrew word that is translated into our English word "helper" is not a wimpy word.

It is the word *ezer*, meaning to aid or provide needed help. In fact, it is the same word used in reference to God as a "helper" to His people in several passages (Exodus 18:4; Deuteronomy 33:7, 29). That's when I realized that being my husband's "helper" was not an insignificant assignment but one of eternal consequence.

IT TAKES THE PASSION OF A FIERCE WOMAN TO ENCOURAGE A MAN WHO'S DROWNING IN A PIT OF SHAME AND DESPAIR.

God didn't create woman to fill a "no big deal" role. Men and women are created with equal worth and value, given equal access to God, and both live with the purpose of glorifying Him. Neither role is inferior or superior. Each comes with its own challenges, and in order to serve well in her role, a woman must be fierce. Not destructively fierce but *beautifully* fierce.

The same fierceness that the unnamed Gentile woman exemplified as she entreated Jesus to deliver her demon-possessed daughter is the fierceness required to fill this role. It takes a fierce woman to live out the helper role determinedly and not allow her own selfish pursuits to take her off course. It takes the creativity of a fierce woman to discover how to motivate the men around her to live out God's calling on their lives. It takes the passion of a fierce woman to encourage a man who's drowning in a pit of shame and despair. It takes the perseverance of a fierce woman to hang in there with her man when the going gets tough.

It takes a woman like my friend Jan, whose husband of two years dropped her off at work one day with the words, "I love you, but I don't want to be married anymore. Marriage is just too hard." Jan didn't give up on marriage or toss her vows out the window. She didn't run to find another relationship, or try various manipulation tactics or issue threats, but she clung to her relationship with Christ. She fiercely stood in faith for her marriage. She persevered in waiting, praying, and trusting God.

After four long years of separation, while receiving guidance and counsel from spiritually mature individuals and making some tough choices personally, Jan and Scott began corresponding. They began to rebuild their friendship and eventually remarried. They've enjoyed a healthy, loving relationship for the past thirty years. If Jan had not fiercely stood in faith for their marriage, if she'd given up or moved on to another man, their marriage would have ended as just another divorce statistic.

It's a woman like Hayley, whose fierceness was seen as she faced her greatest fear and courageously stood where many women give way. When she was barely in elementary school, her parents divorced and she was basically lost in the shuffle between Mom's new husband and Dad's new wife. By the time she was a young woman, her only real companionship was found in her relationship with Christ. Because of the pain and rejection from her parents, abandonment was a lifelong fear, but Christ was the One who never let her down, who promised to be her unshakable constant.

Hayley didn't follow the typical modern romance path. She waited. She entered the dating years with the same perspective she took in all areas of her life: seek God, walk in obedience, and trust Him to provide. And He did. Kevin, her best friend in the church youth group, became her husband. He was a man after God's heart. They entered their wedding night without the shame and guilt of past sexual encounters. They had saved themselves for each other and for that night.

Just four years into the marriage, Hayley's life was shattered again with the pain of betrayal and rejection. I'll never forget the look of sheer terror on her face as I sat with her during the aftermath of shock from discovering Kevin's affair. The one person she'd confidently relied on for constancy had broken the trust of marital fidelity. Her childhood fears engulfed her like a flood.

I watched Hayley endure nightmarish episodes as the graphic details of her husband's infidelity surfaced. As the affair became public, she took on the shame and humiliation brought on by his sin. Broken and confused, she tried to make sense of it all. "I've been faithful and kept myself pure, but I'm having to deal not only with the rejection, the loss of our relationship, but also with the lifelong consequences of his immorality." The injustice was baffling, the betrayal brutal.

If you've walked this same path, you understand the temptation to run from public glare, to curl up in crumpled defeat, to close your heart and never open it to trust again. You understand the mental battle with rejection, the taunting words in your head that tell you of your worthlessness and encourage you to give in to despair. But Hayley stood for her marriage when every fiber in her being screamed, *Run!* She washed herself in God's Word. She used her knowledge of His truth to battle the lies running through her head. She faced the public stares. She followed godly counsel, rejecting the world's shortcuts.

Before Kevin came to the place of repentance and honesty about his sin, Hayley supported the elders' decision to proceed with church discipline for Kevin although it meant she would endure embarrassment and the humiliation of public scrutiny. And when her husband came to true repentance, Hayley worked her way through the rugged terrain of hurt and resentment to reach the place of forgiveness. She leaned hard into Christ and stepped into a position to start rebuilding her marriage with the man who'd broken trust and wounded her deeply. She went beyond just forgiving Kevin; she committed herself to helping him recover his walk with God. Hayley demonstrated the tough courage and faith of a fierce woman fulfilling the "helper" role as a soft warrior.

You see, Hayley's fierceness could've driven her to bitterness and revenge. She could have chosen to manipulate the situation to her advantage or poured all her energies into making Kevin's life as miserable as possible. Even now she could choose to dangle Kevin's past infidelity over his head as a means of control. But instead, her fierce loyalty to Christ drove her to grant Kevin the same forgiveness she'd been given (Ephesians 4:32) and to display to others the reality of God's grace. Rather than hammering him as a moral failure, she seeks to use her power of influence to inspire Kevin to live out his calling as a godly husband and father.

More than a decade later, Hayley and Kevin are taking the lessons learned from their season of brokenness and encouraging other couples who face some of the same marital challenges. What looked like the destruction of their marriage has become a platform of ministry to others. In our culture of divorce, their story is rare, but it doesn't have to be. A fierce woman's courage and determination to fight for her man and her marriage may make the difference.

IRON SHARPENING IRON

Your role as helper is to aid your husband in becoming all that God has created him to be—to be his iron sharpening iron (see Proverbs 27:17). Deep down every true man of God wants to do the right thing: he wants to be the spiritual leader; he wants to live all out for God's glory; he doesn't want to waste his life. When all is said and done, he wants to hear those words, "Well done, good and faithful servant." He wants you to be able to believe in him, to be able to say with all sincerity that you are confident in his leadership because you know he's a man who walks with God.

You may be thinking, "Not my man—his biggest dream is Sunday afternoon football with no interruptions!" Maybe that's all you can see from the outside, but don't discount your power of influence, as a Spirit-controlled woman, to stimulate his passion for Christ.

This is no job for weak-willed women. It takes intentional dependence on the Spirit, immense self-control, and wisdom from the Word to learn the difficult art of challenging your husband to godliness without demeaning him. To encourage him to continue pushing the envelope in spiritual growth without nagging, belittling, or preaching. (See: Challenging Your Man to Robust Christianity in the appendix.)

> **FIERCENESS CAN BECOME AN ASSET OR A DETRIMENT IN MARRIAGE.**

Every life we touch is affected by our fierceness, but the one who is most benefitted or harmed by it is our husband. Fierceness can become an asset or a detriment in marriage. I've had the privilege of listening to many women as they open their hearts to share some of their most private thoughts. They uncover hidden wounds, revealing deep fears and painful struggles within their marriage. And although admittedly we women are complicated creatures, and the details of our situations are varied, there seems to be a commonality in what is voiced. Women struggle with their fierceness and its effects. For some men, the fierceness that attracts them can also become a source of fear and intimidation.

Often when wives exert the strength God placed within them, the husband caves to passivity or rises in aggression. I've seen the pattern repeated far too frequently and watched it squeeze the life from many a vibrant relationship. I personally experienced the damage in my own marriage. Qualities my husband admired when he met me became painful wedges driving us apart after we were married. For several years we were trapped in a destructive cycle.

Looking back to that season from today's position of joy brings fresh gratitude, but also a burden for women suffering in isolation and hopelessness. That's why I've written this book.

As you and I spend time together in these pages, we'll check out the destructive elements of fierceness but we'll also see how to cultivate characteristics of the beautifully fierce woman. We'll consider common barriers that develop in marriage relationships and see how to bring down those isolating walls to build unity. I'll share some practical ways you can show appreciation to your husband as well as give you components for building a platform of influence. I'll give you some guidelines for confrontation when your husband is trapped in a sinful addiction. Finally, I hope to give you a vision for what God could do that goes beyond what you may have ever imagined.

Please hear me as one who hurts with you and is praying for you as you enter this journey. I'm opening my heart to you in much the same way that I would if we were sitting at your kitchen table with mugs of hot coffee. I'll be transparent with you, but I'm ashamed of much of what I'm going to tell you. At the same time, I'm also excited for you to hear about the changes we've seen in our marriage, and my prayer is that it will bring hope and encouragement. But more than that, I'm asking God to meet with you as you grapple with the issues I share.

A fierce woman. That's what I was and still am. My fierceness drove my husband to a crisis of faith and a season of silence and depression. But there is a beautiful fierceness God provides in order for women to fulfill His calling on their lives, to be the soft warrior and "iron sharpening iron" in their husband's life . . . and that fierce woman can be you.

❊ HEART ISSUES ❧

1. Do you see yourself as a fierce woman? Which of these qualities might be descriptive of you?

> Determined Faithful Disciplined Courageous
> Aggressive Decisive Loyal Intense Impatient
> Passionate Bossy Cold Intimidating Devoted
> Controlling Manipulative Heroic Persevering

2. Jesus commended this determined woman's faith (Matthew 15:21–28). What would be your typical reaction to this kind of rejection? Are you facing a similar struggle, and if so, how is your response demonstrating the beauty of fierceness?

3. How are you fulfilling your role of influence in your husband's life? Is he being harmed or blessed by your fierceness?

And Then There's the Scary Side

"A loving woman finds heaven or hell
on the day she is made a bride."

— MARY LATHRAP[1]

I stared blankly out the car window at traffic passing by through the lazy intersection. Outwardly I displayed no shock. I was past that. Finally, he'd voiced what I instinctively knew and had felt for some time.

"I don't love you."

So this is it? Five years into a union that held high hopes for marital bliss and this is where we are?

My conversation was internal. Outwardly, a long silence followed the crisply delivered words. What was there to say or add to his announcement?

I looked at the beautiful result of a wildly romantic night in

Wichita Falls—our little girl. Watching her sleep contentedly in her car seat, I wondered how long it would take this newborn to discover that no love exists between her parents.

Divorce would not be an option for us. I knew that. So where does this leave us? What's "Plan B"?

When I met LeRoy, he was a confident, self-assured, college student. He smiled easily and laughed freely. We'd talk nonstop for hours, baring our hearts and sharing personal dreams. Childishly, I entered marriage expecting it to be something like a romantic fifty-year date. He entered marriage thinking it would be a breeze. As he puts it, "Going into marriage, I thought, *Well, I'm a great guy and will make a good husband. Any woman would be glad to have me. This is going to be great.* I figured it would require little or no effort since we were both believers, both loved the Lord, both loved the Word. A good marriage was inevitable. I thought we'd enter into it, and it was going to be great from that point on."

But once we were married, he changed. My once outgoing, confident lover gradually began to lose his smile. He no longer carried himself with the same self-assured air. He retreated into a cave of dark solitude. The more I attempted to pull him out, the deeper he retreated.

The walls between us grew thick.

I remember one day thinking, *How long has it been since I've seen him smile? He's so cold and silent. I can't even remember what his laugh sounds like!* I reached the point where I gave up hope of experiencing happiness in marriage.

LeRoy explains, "Like most young couples, we entered marriage with unrealistic expectations. Christian couples who know the Lord and have a heart for God but come together with different backgrounds and personality types have real challenges. God was bringing the perfect storm into our lives through our marriage. It wasn't a storm meant to destroy—but it was the perfect storm of God's purifying and refining grace. We didn't know it then, but we can look back now and recognize His hand at work in the pain." No couple starts off marriage planning to spend their lives as strangers or in daily warfare, but that's the miserable state where many exist. The drift

I NO LONGER RESPECTED MY HUSBAND. IN FACT, I DIDN'T EVEN LIKE HIM.

doesn't occur overnight, but at some point intimacy is lost, and the couple realizes that somewhere along the way they've settled into functioning more like roommates than lovers.

I'm afraid our experience could be retold, with basically the same script, hundreds of thousands of times by couples who are left injured, bewildered, and confused, searching for answers to what went wrong. How can the same two people who once stood at a marriage altar with hearts and hands joined, vowing to love and live with one another "until death do us part," come to this place in their relationship?

My kind and gentle husband was bitter and frustrated from years of walking through an emotional minefield, never knowing what to expect: a heated outburst, an icy response, or a verbal onslaught. Our conversations were brittle and brief. I no longer respected my husband. In fact, I didn't even like him. I knew that my feelings for him were wrong and I struggled with my attitude, but I justified my resentment every time I saw his dark expression. I kept thinking, *If he would just realize how much he's hurting me and be willing to change—we could have a happy marriage!*

We were caught in a vicious cycle of pain. Neither of us understood what was happening or why we couldn't seem to fix it but we both knew we were miserable. After stating his feelings in the car that afternoon, we faced the fact that the only bond holding our marriage intact was our individual commitments to Christ.

Although we were immature spiritually, divorce was never an option in our minds, so we settled into a season of dark misery.

I was isolated in my pain. Some women take their marital problems to understanding friends, but for years I kept silent. Although I was angry and hurt, I thought it would be disloyal to talk about my husband, so my journal became my place to vent:

"His cold responses leave me stunned. He seems to live with a simmering resentment toward me . . ."

"How can I reach him? There must be a key to this . . . why can't we communicate without friction? Why is he so easily offended?"

"He can't speak to me without using cutting words or sarcasm . . ."

"All I want is for him to love me . . ."

"The pain is too much . . ."

Several years passed living with walls of separation. At times I believed I hated him, but because of my commitment to Christ, I determined that no matter how hard things were, I wouldn't leave him.

We didn't struggle with the issues that destroy so many marriages: substance addiction, financial conflicts, terminal illness, immorality, physical abuse, pornography. We were simply trying to cope with natural feelings and emotions in self-centered ways. We had the resources to build a loving, harmonious relationship, but in ignorance we wandered through marital meltdowns. For years I was resigned to the fact that things would never improve. My husband, convinced things would never change, entered a long period of severe depression.

> **YOU SEE, I THOUGHT MY JOB (THE "HELPER" ROLE) WAS GOD'S WAY OF USING ME TO *HELP MY HUSBAND IMPROVE*!**

When we counsel couples, my husband now admits that he started out our marriage with a smug attitude, confidently assuring himself that he was going to be a great husband and therefore we'd have a great marriage. From my perspective, he had plenty of room for improvement—and I spent a good deal of energy attempting to shape him into the man of my dreams!

You see, I thought my job (the "helper" role) was God's way of using me to *help my husband improve!* I could "help him" with his grammar, correct his awkward clothing choices, or instruct him on the proper way to hang his bath towel. With "helping him improve" as my job description, I became his worst nightmare . . . criticizing where he parked the car, decisions he made in the home, pointing out how he could've made a better choice. And with my fierce determination to do my "job" well, he retreated into his own silent world. He clung to passivity as the only safe solution.

FIERCE WOMEN/FEARFUL MEN

I've often seen fierce women produce fearful men. That may not be the case in your home, but that's what happened in our relationship. We both laid the blame on the other, and neither of us realized how our individual actions contributed to this destructive cycle. I was trying to mold him into the man I wanted him to be, and he was running for cover! I expected him to fulfill unspoken desires, and he was scratching his head in confusion. I wanted him to relate to me emotionally (more like a girlfriend), and he was struggling to live out his manhood. I was trying to exert my strength to control him, and he was using passivity in defense.

We were in the grip of the same destructive cycle that plagued the first couple and has been repeated for thousands of years since. It's the warping of the gender dynamic where the wife's strengths transform into this scary fierceness. She takes charge while the passive husband sits on the sidelines. It's been happening since Genesis chapter 3.

When my young husband realized we were caught in this destructive cycle, he went to a well-meaning counselor who suggested he just needed to "pull himself up by his bootstraps" (whatever that means) and take his stand like a man. He needed to tell his wife to hold her tongue, even if she had all the right answers, so he could assert himself as the leader.

Neither of us took too well to this counsel. It sounded like putting a false front on a house where the foundation had already given way. We were imploding and in need of real help, and for me to carry on the charade of a mealy-mouth, empty-headed, shrinking violet . . . well, it just didn't seem like the answer!

I've since learned that I didn't need to put on a "weak appearance" in order to encourage my husband's leadership. I didn't need to lie down as a ready doormat to improve our relationship or fulfill my role as helper. No, I've learned that my fierce strengths were placed there by my wise Creator. *The problem with our marriage wasn't my fierceness, but the problem was my understanding of what I should do with that fierceness.* And my fierce displays were resulting in a very passive, even fearful, husband.

The cycle works like this:

WIFE HAS STRONG DESIRES
AND "EXERTS HER FIERCENESS"
IN ORDER TO OBTAIN THOSE DESIRES . . .

↓

AND/OR ⇄ AND/OR ↺

| HUSBAND RETREATS IN FEAR . . . | HUSBAND IGNORES WIFE AND PICKS UP THE NEAREST BRAIN-NUMBING OBJECT AVAILABLE (MEDIA REMOTE, NEWSPAPER, LAPTOP) . . . | HUSBAND FEARS DISAPPOINTING WIFE AND GOES TO ANY LENGTH TO MAKE SURE SHE GETS WHAT SHE WANTS . . . | HUSBAND FEELS INTIMIDATED AND LASHES BACK IN ANGER RESULTING IN VERBAL OR PHYSICAL INJURY. |

All the above reactions are wrong. The wife's destructive fierceness is wrong. But if you were to catch a couple in the midst of this downward spiral, each would probably justify their own actions. Whether he comes across as a cowering wimp or an abusive tyrant, in all of the examples above, the husband's response is driven by fear.

I was in conversation with one couple who've enjoyed a long marriage, but, just as most of us, they've experienced their ups and downs. We were discussing this relational dynamic when the husband commented on his wife's ability to affect him: "Oh, she only has to give me a certain look and she can bring me to my knees!" I watched her give him a bewildered look and ask in shock "I can?" He was a successful, seemingly confident man, but he readily admitted how his wife's disapproval could strongly derail him.

I don't think most of us realize how much we affect our husbands, and I think we're often unaware of when our God-given strengths transform into this destructive fierceness. I know I was. I really thought my husband was the problem in our relationship. You may not relate to many of these characteristics, but perhaps you identify with a few:

Characteristics of a Destructive Fierce Woman:
* She's established herself as her own authority. Her identity flows from the faulty perception that she's in charge of her life and her independence is her highest value.
* She's always pulled by the lure of "more." Her desires are never satisfied.
* She's unaware that ingratitude, pride, and fear are the driving components of her life.
* She's obsessive about things that matter to her. She lives with a self-centered agenda.

* She longs for love and affection but can come out
  swinging if rejected!
* She goes to battle often, mistaking her belligerence for
  heroism.
* She grabs for power, and no one and nothing prevents
  her from getting her way.
* She uses her strength to bully others. She may not
  recognize it as bullying, but her continual criticisms,
  negative perspective, and harsh tones can eat away at
  others like acid.
* She's harsh and blunt in her honesty and proud of it.
* She is often involved in conflicts with others.
* She may claim God's Word as her ultimate authority,
  but her study is merely academic; it doesn't affect how
  she treats others.
* She usually has no trouble confronting, but her motive
  is for personal gain or comfort and her approach is
  demeaning.
* She walks in arrogance and pride but is blind to her
  lack of humility. She views meek behavior as a sign of
  weakness. She sincerely believes her personal conflicts
  stem from others' ineptness, lack of spirituality, or
  inferior behavior.
* She craves power over others and has mastered the art
  of controlling them through subtle manipulation.
* Although she may not admit it, her life is devoted to
  selfish pursuit. She's only satisfied when she gets her
  own way; she's unhappy with anything less.

Wow, she sounds pretty intimidating. I wouldn't want to cross
her. You may not realize it, but you could have more in common

with this woman than you think. I know I did.

Does your husband ever make comments that indicate he feels he can never measure up to you? Do the men you come in contact with seem to "shut down" when you're in conversation? Has your husband ever complained that your silence has a chilling effect? Do you have a certain look that can bring him to his knees? If so, you may be caught in the Fierce Woman/Fearful Man cycle.

When I was in my early thirties, I was invited to serve on the board of trustees for one of the most prestigious theological seminaries in the world. At the time, I was the only woman serving with sixty-three men. Occasionally, people who didn't know me well would ask LeRoy how I handled being the only female serving on a board with that many men. His quick reply was always: "Oh, I'm not concerned for Kim—I'm concerned for those sixty-three men!" He laughingly joked about my ability to intimidate men, but it really isn't a reputation I'm proud of now.

What is driving the destructive fierce woman? What is it that causes our beautiful fierceness to go bad on us? What's up with that? I think there may be a few things involved: ingratitude, pride, fear, and the desire to control. Let's take a look at where all the trouble originated and see how it applies to our marital relationships.

Okay, I'm placing a reader warning here before we go any further: *Familiar Passage Alert!* I'm about to take us to a passage you may already know well, one that I think probably every Christian book on marriage cites, but please don't close the book or kick into autopilot; hang in here with me because it's important to get a handle on this.

A DANGEROUS CONVERSATION

In chapter 1, I mentioned that Eve was created as Adam's helper. In an intimate garden wedding, we see the romantic joining of two into one and the next thing we know, Eve is hanging out in a dangerous location—near a forbidden tree. Apparently Eve was no pushover or fainthearted wallflower. She was bold enough to hold a conversation with a talking serpent but foolish enough to make an independent and rebellious choice. Let's take a minute to listen in on their conversation and see if it helps us understand our ugly fierceness a little better:

"Now the serpent was more crafty than any other beast of the field that the Lord God had made. He said to the woman, 'Did God actually say, "You shall not eat of any tree in the garden"?'" (Genesis 3:1).

Can you believe this? By subtly misquoting God's Word, the serpent starts the conversation by throwing in a negative view of the Creator. He has the gall to imply that God is unfair or too restrictive and is withholding something she deserves. I doubt Eve would've ever considered being dissatisfied with what she'd been given without his presenting the temptation. I would think with paradise literally at your feet, it might not enter one's mind to want "MORE!" But with the serpent's insidious suggestion, the longing for more was a desire conceived. The longing lured and enticed Eve until it gave birth to the sin of idolatry, which brought death.

> THE ROOT OF SELF-PITY IS THE PRIDE OF THINKING I DESERVE "MORE!"

James describes the progression this way: "But each person is tempted when he is lured and enticed by his own desire. Then desire when it has conceived gives birth to sin, and sin when it is fully grown brings forth death" (James 1:14–15).

"MORE!"

Do you recognize the serpent's fatal line of attack? It's the same old thing the enemy uses on me. And if I'm not careful, it'll lead me straight to idolatry. Whenever I covet the good stuff I want but am not receiving, my pride jumps to its feet to demand "MORE!" It then shows up in ugly behaviors like self-pity. I'll end up thinking, *Look at what all I've done, how hard I've worked . . . I don't deserve this kind of treatment!*

The root of self-pity is the pride of thinking I deserve "MORE!" I deserve more . . . bigger . . . better! It's ingratitude coupled with greed. It's discontentment birthed by longing for the forbidden or denied. I often delved into the deep abyss of self-pity as I focused on LeRoy's inattentiveness or was crushed from the disappointment of unmet expectations.

On the third night of our honeymoon, my husband woke up to the pathetic sound of a crying new bride. When he asked me what was wrong, I spilled out my complaint: "You fell asleep on me!" Rather than being thankful that this worn-out man had driven hundreds of miles to get us safely to our destination (um . . . to be honest, while I *napped*), I focused on my hurt and took offense at his seeming insensitivity.

I was lying there beside him, in the dark, longing for what I wanted but wasn't getting. I deserved "MORE!" attention . . . "MORE!" cuddling and quality time . . . "MORE!"

Through sobs I poured out my injury. He merely groaned, rolled over, and was soon snoring again. We laugh about it now, but it serves as a silly example of the repetitive cycle of pain we were about to embark on for the next several years.

"And the woman said to the serpent, 'We may eat of the fruit of the trees in the garden, but God said, "You shall not eat of the fruit of the tree that is in the midst of the garden, neither shall you touch it, lest you die"'" (Genesis 3:2–3).

Whoa. We've got a major problem here. Eve doesn't have the instructions exactly right. According to Genesis 2:16, God told

Adam that he couldn't eat from this tree . . . but where did Eve get the idea she couldn't even *touch* it?

All we can do is speculate. Maybe Eve exaggerated (something self-pity tends to promote). Perhaps she wasn't listening well when Adam relayed the instructions from God. Then again, maybe Adam miscommunicated (I started to say he wouldn't be the first man to do this, but then I realized—oh yeah, he would be!). Whatever the reason for her confusion, Adam should have straightened things out. He should have been the man and stepped into the fray here rather than let Eve do all the talking. He left her in a wide-open, vulnerable, position. And she was about to be hit with the enemy's best shot:

"But the serpent said to the woman, 'You will not surely die. For God knows that when you eat of it your eyes will be opened, and you will be like God, knowing good and evil'" (Genesis 3:4–5).

Don't miss this—he just called God a liar! He takes a swing at Eve's faith by accusing God of not being trustworthy. If she can't trust God, then what use is there in obeying Him? Why put yourself through such a rigorous chore of self-denial? And hey, who wouldn't want to experience all there is to see and know out there . . . why should God hold on to all that omniscience for Himself? (*Ahem* . . . wanting "MORE!" again.)

Let's do a quick recap of what we've been watching happen here: Satan, in the form of the serpent, crafts suggestive insinuations to supplant Eve's trust in God's goodness. He attacks God's truth through half-truths and subtle accusation using a question. He raises suspicion about God's character and intentions. His implication is that God isn't being totally honest with Eve, therefore, He's not trustworthy. And he dangles this big carrot of "special sight/ secret knowledge" in front of her face.

His temptation skillfully works the two-pronged fork of pride and fear, weaving into the conversation bits of doubt intended to cloud her mind with questions such as, "Why has our Creator withheld this most exquisite tree from us? What else is He keeping from us?"

His artful tongue piques the lust of her flesh, "We deserve this fruit. The forbidden must hold the greatest pleasure, and He's denied us of it! I want the same knowledge He has."

The pride of life raises her voice, "I can decide what's best for me. I don't need God to run my life!"

Fear rushes in like a flood. "If God has lied to us, we can't trust Him! I don't want to miss out on all there is to experience."

And as she raises her hand to place the forbidden fruit to her lips, her mouth opens to receive the promised death.

PLUNGING INTO DEATH

When a woman is convinced that she knows what's best for her life, when she feels vulnerable and unprotected, she usually takes things into her own hands and forges ahead despite the risk. That's exactly what Eve did. She operated under the delusion that God was withholding something good from her—that He was untrustworthy. She feared she was missing out, and her husband left her totally unprotected as she was in the throes of temptation.

EVERYTHING IN PARADISE IS CHANGED. FOR THE FIRST TIME, FEAR ENTERS THE GARDEN.

Turning her back on God, she took a giant leap of independence. She plunged headlong into disobedience and took the rest of her daughters down with her (that's you and me). We may want to lay the blame on Adam's passivity, the serpent's subtlety, or temptation's power, but Eve is responsible for the choice to commit treason against her faithful Creator.

Rather than serving her husband well as his helper, she influenced him to join in her corruption:

"So when the woman saw that the tree was good for food, and that it was a delight to the eyes, and that the tree was to be desired to make one wise, she took of its fruit and ate, and she also gave some to her husband who was with her, and he ate" (Genesis 3:6).

Life stops. Death begins.

If we were watching this scene in vibrant Technicolor, at this point I'd expect to see the dark shadows of black-and-white flow from the freshly bitten fruit, covering and gobbling up each color-tinged pixel, like a wave rolling across the field of vision until all color is obliterated by charcoal shades of grey, with drab bits of white. Everything in paradise is changed.

For the first time, fear enters the garden:

"And they heard the sound of the Lord God walking in the garden in the cool of the day, and the man and his wife hid themselves from the presence of the Lord God among the trees of the garden" (Genesis 3:8).

The ruling couple stands shivering in shameful fear of their Creator. Instead of enjoying a fun day together, seeking out new adventures and running to greet the Father, darkness invades their relationship and they run for cover.

Rather than bringing freedom and the promised God-like power, their disobedience has introduced the first couple to craving's bondage. Their exposure to sin has forever marred them, and they will never be the same. Every marriage since that day has groaned under the effects of their fall.

A STRANGE TRANSFORMATION

When I was a little girl, I was fascinated by a couple who would occasionally drop by my parents' home for a visit. Although elderly, the wife was still an elegant beauty. I'd pull up a chair in the kitchen beside my mom and we'd eagerly listen to her stories of travel and adventure. She was well respected in the world of education and seemed to have a firm grasp on any topic at hand. Her clothing style was fashionable, classic, and refined, her vibrant personality captivating.

While we hung on her every phrase, the men visited with her husband in the next room. He was equally impressive. He was a man's man, having flown several missions in World War II. His old war stories held everyone's interest. He talked and laughed easily and was quite likable.

They were an enjoyable and admirable couple—as long as they were in separate rooms. But as soon as they came in contact with each other, a strange transformation occurred. Her generous smiles and gracious tone turned to ice. His ease of conversation left him and he fell mute, eyes downcast. The thick tension between them was obvious.

Each of them, highly respected by their peers, seemed to view the other with contempt or disgust. She would verbally skewer him in front of us, criticizing his driving, his choice of hotels, or his lack of taste. While in the middle of a story, she would correct minor details as he spoke or challenge his portrayal of the event. He would seemingly never hear a word she said, often silently retreating from the room in the middle of her lambaste.

I didn't see them often, but when I did, the bitterness and resentment between them never wavered. It puzzled me that two very likable people seemed to dislike each other so much. I was amazed when they remained married (totally miserable with one another but married) into their final years.

Remembering this sad couple, and seeing many similar marriages, causes me to wonder . . . I wonder how many couples are truly enjoying each other.

How many marriages consist of couples existing as housemates or enemies? How many wives are filled with bitter resentment while their husbands are indifferent to their needs? How many would say their marital unhappiness is the other's fault?

BLINDED BY THE FALL

You and I struggle as a result of Eve's fall. Her beautiful fierceness turned ugly and perverted as she dined on stolen fruit. The sight she desired became a blinding shroud. We are all born with this same blindness. I spent years in marital misery before I recognized my own ugliness and how it affected our relationship. Before my eyes were opened to what I really looked like, I was self-satisfied and blind to my need.

Through a painful process of discovery, I began to realize that our marital problems were not all my husband's fault. In fact, much of the blame fell to me. But it took a lot of painful face-planting events before I admitted this. By face-planting, I mean God used difficult and humbling situations to bring me to a state of brokenness over my sins; events that eventually brought me to a point where I fell prostrate before Him.

I started noticing how most of my husband's comments to me were filled with sarcasm and thinly veiled resentment. He seemed to be angry with me all the time for no apparent reason. He never asked for, or wanted, any input from me. He rarely touched me. I seemed to be a constant irritant to him.

But then I also noticed it wasn't just my husband reacting negatively toward me: a lot of men I had contact with seemed defensive in conversation with me. I couldn't understand what the problem was. Conflicts with people seemed to be a regular part of my life. What was wrong with these people?

I was in my midtwenties. My husband was the senior pastor of a growing church in the Midwest and we were *busy*. I loved ministry and I thought I loved people. I mean, isn't that what ministry is all about: loving God and loving others? But in the midst of all my good "kingdom work," I was stopped short when I was confronted by a staff member's wife. It was one of the first conversations that caused me to pause (but only briefly) to consider that I might need to evaluate my treatment of others.

> A DEAR FRIEND HAD THE COURAGE TO ASK ME A PENETRATING QUESTION. "DO YOU THINK YOU INTIMIDATE YOUR HUSBAND?"

Looking back now, I don't know how this young woman had the nerve to approach me, because back in that day I was one intimidating fierce woman. Her voice was shaking as she timidly ventured an attempt at confronting my cold and businesslike demeanor. "You just don't seem to care about people. You seem so hard and matter of fact. I mean, for instance, I've never even seen you cry . . ."

Her stab at confrontation wasn't enough to effect any real change, however. I embraced my fierceness, pitied her ignorance, and breezed out of the room to move on to more important matters. I thought she was just whining. I left the conversation fairly unfazed.

Interestingly, almost ten years later, I was faced with a similar rebuke from another woman in leadership. Her words cut through me, reaching the heart: "You just walk over people." This time the confrontation came in the midst of great personal brokenness. God was already opening my eyes to the ugliness of my fierceness, and I took to heart her accusation.

Not long after receiving that blow to my pride, a dear friend had the courage to ask me a penetrating question. "Do you think you intimidate your husband?" My first response was to laugh. But her question wouldn't leave me alone. I played and replayed it . . . and started to wonder if this wise sister recognized something in me that I had missed but needed to see.

God used these confrontations on my journey toward broken-ness and deliverance. When my eyes were finally opened to the depth of my own need for change and the responsibility I bore for our estrangement, I was broken. I laid it all down. I asked for LeRoy's forgiveness. That was a turning point in our marriage. Things didn't suddenly become easier. Our marriage didn't change overnight. But my heart changed and eventually our marriage changed as well. I'll share that part of our story in more detail as we go along.

You may be ready to close the book now, repeating words similar to mine: "He's the one who needs his eyes opened, not me! If only he would be more loving, open up, communicate . . . we could have an intimate and enjoyable relationship . . . if only he would change . . ." How often I sang that same song. All the while, intimacy continued to steadily erode.

Every couple's issues will be different, and the specifics of the relationship struggles will vary, but when it comes to marital conflict, there are no innocent bystanders. There is always the need for growth in both partners. In the years I've spent talking with women on this topic, I've found that no matter how desperate the situation, admitting when you're wrong and consistently demonstrating love results in positive changes. Our marital transformation has been a journey of bringing down walls and a process of building unity. Stopping the blame game is where that starts.

✣ HEART ISSUES ✤

1. When walls of separation begin to develop in a marriage, what is the natural tendency? The harmony and union God created for man and woman to experience were fractured with the fall of mankind in the garden. That's when the battle of the sexes began! Recount what you see happening with the first couple (Genesis 3:7–13).

2. Are you blaming your husband for the walls? Have you told yourself repeatedly, "If he would only change . . . be more compassionate . . . listen . . . care . . . consider my feelings . . ."?

It's usually easier to see the need for improvement in our husbands than in ourselves. Carefully read through the chart contrasting the characteristics that define the Beautifully Fierce Woman and the Destructive Fierce Woman (see the appendix). Which of these more closely describe you? Is it possible you and your husband are caught in the Fierce Woman/Fearful Man cycle?

If you are serious about bringing down the dividing walls and destroying the barriers in your relationship, you're going to have to get honest with God and with yourself, and admit it's not all your husband's fault. I'm challenging you to stop, take a deep breath, and state the truth out loud: "It's not all his fault."

3. Spend a few moments in 1 John 1. Notice the contrasts: light and darkness, deception and truth, lying and confession. Ask God to open your eyes to what He wants you to learn in our time together in these pages. Ask Him whether there is something you need to confess before we go any further. Specifically, find encouragement in the truth of verse 9.

CHAPTER

3

Where Is the Man I Married?

"As far as I can tell, real men don't have a problem with smart, successful women. But they do mind being castrated. It's a guy thing."

— KATHLEEN PARKER, SYNDICATED COLUMNIST[1]

Hey, why'd you take the expressway at this time of day? Don't you know this is the worst time to take that route? Why didn't you go the back way—*we'll be late!*" Another husband crumples in defeat under his wife's correction. Once again his mental recording plays in his head: *Why even attempt to make your own decisions? You never make the right one; you'll never measure up to her expectations . . . why even try?*

If we could hit rewind and begin this woman's day with the question, "Are you planning to emasculate your husband and shut him down with your opinions today?" she'd probably reply with something like, "No way! I want him to be the leader in our relationship. I'd never treat him that way." Another couple caught in the Fierce

55

Woman/Fearful Man cycle. I don't think any of us ever plan emasculation; it just seems to happen before we know it. Ever been there? Why do we do that?

I'm not talking about sharing healthy observations or positive, constructive criticism with our guys. And I'm not advocating ignoring sin or neglecting biblical confrontation (as you'll see if you hang in here with me through the book). What I'm talking about is that irritating tendency to view his decisions through the narrow grid of my tightly held opinions. It's that kind of critical spirit that rears its ugly head to dismantle a husband's confidence and cripple his desire to lead.

Early in our marriage, I often found myself questioning, "Where is the man I married?" I often hear women complain about their husband's passivity and lack of leadership, followed by the question of why this happens. We leave the wedding altar, and some pitiful deadbeat-loser-guy invades the body of our robust champion. And this scenario isn't one or two isolated cases—it's happening in droves!

It seems we're watching the extinction of real men.

Surely you've seen him trudging behind his wife in the mall. His eyes are glazed over and downcast. He seems to be in an almost comatose state. He's the "neutered man." At one time he may have seen himself as a man's man, a leader, flexing his skills and strengths, willing to take risks to achieve and explore; to conquer new territory and hurdle obstacles. That was before his body was invaded by Mr. Passive.

Now, he no longer tries.

He's lost his zeal for living and his confidence as a man and leader.

His "risk taking" is limited to the occasional feeble suggestion he offers his domineering wife.

WHIPPIN' MY MAN INTO SHAPE!

Whether single or married, most women struggle with this issue of control. We have an underlying drive to manipulate the men around us. We may not express it overtly, with harsh tones or verbal jabs; some of us may take the more subtle route—raised eyebrows and manipulative silence. Yet either way, men can become paralyzed by fear when faced with a controlling woman; they cave to a common default position: passivity.

One definition for emasculation states: to deprive of strength or vigor; weaken.[2] The fierce woman can suck the heart right out of her man through emasculation *or* she can put steel in his spine through admiration and appreciation.

But why does emasculation come so easy?

We'd probably all agree with the source of our desire to control, and chalk it up to that catch-all sin: PRIDE . . . But I'm wondering if it also has something to do with the way we are wired: as *helpers*!

We girls love the helper role! That's what gives me permission to whip my man into shape! Our intentions are honorable. The motive is to help our men improve. (I think I know the best way, and surely it's helpful to let him know the "best way," right?) But the end result is *not* helpful to a man who desperately needs to be given room to lead!

THE DESIRE TO CONTROL

Eve's choice of the forbidden led to her curse, and every woman since Eve has had to contend with it.

"To the woman he said, 'I will surely multiply your pain in child-bearing; in pain you shall bring forth children. Your desire shall be for your husband, and he shall rule over you'" (Genesis 3:16).

When I was younger, I thought the phrase "Your desire shall be for your husband" referred to having some kind of insatiable desire for my husband either emotionally or physically. But when I dug a little deeper and checked out some reputable commentaries, I discovered the curse contains an interesting Hebrew word found only one other time in Scripture.

In Genesis 4:7 we find the other time the word translated "desire" is used, and it's in reference to sin wanting to dominate or overpower Cain: "If you do well, will you not be accepted? And if you do not do well, sin is crouching at the door. Its desire is for you, but you must rule over it." According to Pastor John MacArthur:

> Because of sin and the curse, the man and the woman will face struggles in their own relationship. Sin has turned the harmonious system of God-ordained roles into distasteful struggles of self-will. Lifelong companions, husbands and wives, will need God's help in getting along as a result. The woman's desire will be to lord it over her husband, but the husband will rule by divine design (Ephesians 5:22–25). This interpretation of the curse is based upon the identical Hebrew words and grammar being used in Genesis 4:7. . . to show the conflict man will have with sin as it seeks to rule him."[3]

The flipside of the woman's calling to be a helper is the curse of . . . controlling. We want to control our husbands. The good stuff God put in us, which makes us a beautifully fierce woman and an effective helper, gets perverted and twisted into this dangerous tool of domination that we use to "whip the man into shape."

For example, a Fierce Woman's:
Power of Influence can evolve into the Power of Pressure
Gift of Encouragement can morph into the Habit of Nagging
Keen Intellect can degenerate into a Sense of Superiority
Passionate Exuberance can become Overwhelming Intensity
Godly Wisdom can become his worst nightmare as an
    Intimidation Factor

Remember the beauty of fierceness in the first chapter? Well, here we have its evil twin: unrestrained, ugly fierceness. And it can be as deadly as beautiful fierceness can be empowering. When a woman applies pressure to her husband, nags him, intimidates and demeans him, he'll look for a "safe place" for relief.

One husband told me, "Men gravitate to those who make him feel like a winner. No guy will keep playing a game that he's losing all the time . . . if he feels he's losing at home,

OFTEN, THE DESIRE TO CONTROL STEMS FROM A WOMAN'S DEEP LONGING FOR AFFECTION.

he'll start looking for some place where he feels respected. We need to know that we're succeeding in what we're doing."

Often, the desire to control stems from a woman's deep longing for affection. She desires a man who will passionately pursue her and is willing to fight for her heart. Other motives for controlling might include the fear of loss or harm, the desire for safety and security, the need to fix a problem or find a solution, the hope for improvement of people or circumstances. We forget that we can't "make" our husbands into the romantic man of our dreams.

Perhaps you'll recognize some of the following statements. How often have you said something similar? (This is pretty much a list from my personal bio—and notice all the exclamation points.)

"I'm just trying to help you!"

"If it's going to be done right, I'll have to do it myself!"

"If I don't take charge, it won't get done!"

"That's the last time I let down my guard!"

"I'm just trying to protect you!"

"I guess I'll have to be the one to take the bull by the horns!"

I've not really said all these things out loud (well, some I have), but my actions can communicate these messages. I've noticed there seems to be an epidemic of women saying the same thing. Look around and you'll see many couples caught in the Fierce Woman/ Fearful Man cycle. And it's not just controlling wives who are demeaning their husbands; it appears our culture is bent on sending the message that men are merely here for comic relief.

MEN ARE THE NEW WOMAN

In Maureen Dowd's book *Are Men Necessary?: When Sexes Collide*, she chronicles men's fear of relationships with "alpha women" and suggests that many women who came of age in the "women's lib generation" have ended up unmarried and childless because they're successful.[4]

Syndicated columnist Kathleen Parker takes issue with this premise. Parker states, "Men haven't turned away from smart, successful women because they're smart and successful. More likely they've turned away because the feminist movement that encouraged women to be smart and successful also encouraged them to be hostile and demeaning to men."[5]

Parker illustrates how men have been characterized for the past thirty years: "male chauvinist pigs, deadbeat dads, or knuckle-dragging abusers who beat their wives on Super Bowl Sunday." She goes on to describe the irony of what we women have asked of these same "male chauvinists."

"At the same time women wanted men to be wage earners, they also wanted them to act like girlfriends: to time their contractions, feed and diaper the baby, and go antiquing."[6]

But woe to the man who might "lapse into guy-ness," then it's *hit the road, buddy*! Parker continues by pointing out the broader effects of male bashing, extending beyond our personal relationships to the culture at large:

"Meanwhile, when we're not bashing men, we're diminishing manhood. Look around at the entertainment and other cultural signposts and you see a feminized culture that prefers sanitized men—hairless, coiffed, buffed and, if possible, gay."[7]

It sounds like you only have to flip on the nightly television programming to see one of these cultural signposts. I ran across an article touting "A New Generation of TV Wimps." It clued me in on a huge cultural shift that has occurred in the way men are portrayed since my childhood days of TV watching.

From what I read, it seems there is an abundance of television sitcoms that center on lead male characters struggling with the changing dynamics of men as they relate to the successful women surrounding them. According to one executive producer, "Manliness is under assault."[8] Today's men in the media are seen as inept buffoons and fearful wimps in need of mothers. The accomplished women they've married (for some unknown reason) put up with these immature sluggards, and the conflicts that arise from this pairing produce modern "entertainment."

WE'RE WITNESSING A KIND OF REDEFINITION OF "MALENESS."

We've come a long way since men like my grandmother's hero, Matt Dillon (the marshal from *Gunsmoke*), who protected Dodge from any ne'er-do-well. In previous generations, the common male stereotypes in the media were wise (Jim Anderson of *Father Knows Best*), dependable (Pa from *Little House on the Prairie*), and provided strong leadership (Captain Jean-Luc Picard, who could tackle any mission in space).

It's not only happening in the entertainment industry. We're witnessing a kind of redefinition of "maleness" as men are moving into the women's department in the fashion world. I was a little taken aback when I read an article promoting "Fashion Trends That Prove Men Are the New Women."[9] Huh? (Did your mouth drop open? Mine did when I read that title.)

Some of the trends noted were "guy skirts," patterned silk "man-tyhose" (think really decorative pantyhose on men's legs . . . sorry to put that thought in your head), and the man version of the bikini, a "mankini" (I can only imagine what John Wayne would say to the guy wearing this thing).

An article from the *Wall Street Journal* points out how the rise in this type of apparel for men is being accommodated by linguists. Five years ago the English Oxford dictionary included "manbag" (um . . . that's a man's *purse*) as a word.[10] It appears you can place the word "man" as a prefix in front of any inherently feminine object and—Presto! You have a fashion craze.

I thought at least eyeliner would be off-limits (surely there's something still reserved for women only . . .); then I saw that "guy-liner" is now a hot item. Wow . . . is *nothing* sacred anymore?

What's happening here?

How've we reached this point?

If art reflects culture, then we're in need of a "True Manhood Revolution." If art *shapes* culture, then we're in need of some men exhibiting true masculinity to counter what Hollywood and the fashion world is pumping out.

All of this "gender flipping" is sending confusing messages to a young generation struggling to know how to live as men and women. While I was working on this chapter, a desperate young woman posted this comment on one of my blog articles: (I've left her words and misspelling intact.)

"Im addicted to lesbianlism &masturbation even though i have a boy friend. oh!God im so confused."

Her cry represents so many in her generation who are drowning in a moral morass. I fear this is a trickle-down effect from decades of messed up marital relationships where the roles have reversed, respect and kindness have gone by the wayside, and divorce is the norm rather than the exception.

Laura describes herself as coming from a long line of (destructive) fierce women. She once viewed men as worthless and easily expendable. Her marital relationship is a graphic example of this cultural trend. She shared with me how her destructive fierceness affected her role as a wife:

> During my college years, I joined the National Organization for Women, read every feminist tract and book, and went through men—I was belligerent and cruel, I enjoyed the power. Because of my fierceness, I excelled in corporate America. My career progressed, which reinforced the value of my attitude and approach. Making an obscene amount of money and feeding my self-reliant spirit, I concluded marriage was simply unnecessary.
>
> When I reached my midthirties, marriage became attractive, if for no other reason, I deemed it time. Everyone else was doing it, so not one to be left out, I married a non-Christian man. I left him twice in our first year to year and a half in marriage. As he lost his job and was unwilling to find another, I handled all the finances, giving him a monthly allowance. I even demanded an accounting; he would hand over receipts with the exact reason for the purchase detailed on the back.
>
> As with the men in the workplace, I competed with my husband. And if there was any respect in the beginning of our marriage, there was none at the end. I found him weak and pathetic. I could barely tolerate his presence and the man knew it. I sought my freedom by divorcing my husband.

Laura's story is typical of so many marriages today—couples confused by their roles and grappling with how to harmonize and appreciate gender differences. We are witnessing the loss of courageous men. Men are struggling to understand what true manhood looks like and are groping for answers in how to live it out. At the same time, women have lost respect for men in general.

Hanna Rosin, in her article "The End of Men," raises the question of where we're heading with the current cultural trend:

> For the first time in American history, the balance of the workforce tipped toward women, who now hold a majority of the nation's jobs. The working class, which has long defined our notions of masculinity, is slowly turning into a matriarchy . . . Women dominate today's colleges and professional schools—for every two men who will receive a B.A. this year, three women will do the same.[11]

So What Can You and I Do?

You or I may not be able to produce a powerful media piece to counteract the damage of the cultural trend of male bashing, and we may not have the answer to fix the matriarchal trend in the world of economics and education, but here are a few things we can do:

* Intentionally encourage the men around us as we see them striving to live out biblical manhood in a culture that views men as a joke.
* Determine to be a change-agent in female conversations when man-bashing starts, by reversing the negative tone and direction through encouraging women to be supportive of their man.
* Never demean men (husbands, sons, brothers, or coworkers) privately or publicly.
* Provide masculine role models for sons or young men in our sphere of influence.

* Read good resources that promote biblical manhood and womanhood.
* Be informed and educated to protect our hearts and minds from the culture's relentless unisex noise.
* Ask our husbands what we can do that will encourage them to express their masculinity.

Why Does This Matter?

It matters because the demeaning of men, whether in the home by a wife or on the larger scale of a culture, erodes God's sacred and mysterious picture in marriage. God has purpose in His creation of male and female. "So God created man in his own image, in the image of God he created him; male and female he created them" (Genesis 1:27).

He didn't create genderless beings. Masculinity is tied to the role and responsibility that God has given to men. Masculinity is to serve as a reflection of the warrior role of our eternal Bridegroom. The denigration of masculinity mocks God's purpose in creation and it mars the sacred metaphor of marriage.

MARRIAGE IS MUCH BIGGER THAN THE TWO PEOPLE IN A PARTICULAR MARRIAGE.

Ephesians 5:22–33 helps us to see and understand God's purpose in creating man and woman and uniting them in marriage. Marriage was not created for man and woman. Marriage was created to display the gospel. It's not all about us.

Marriage is like a metaphor. God uses this sacred relationship as a parable or a model that represents something more than a man and a woman becoming one flesh. It represents the relationship between Christ and the church. That's the deepest meaning of marriage. It's meant to be a living drama of how Christ and the church relate to each other.[12]

I'm not saying we aren't supposed to get anything out of marriage for ourselves or that God doesn't intend for us to experience personal enjoyment or benefit—not at all. I'm just trying to underscore the point that marriage is much bigger than the two people in a particular marriage. It goes beyond that. We're not operating in a vacuum. God wants every marriage to be so characterized by unity, tender moments, lots of laughter, adventure, excitement and passion, humility and self-sacrifice, forgiveness and grace that when people see it, they can step back and say, "Oh, that's what real love looks like. I get it."

And the real love they see going on between us, as husband and wife, is ultimately to point them to the love relationship between Christ and the church. But when the husband mistreats his wife, or when the wife dominates her man, or when they flip the gender roles, we've got a mess on our hands. We're sending a confusing message. We've missed the opportunity to showcase the gospel through our marriage.

She's Outdone Me Again!

"Hey, you've got to see this! She's one *fierce woman*! Man, I feel for her husband." LeRoy called me over to check out the article he was reading in our local newspaper.

I picked up the paper and was immediately struck by the picture. I understood why LeRoy was feelin' it for the guy. The picture captured the riveted expressions of fans at a minor league baseball game. They were all watching a young mom, one arm wrapped around her eight-month-old baby boy (eating a biscuit), her other arm extended into a high stretch for the foul ball.

The picture was shot at the exact moment she snagged the ball in her baseball-gloved hand. Every eye in the stands was glued to the catch. But underneath her long-armed stretch stood her husband who, with both hands (one in a baseball glove), was reaching for the ball as well. She actually had to stretch high over his head to catch the ball; its trajectory was headed straight for him.

When a reporter asked her about cutting the ball off from her embarrassed husband, she explained indifferently that she already had it in her glove, and that possession was nine-tenths of the law. Someone asked her about the widespread attention the picture was getting and she responded that she loved seeing the reaction on her husband's face. The reaction she was referring to was an obvious "She's outdone me again!" look.

I've seen it often.

I've mentioned my own scary fierceness and how it affected my husband. It wasn't until I realized my treatment of him was tied to glorifying God that anything changed in our marriage. When that truth came crashing into my life, along with the realization of my ugly behavior, it broke me. It broke me big-time.

I realized I was guilty of presenting a faulty view of the love relationship between Christ and the church. I was guilty of marring this beautiful picture by my destructive behavior. I had to change how I treated my husband for the sake of the gospel.

For the sake of God's glory.

I've referred to my demeaning treatment of him as "emasculation." Practicing emasculation is typical when caught in the Fierce Woman/Fearful Man cycle. This one word could be the topic of an entire book! But I'll sum it up in this chapter by giving you this acronym. If you find it helpful, you might put it on your refrigerator as a reminder. If you think it's cheesy . . . well, just hang in here with me and give me grace.

EMASCULATION:

Ego-deflating treatment:
* Criticism that demeans
* Comparison
* Questioning his decisions regularly
* Mothering/smothering
* Dream destroying

Manipulation:
* Behavior modification (similar to puppy training techniques)
* Exerting pressure (to get my way or get him to take care of responsibilities)
* Hidden agenda behind syrupy sweetness and batting eyelashes
* Withholding sex or using it for bribery

Aggression:
* Taking forceful action to get what you want
* Pushy attitude, tone, and words
* Hit-n-run tactics (setting up an emotional minefield for him to weave his way through)

Selfishness:
* Self-focused/self-absorbed
* Self-serving
* Prone to self-pity

Controlling:
* Dominating
* Fearful of outcome if not calling the shots
* Attempting to change husband

Unrestrained words:
* Too much talking
* Tone plus facial expression/body language that

communicates he's an idiot, worthless, or can never do
anything right
* Using words as weapons

Leaving your husband hungry for attention:
* Ignoring his needs
* Not making him a priority
* Letting yourself go

"Anything you can do, I can do better":
* Competitive rather than supportive
* Superior attitude
* Intimidating

Taking charge:
* Impatient, unwilling to wait for husband to act
* Taking over his areas of responsibility
* Saying he's the leader while you make all the decisions

Independent living:
* Pursuing separate interests
* Living in your own world (romance novels, Facebook,
Internet, friends, church)
* Keeping secrets from him

Obnoxiously opinionated:
* Convinced yours is the only way
* Treating preference issues as absolutes
* Unteachable and unwilling to listen

No margins:
* Spending time with your man is squeezed out by your
over-filled schedule
* He's not an important priority to you and he knows it
* No time to build an intimate emotional bond through
date nights or weekend excursions

So I've given you the bad news. Our curse is our desire to control. Before we close this chapter, let me leave you with the good news. There is victory. You can break out of the destructive cycle. We don't have to emasculate our men. We can learn to treat them with honor and respect. We can give and receive love the way we were created to experience.

Remember where we left Adam and Eve?

Hiding in the garden . . .

The time arrives for a walk and conversation with God, but the first couple is hiding—shivering in newfound nakedness and fig leaves. Imagine their encounter with Him after their betrayal.

"Where are you?"

The Creator calls out for Adam, not because He couldn't find him but as an appeal for confession. The sordid scene of rebellion and betrayal is laid bare before His all-knowing eyes. Stripped of purity's glory, our first parents stand guilty, waiting for their judgment.

But with the curse comes grace.

Mercy flows as God communicates the gospel message. Planted within the serpent's curse lies redemption's first promise; whispers of Bethlehem's holy Child. From woman's seed, deliverance will one day come. The Christ will crush Satan with a fatal blow (Genesis 3:15; Hebrews 2:14–15; Revelation 20:10).

The shadow of the cross falls upon the guilty pair as the first blood is shed—a sacrificial animal, slain to provide garments to cover man's nakedness. This redemptive act points to the Lamb "slain from the foundation of the world" whose holy blood would serve as man's only atonement (Genesis 3:21; 2 Corinthians 5:21; Revelation 5:6–14).

You may not be aware of it, but God is involved in your life. He sees you. He knows what you're facing today, and He cares. He desires to speak to you through His Word, to communicate His truth, to give encouragement and guidance. He longs to have fellowship with you. He delights in bringing beauty out of the ashes of broken marriages.

I'm not making the assumption that you already have a real and personal relationship with Christ. All this stuff about a "personal God" may seem strange to you. You might even fear holding a conversation with Him. You may want to hide from Him because you know you're unworthy (as am I) to rub up close to a holy God . . . but now we reach the heart of the gospel.

The word *gospel* means "good news," and this is the good news—Jesus Christ came to suffer the penalty for our sin and cleanse us from all unrighteousness, so that we could enter into relationship with Holy God! He extends this offer of friendship to you:

"These things I have spoken to you so that My joy may be in you, and that your joy may be made full. This is My commandment, that you love one another, just as I have loved you. Greater love has no one than this, that one lay down his life for his friends" (John 15:11–13 NASB).

Don't miss this next part!

"You are My friends if you do what I command you. No longer do I call you slaves, for the slave does not know what his master is doing; but I have called you friends . . ." (vv. 14–15).

Let that soak in. Amazing love.

This beautiful invitation to friendship is straight from Jesus' mouth as He spoke with His disciples shortly before His death. While preparing them for His departure, one of the topics He covered was—*friendship*! He loves us. He laid down His life for us. He desires a personal relationship with us and He invites you to be His friend.

Entering into this love relationship involves admitting your sinful condition and your inability to approach a holy God on your own. As you express your need for His forgiveness and turn from your sin, confessing your need for Him, He will cleanse you, His Spirit will fill you, and your new life in Christ can begin (Romans 3:21–24; 5:6–15; 1 Corinthians 6:19–20; 1 John 1:9).

Only then can you have the needed foundation to experience and share love.

Only with Christ as the object of your love can you receive and give love to others.

> BECAUSE OF CHRIST'S REDEMPTIVE WORK ON THE CROSS, WE CAN GIVE AND RECEIVE LOVE THE WAY WE WERE CREATED TO EXPERIENCE.

Love's deepest mystery is the passion of Christ as He pursues His bride with white-hot devotion. He wants to capture your heart. As the Bridegroom, He's orchestrated a divine rescue. The love demonstrated at the cross held no selfish gain. He desires to woo you and win your heart. He extends an extravagant offer of love. By laying down His life, He offers you deliverance from the domain of darkness. He delights in transforming ugly, destructively fierce women into beautiful soft warriors.

Surely you've struggled with the desire to control, as I have. We don't want to emasculate our men, but we do. We don't want to live as the destructive fierce woman, but we do. But the good news is: There is victory!

Because of Christ's redemptive work on the cross, because grace flows when we humble ourselves and cry out to Him for help—we can give and receive love the way we were created to experience. You, who are restless and weary of heart, find your heart's rest here. Christ offers true love to you. You may never have known or even imagined a love of this proportion. We, who are helpless, can find our need fully met in this Man.

You may be longing for love, wandering through a wilderness of pain and isolation, I assure you—no love relationship can compare to the one He offers. The pursuit of love must begin here.

Our first experience of true love originates at the cross.

✳ HEART ISSUES ☙

1. Does your husband seem like a different person than the man you married? I wonder whether you seem different to him. Have the gender roles flipped, become confused or blurry in your relationship? Would your husband say he tends to take the lead at home? Are you guilty of attitudes or statements similar to those I listed as part of "my personal bio"?

2. Are you, even unwittingly, contributing to the emasculation of the men around you? How can you counteract this cultural trend? Since we've addressed issues your husband is dealing with in a culture in which masculinity is under attack, you might consider asking him to read this chapter and discuss his thoughts on ways you can encourage him in living out biblical manhood.

3. Prayerfully read through 1 John 3 before answering the following questions:

   According to 1 John 3:5 and 8, why did Jesus come?

   What is the "test" of Christianity in verse 10?

   What is the proof of a person's new life in Christ according to
   1 John 3:14–15, 23–24?

   Does your treatment of your husband shine as a "proof" to
   others of your relationship with God?

   What does verse 18 tell us to do? How will you fulfill this in
   your relationship with your husband today?

Have you entered into the love relationship with Christ described in this chapter? If not, or if you're unsure whether you have, please read the verses referenced and consider turning to Him for salvation today.

The Deadly Three

"She had wandered, without rule or guidance, into a moral
wilderness. Her intellect and heart had their home,
as it were, in desert places . . ."

— NATHANIEL HAWTHORNE IN *The Scarlet Letter*

From childhood, Anne was well versed in right and wrong.
She was "starched Sunday best," proper and moral through
and through. If you knew Anne back then, you would never
have imagined the detour her life would take. Those who know her
story now are amazed that her marriage withstood it. Please pull up
a chair; with her permission, I'll share it with you.

Anne's childhood was solid and loving, her parents committed believers. She was surrounded with the comforts of a fulfilled
American dream. When she graduated from her Christian high
school, she went on to get her degree at a well-known Christian

college. While there, she fell in love with a young man who had a passion for missions.

After she and Gary married, their family grew quickly. Gary served on a church staff for a bit. Following that, he taught in a Christian school. He toyed with the idea of medical school. Job instability and frequent moves characterized their early years before they made the decision to prepare for the mission field.

Anne and Gary spent exhausting months traveling to various churches sharing their vision, and raising financial support in order to fulfill their calling to foreign missions. When they finally raised enough funds to support themselves, they headed out, with several little ones in tow. Once they reached their new home, there was plenty of work waiting for them.

Their first priority was learning the language of the people they would be ministering to, which involved daily four-hour tutoring sessions. Life was filled with hard work and ministry opportunities, and although Anne was putting her heart into it, something was missing.

She felt trapped and isolated. She longed for more. More of an emotional connection with Gary. More understanding from him. More intimacy. Although the house was full, with children and a husband, Anne was empty.

THEY BEGAN TO FORM A TENDER FRIENDSHIP THAT RIPENED INTO A DEEP EMOTIONAL BOND.

Her view of Gary became critical and negative. Why couldn't he relate to her emotional needs? Why couldn't they connect at a deeper level? She wanted more from him. Needed more from him. She needed someone.

She and Gary met Celeste, a young woman who was a new believer. Her circumstances at home were difficult and she was in need of income. At the same time, Anne was struggling under the heavy load of language study and could use some help with the children and home responsibilities. They knew the young woman needed discipleship as well, and saw this as a ministry opportunity. Anne could disciple her, be a role model and friend to her.

Celeste came to their home as a needy twenty-year-old. She'd never had a good relationship with her mother. She was lonely. Her background was characterized by sensuality and emotional hunger. Unwed and pregnant at fifteen, Celeste was forced into an abortion and still suffered from the loss.

Anne's heart went out to her. Over the next several months, she invested time and energy into Celeste. The women grew to know and care for each other. Celeste shared her deepest struggles and turned to Anne for the love she'd never received at home. Anne thought, *She's never had anyone truly care for her. I can help Celeste in a way no one else can . . . she needs me.* Anne found the young woman's company enjoyable, and they began to form a tender friendship that ripened into a deep emotional bond. Anne saw that she could fill the role in Celeste's life that no one else had and could give her the love she'd never known. Anne began filling the empty places of Celeste's heart with her affection.

The relationship became a satisfying outlet for Anne's cravings for emotional connection. As the bond between Anne and Celeste grew more intimate, the divide between Anne and Gary became deeper. As her affection and attachment to Celeste intensified, her need for connection with Gary waned. Her irritation with him grew almost daily. *Why can't Gary relate to me more like a woman? Women understand each other so much better. Two women can relate much better than a man and woman. We know what the other wants and feels.*

What subtle lines does one cross before reaching for the forbidden? When a woman crosses the line into immorality, it's not with one giant leap but it's with smaller, less defined steps.

Anne's first line into the forbidden wasn't crossed when her treatment of Gary grew hostile and disrespectful. It wasn't crossed when her loyalty to Celeste became greater than her loyalty to Gary. It wasn't crossed when she and Celeste held each other in a long, tender embrace or when they exchanged their first passionate kiss as lovers. No, the first line into the forbidden was crossed long before: the opening of the mind; the shifting of the heart; the turning of the back.

These are the subtle lines Anne crossed. Her mind opened to fantasizing about a relationship that was beyond what Gary could give. She wanted more. Her heart shifted from him to someone she thought could meet her deepest needs. She turned her back on Gary, on her views of morality, on God.

Immorality springs from an idolatrous heart . . . it is the heart seeking satisfaction in places other than in Christ. It is the subtle exchanging of One for another, the exchange of God for something less . . . far less.

When I first met Anne, she was fresh into the process of repentance and brokenness. A friend introduced us and recommended me as one who might help her in the difficult challenge of rebuilding her relationship with her husband. She has graciously agreed to allow me to share her story with you, because she desires God to receive glory from the amazing work of transformation He's done in her life and in their marriage.

LONGING TO BE LOVED

All women long to be loved. It is a natural and good desire, but it can become a perverted demand. The longing for my husband's love and affection was the primary factor in developing my destructive fierceness. I was hurt every time I felt he somehow neglected me or failed to demonstrate love and affection. And in my pain, I lashed out in ugly retaliation, hoping to get his attention, hoping he'd recognize my need for him to come to my rescue.

I wonder if Eve felt unloved in her unprotected state. This is only speculation, but I wonder if she was hoping Adam would intervene in her conversation with the serpent. Was she waiting for him to take his rightful place of spiritual protector? Was she hoping he'd step in to rescue her from herself as she grabbed for the forbidden?

Rather than lashing out at the husband, some women retreat into their private world of romance novels or mental fantasy when they feel neglected. Every day, lonely wives make connection with a potential lover via the Internet's many social media sites. Other women try to stifle their longing for love with food, prescription drugs, or some other addiction.

I've spoken with women who've turned to alcohol, cutting, masturbation, even crystal meth to satisfy longing. The drive to fill your life with pleasure isn't wrong. But attempting to substitute the Living Bread with addictive substitutes is like filling your mouth with gravel (Proverbs 20:17). You may be flirting with the lure of an attractive substitute, a seeming "innocent" Facebook connection or spending long hours in erotic fantasy through the pages of a magazine or novel, thinking, "I can handle this . . ." and all the while chains of enslavement are silently encircling.

INGRATITUDE: THE DEMAND FOR "MORE!"

Remember how we saw Eve lured by the desire for "MORE!" in chapter 2? Where did that start? I think the starting place is familiar to all of us. It is in the desert place of ingratitude. She had paradise but wanted "MORE!" She had a relationship with Adam but wanted "MORE!" She experienced all the good things God provided but wanted "MORE!"

Eve's ingratitude took her from the lush gardens of peaceful contentment and drove her into the wilderness of desolate places: always seeking; painful longing; insatiable hunger; empty dreams.

While in the car driving to my first meeting with Anne, I called my husband to have him pray for me. Before we hung up, I asked him to give me one word from a husband's perspective; one word of counsel that I might need to give to Anne. The word he spoke was *gratitude*.

Ingratitude is the open doorway to immorality. It is exchanging the truth about God for a lie:

> For although they knew God, they did not honor him as God or give thanks to him, but they became futile in their thinking, and their foolish hearts were darkened. Claiming to be wise, they became fools, and exchanged the glory of the immortal God for images resembling mortal man and birds and animals and creeping things. Therefore God gave them up in the lusts of their hearts to impurity, to the dishonoring of their bodies among themselves, because they exchanged the truth about God for a lie (Romans 1:21–25).

Notice the description of those who turned to immorality—specifically homosexuality, in this passage from Romans. They did not honor Him as God or give thanks. They grabbed His position of deity for themselves and were ungrateful for what they'd been given.

"MORE!"

Nancy Leigh DeMoss makes the connection between ingratitude and immorality in her book *Choosing Gratitude: Your Journey to Joy*:

> Ungrateful people are bent on gratifying themselves. They tend to focus on "my needs," "my hurts," "my feelings," "my desires," "how I have been treated, neglected, failed, or wounded." An unthankful person is full of himself, seldom pausing to consider the needs and feelings of others.

Incidentally, I believe this is why a common end result of ingratitude is the sin of moral impurity. A person who is wrapped up in herself, whose whole world revolves around getting her own needs met, is prime bait for a tempter who thrives on accusing God of being unfair and ungenerous. An ungrateful heart is quick to notice when self is feeling unsatisfied, and is vulnerable to resorting to sinful acts and behaviors in an attempt to eliminate pain and experience personal pleasure.[1]

Ingratitude stems from not drinking deeply of Christ. The woman in John 4 who had been seeking all her life for love, searching for someone who would fill the empty places of her heart, only found it in one Man. He is the only cure for ingratitude. He is the only complete satisfaction to the insatiable longing to be loved. He is the quenching for a parched heart.

BUT GOD INVITES US TO WALK WITH HIM IN THE SUPERNATURAL.

If Anne and I could sit down at your kitchen table for a visit, she would tell you what she now conveys to women struggling with an unsatisfied longing for love in their relationship with their husbands. "The answer to my cravings was falling in love with Jesus and having my affection completely set on Him. Satisfaction in Christ is it. Before, I only had head knowledge; now I have a deep love relationship with Him."

Her choice to look to anything other than Him for true pleasure reminds me of one of my favorite quotes from C. S. Lewis: "We are halfhearted creatures, fooling about with drink and sex and ambition when infinite joy is offered us, like an ignorant child who wants to go on making mud pies in a slum because he cannot imagine what is meant by the offer of a holiday at sea. We are far too easily pleased."[2]

God isn't opposed to desire or pleasure. He created us with a huge capacity for both. The problem isn't that we have strong desires; the problem is that our desires are too small. Too ordinary. Too halfhearted.

When my desires are coming from my flesh rather than His Spirit, they are base and natural. But He invites us to walk with Him in the supernatural: "But I say, walk by the Spirit, and you will not gratify the desires of the flesh. For the desires of the flesh are against the Spirit, and the desires of the Spirit are against the flesh, for these are opposed to each other . . ." (Galatians 5:16–17).

This passage goes on to describe the desires of the flesh: "sexual immorality, impurity, sensuality, idolatry, sorcery, enmity, strife, jealousy, fits of anger, rivalries, dissensions, divisions, envy, drunkenness, orgies . . ."

When we first answer the call to an attractive offer to fulfill a craving, or think we've found the object that will finally satisfy our desires, we're usually unaware of the enslaving cords of bondage as they begin wrapping around our hearts and minds. Consider the following descriptions and ask the Holy Spirit to alert you to anything in your life that might have the potential to be a fleshly addiction.

Desires That Enslave:
* Spring from self-centered thoughts and motives
* Are shrouded in secrecy or fulfilled under cover of darkness
* Can lead to crossing lines that expand far beyond God's clear direction
* Carry with them the fear of being caught while gratifying them
* Have an addictive pull
* Require layers of justification based on your "unique" situation or need

* Are "all about me"
* Prevent sincere worship

Gratification of these Desires:
* Involves anything that is morally corrupt, spiritually perverted, and is physically harmful or addictive
* Leaves you with feelings of guilt and shame, but always hungry for more
* Brings harm to others

In contrast to the desires of the flesh and the destruction they produce, Galatians 5 describes the fruit produced by the desires of the Spirit: "love, joy, peace, patience, kindness, goodness, faithfulness, gentleness, self-control . . ."

Desires That Lead to Fruitfulness:
* Spring from God's passion for His glory
* Can be openly shared with others
* Lead to fulfilling God's purposes for your life
* Carry with them a profound sense of joy and anticipation for the future
* Are cultivated by abiding in Christ
* Are beyond ordinary
* Are "all about His glory"
* Lead to worship

Fulfillment of These Desires:
* Brings spiritual growth and greater freedom
* Inspires others to gain a closer walk with Christ
* May involve hard work, long hours, even tears

In Numbers 14:21 God lays out His one all-consuming passion and desire for us and invites us to join Him in fulfilling it: "But as truly as I live, all the earth shall be filled with the glory of the Lord" (KJV). True joy is only attained when our hearts beat with God's desires, when we love His will more than our own, and when His desires fuel our desires. God is leading a holy expedition and bids us to come. What a privilege! To be asked to join His sacred mission; to receive an invitation to go beyond the flesh and to live out His kingdom purpose.

I get inspired when I think about how He wants to accomplish that monumental work. It's amazing to consider. He takes broken, ordinary, needy, little people—like you and me—and He woos us as a bridegroom, purchases us through His own bodily sacrifice, and then fills us with Himself. As He transforms us from our ugly yuck into the beautiful image of Christ, others stand amazed and have to admit "Only God could do that!"

He gets the glory and that's what it's all about.

But that's what my pride often prevents.

PRIDE: IT'S ALL ABOUT ME!

When I focus on what I want or on what God's *not* doing for me, rather than focusing on living out His desires, the pursuit of His glory fades from my mind. Eve paused to consider that God may be withholding something good from her, and her pride was wounded. Although she and Adam had free run of paradise and had more food choices than those on the best buffet—she became discontent and ungrateful. She forgot about God's desires and got all tangled up in hers.

When Eve listened to the serpent, ingratitude took hold. Her reaction was to pull away from all she'd been given, to yearn for the forbidden. Her independent decision placed her in opposition to God and aligned her with His enemy.

She pushed past God's instructions, past Adam's leadership, and exalted herself as deity. The ugliest and most bizarre component of the rebellious fierce woman is her pride. It is ugly because it is self-promoting and self-glorifying. It is bizarre because it sets up self as its own authority—the created exalted over the Creator. Bizarre.

AT ONE TIME OR ANOTHER, WE'VE ALL SHAKEN OUR FIST AT GOD.

Anne told me that part of the satisfaction in her relationship with Celeste came from feeling needed. She enjoyed the sensation of meeting needs in this woman that others couldn't meet. She stepped into the Savior role and found the spot pleasurable.

At the same time, Anne's pride fueled her anger against her husband and God. She told me that she struggled with God's plan for marriage being limited to a male/female relationship. She expressed her frustration with His heterosexual design: "Men can't relate to women as well as other women; why couldn't God design marriage to be between two women?" She was angry with God for setting things up this way. She said she felt like shaking her fist in the face of God and telling Him, "I don't like Your plan for my life—I don't like how You set things up and limited marriage to heterosexual unions only!"

Your pride may not look like Anne's, but at one time or another, we've all shaken our fist at God—perhaps not literally but figuratively by our resistance and rebellion against His way of doing things. Our pride treats God like He's not worthy of His position; He's not intelligent enough to run my life, and if His plan conflicts with mine—He needs to get out of my way.

The same pride that turned Lucifer's heart to self-worship is what drives the desire for all love and affection to be laid at your feet (Isaiah 14:12–14; Ezekiel 28:12–17). When a woman becomes obsessed with getting love from her husband, it should serve as a red flag, warning her that she's in dangerous waters. She's headed toward disaster. She's asking her husband *to give her what only God deserves,* and she's seeking from him *what only God can give.*

Pride is like an oozing canker sore in a marriage relationship; it's always festering, and when it's bumped, it spews its poison and pulsates with pain. A woman whose pride is wounded can be dangerous. She lashes out in self-defense, determined to take her offender down. Her husband forgets her birthday . . . fails to notice her new hairstyle . . . is glued to the television while she aches for conversation . . . her pride will not put up with this kind of treatment. She deserves better; she pulsates with pain and she'll *make him pay!* Pride perverts the beautiful strengths of fierceness into a harsh, self-centered and demanding ugliness.

Patterns of Pride:

* My desire to be loved consumes my thoughts and drives my emotions.
* Convinced if he really cared, I wouldn't have to tell him what I want—*he'd instinctively know!*
* Feeling justified in handing out emotional punishment when he's hurt me.
* Giving off a superior attitude that conveys "Anything you can do—I can do better!"
* Viewing my husband through the eyes of an "inspector" rather than the gracious eyes of a lover.
* Being more concerned about winning the argument than crushing his spirit.
* Never in doubt that my way is the best way.
* Talking to my husband like I'm his mom rather than his lover or friend.

* Convinced our marital problems are his fault. He's the one who needs major change.
* "I'm to be prized, adored, and served." (These expectations may never be voiced, but lie beneath expressions of anger when these desires go unmet.)

I'm not placing all the blame on a wife in a situation similar to Anne's. I've never seen a marriage where only one partner had pride issues. There are always two who contribute to the problems in a marriage, but I'm only addressing wives. I'm hoping to help you see how your fierceness can be used to have a powerful influence in the most desperate of marital struggles but also how pride can serve as a destructive component in the relationship.

In the early years of our marriage, my husband and I were both operating in pride. If anyone had suggested "pride" as an underlying root issue, we would've quickly defended our actions and pointed the finger at the other partner as the source of the problem. Why is the ugliness of pride clearly visible when we observe it in others, yet cleverly hidden from sight when it resides in our own hearts? Pride will be the default position unless a couple learns to recognize it and battle it.

FEAR: FALSE EVIDENCE APPEARING REAL

Fear is one of woman's most cruel companions. Pride and fear work in tandem. They are powerful weapons wielded by a deceptive enemy. Someone told me that you can view the letters of fear as the acronym:

F: False
E: Evidence
A: Appearing
R: Real

That's where the enemy of our souls gets us. He throws out these believable sounding whispers, "God's withholding . . . He doesn't want you to have the good stuff . . . He'll let you down . . . He doesn't care about you . . ." and we cave to fear. Our fear that God is not who He professes to be is based on the enemy's lies. Our fear that our husband is not what he professes to be may be based on past experience or merely empty suspicions, but the truth is—man will always disappoint. That is why our ultimate trust rests not in our husband but in God's faithful character.

Illegitimate fears are born from a faulty view of God. These fears need to be countered with the truth of His Word. We live in a world filled with suffering and evil and the only way to safely navigate such fear-filled terrain is by placing our trust in our faithful Creator (1 Peter 4:19).

A woman longs for safety and protection. A wife needs the assurance that her husband is a faithful protector, that he's trustworthy; he'll watch out for her and cherish her. Adam failed in this regard. A careful reading of Genesis 3 reveals that he was apparently right there with Eve while she held the conversation with the serpent. He was watching passively on the sidelines as she caved to temptation— then he joined in with her. His failure to stand up to the threat of evil had catastrophic results. We've all experienced similar disappointments because no man will perfectly fulfill his role as spiritual leader and loving protector—but the question is—who are we to ultimately place our trust in?

When a woman's trust is violated or she feels her safety threatened, she'll often put up a fight. It's the reaction of the woman when catching her husband viewing porn. She fears she's lost him. She fears what she sees him becoming. She fears what she can't compete with. But her fears may lie hidden under a torrent of angry words— the quickest weapon of defense available.

Her fears are legitimate—her husband is viewing porn. Evil has filled her home, invaded her marriage—but the false evidence that appears real to her is that God cannot redeem this situation and it is up to her to take things into her own hands. She takes on the stance of self-defender rather than following God's scriptural process—allowing Him to be her defender. (See Guidelines When Confrontation Is Necessary in the appendix.)

Often, women who've experienced sexual violations will live with an unspoken vow to never allow a man to overpower them again. They live with the protective shield of simmering anger toward all men whether they realize it or not. My friend Laura (from chapter 3) agrees with this observation. She shared some of her story with me:

> I come from a long line, multiple generations, of self-proclaimin' and livin' Fierce Women. From a very early age, my grandmother and mother warned me—men are worthless; they will let me down, and they are to be used.
>
> "Marry if you must, Laura, but the moment he gets out of line, get rid of him and *quickly*."—I cannot count how many times I heard that mantra.
>
> My grandmother married at least three times, lived with several men, and had two backstreet abortions. My mother managed to stay married to my father for over forty years, although her sister, my aunt, traveled the exact same path as my grandmother.
>
> Interestingly, as far as I can tell, each generation of Fierce Women was sexually abused as children. Once we grew to a certain age, **our fierceness became our protection**. This was a natural evolution for our pain and helplessness since we did not know Jesus Christ. (Emphasis added)

I didn't realize until several years into our marriage that my experience of sexual molestation as a child played an integral role in how I viewed and treated men. My response to men in general flowed from a legitimate childhood fear. I was determined to never allow a man to hold me down or take advantage of me again. This determination produced a shield of protection—verbal fierceness. I might not be able to fend off an assailant physically, but I would be on my guard and ready to take a man down verbally when I felt the need to assert my ground.

I have a news flash. Every man will let us down. Every man will hurt us. Some will even physically or sexually abuse a high percentage of us. The likelihood that you've been raped or sexually assaulted is high. Studies estimate that one out of every five women has been sexually assaulted at some point in her lifetime.[3]

The answer to our fear is not a man's love.

The only answer is to place our complete trust in One who will never disappoint.

If you've suffered abuse at the hands of a man, there is a high likelihood that this has produced a faulty view of God and an unhealthy fear of men. You may be struggling with deep-seated anger and resentment. If you are in this painful place, I encourage you to reach out to a spiritually mature woman or couple who will help you navigate through the lies of the enemy by providing wise biblical counsel. If you've never shared this with your husband, secrecy can be a dividing wall the enemy is using to prevent marital unity and freedom. I appeal to you to contact those who can provide help and healing.

Fears We Face:

* Fear of abandonment
* Fear of the unknown
* Fear of rejection
* Fear of man

* Fear of betrayal
* Fear of suffering
* Past hurts that appear as a menacing phantom to cloud your perspective on the now

And then there are the cruel "What if" fears that tug at the corner of your mind:

"What if he's secretly seeing someone?"

"What if he loses his job?"

"What if the odd mole is cancer?"

"What if he leaves me?"

"What if his choices harm our children?"

INVITATION TO FEARLESS LIVING

God's word to His own is always, "Fear not!" "Do not be afraid." He tells us not to fear the circumstances, the people, or the future. The fear God calls us to withstand doesn't originate with Him or lead us to glorify Him.

Healthy fear keeps us from jumping off bridges and cliffs, or placing a hand on a hot stove. That's not the kind of fear God tells us to extinguish. The toxic fear He opposes rises from the darkness.

It's the fear that comes from the enemy's whispers.

The fear that paralyzes.

It's the fear that causes you to hide behind walls of self-protection.

The fear that causes you to grab for "deity position" because you think you've "got to take care of this!"

The only fear God calls for is a holy fear of Him. He invites us to fearless living based on who He is. Because "He IS," we have no need to fear.

You've never known any other who is committed to be your constant companion, only Him. He's never given up on you. He's never been unkind or insincere. He's never lied to you. He's never been harsh or demanding. He's never let you go. He's never let you down. No one else offers you the steadfast, pure love He gives. He alone deserves your trust.

FAITH MARKERS

When my husband and I were hiking a few years ago, we started out on a clearly marked mountain trail. But as we hiked, there were fewer markers lining the trail. After trudging through the wilderness for several hours, we finally admitted we were lost. Right before dark, we wandered onto a mountain road and flagged down a lone pickup truck to hitch a ride back to our car—nearly twenty miles away! We'd lost our bearings due to a lack of trail markers.

Whenever I find myself wandering through the wilderness of the deadly three—ingratitude, pride, and fear—especially when fear grips my heart, I've learned to depend on "faith markers" to get me back on the trail and out of the woods. One of my favorite faith markers is Psalm 46. It reminds me of God's ability to take care of me. What I mean by that is . . . *if He is powerful enough to make the earth "melt" by merely uttering His voice* (Psalm 46:6) *then I know I'm safe in His hand. Nothing can touch me.*

By "nothing can touch me," I'm not saying I won't experience pain. I have. I don't mean I won't experience loss. I have. I don't mean things will always turn out like I planned. Much of my life hasn't. And I don't mean to imply that I always walk in faith—I don't.

But what I mean is this: When I remember that, while I'm in His hand, nothing can touch me but what He opens His hand to allow, it calms my fears. And, when my pride shouts that I don't like what He's allowed, all I have to do is remind myself of all I know about Him, and that settles it. Focusing on His faithful character then leads me to gratitude.

You may have experienced sorrow because of a loved one's destructive choices. You may know the pain of abandonment, the injustice of sexual assault, or you may be walking through the long journey of a terminal illness. We've all struggled under the challenges that come from living in a broken world. But when we allow Him to hold us through the storm, and remember He's the one who can melt planets, we can have full confidence that He is going to take care of us. There is no need to fear. We can trust Him. We can thank Him.

These are the truths that hold us fast when our world is shaken. Even as I've been typing these sentences, I've received word from a dear friend that an elder in her church died suddenly. Unexpectedly, his life is taken at fifty-nine and his wife left a widow. This is an opportunity to test the waters and see whether there's a safe place to stand. To walk toward Him while all the sea is raging. When life sweeps in like a flood, when the waters of sorrow engulf, Christ is the only safe place.

Many times in the early morning hours, before my eyes open, especially when I've been walking through a season of intense pain or fear, Psalm 46 comes to my lips. Other faith markers that encourage me are journal entries where I've recorded answers to prayer, reading or hearing accounts of God working in other people's lives. Faith markers, like stones of remembrance, help to keep me on track when I encounter any of the deadly three.

Each of the components of destructive fierceness: ingratitude (the desire for "MORE!"), pride, and fear are all interrelated. Left unchecked, these heart issues will lead a woman down a lonely, cruel path. They led to Eve's crossing of the line into the forbidden, and can lead you and I off track as well. But when I recall my faith marker, it takes me to the sanctuary of God's reality. It leads me to moments of worship. It reminds me that He's the One who—with one word—can melt the earth or subdue a raging sea. And He brings me out of the wilderness to the safety of His hand.

He will do this for you as well.

As my husband and I spend time with Gary and Anne today, the brokenness of their past now several years behind them, we are able to observe the power of the gospel at work. As I watch Laura interact humbly with men rather than viewing them as contemptible, it gives evidence to God's redeeming power. Such transformation could only come by God's gracious hand. We stand amazed and have to admit, "Only God could do that." He gets the glory.

⚜ HEART ISSUES ⚘

1. The key to conquering the "deadly three"—ingratitude, pride, and fear—is faith that comes through recognizing and worshiping God for who He Is.

   Remember when I said, "I've learned that my fierce strengths were placed there by my wise Creator. The problem with our marriage wasn't my fierceness, *but the problem was my understanding of what I should do with that fierceness*" in chapter 2? The same fierceness that can bring destruction to your marriage can be applied to getting victory over the heart issues of ingratitude, pride, and fear. Gaining that victory opens the door to experiencing God's beautiful work in your marriage.

   Ingratitude and the craving for "More!" is demolished by gratitude. When I'm thankful for His every gift, ingratitude and evil craving is swallowed in the wake of thanksgiving (see James 1:17; 1 Thessalonians 5:18).

   Pride submits when God is enthroned in His rightful position in my heart. When I surrender to the fact that He is God and I am NOT, my pride bows to His rule (Isaiah 45).

Fear is cast out through love. When I begin to actually glimpse who He is and what the cross means, I know I can trust Him and that love relationship removes my fear (1 John 4:13–18).

2. Read through 1 John 2 with an open and prayerful heart, asking God to use His Word to speak to you. What assurance do we have that we are in a relationship with Christ according to verses 3–5? Personalize verses 9–11 by inserting your name in place of "The one" and your husband's name in place of the words "his brother" in verse 10. Are you demonstrating love to your husband, or would your feelings be more like "the one" in verse 11?

3. Which of the "deadly three" are you grappling with today? Perhaps you're struggling with all three. Ask God to point you to Scriptures that will serve as your own personal "faith markers." I encourage you to record these in a journal. Place the headings: Ingratitude, Pride, and Fear at the top of a sheet and list the specific situations in your life that fit within each category. Beside each situation you listed, record Scriptures that you can use as faith markers (perhaps some from today's first question). Let this be an ongoing project. Add to the page as you find additional Scriptures or faith markers. Memorize and spend time thinking about these passages through your day.

The Life-Giving Trio

"Love is our primary 'affection,'
the fountain of all our other heart experiences."

—JONATHAN EDWARDS[1]

We were still married . . . legally.

Bound by conviction of conscience . . . morally.

Sharing the same roof . . . separately.

I'd almost stopped pleading with God to change my husband. LeRoy only seemed to grow darker and increasingly distant the more I pulled on him for love. I decided instead to pour my heart into my children, friends, and ministry. We settled into separate worlds. It was less painful that way.

Before I take you into the deepest place of our pain, let me answer a few questions people ask when we share our story. We're often asked how we can be so transparent about our marital struggles. A few years ago, my mom and I listened together as this story was aired on the radio. At the end of the program, she asked me if I wasn't a little embarrassed or concerned what people would think of us after hearing it.

My answer to those who question why we tell our story is—*how can we not?* God has been so merciful and gracious in redeeming our marriage, He's given us such joy and rewarded us with the most intimate and pleasurable unity, how could we not praise Him by sharing with others His great work? But also, why would we not reach out to offer help and hope to others who are suffering in places of dark despair, as we once were?

People question why/how we remained in ministry while our marriage was in shambles. First let me say, that only by God's grace, neither of us was involved in immorality or emotional affairs.

LEROY KNEW MY COMMITMENT TO CHRIST BUT SAW THAT IT HAD LITTLE TRANSFORMING EFFECT ON MY LIFE.

As we've counseled other couples through the years, we've discovered that the destructive pattern of relating to each other that we practiced is fairly common, and sadly, we've found that includes many in ministry.

We'd only been married a few years when my husband began to withdraw and shut down emotionally. In LeRoy's words: "Here's the conflict: I admired Kim so much—her walk with the Lord, her commitment to Scripture, and her ability to counsel with people . . . she had so much to offer the body of Christ. I admired and respected these things. But her love for Christ wasn't translating to our relationship. She was often intimidating and impatient with me. In our interactions, I felt I could do nothing right, could never measure up and was totally inept. I became very inward and depressed. I was difficult to live with, resentful, and feeling helpless and hopeless because of the situation."

He entered a long season of depression and eventually a crisis of faith. Rather than having compassion for him, I was repulsed by his depression. I felt like he needed to "get his act together" and be a man! But my reaction only fueled his confusion.

He was bewildered by the fact that I was consistent in Bible study and prayer but also able to treat him with disrespect and harshness. The two didn't add up. LeRoy began to struggle spiritually because he knew my commitment to Christ but saw that it had little transforming effect on my life. At the same time that I was begging God to change him—to "make him a strong spiritual leader"—he was asking God to change me, but from what he could see, his prayers and the Word were having no effect.

"What began to develop in my heart was literally a crisis of faith because I didn't know how to deal with our marriage," he explains. "All of my feeble attempts to deal with it had been unsuccessful. I'd pray and pray and pray but it wasn't getting any better. It was getting worse. I struggled with whether God was even listening or cared. At the same time there was a great conflict because I had a commitment to preach the gospel and to pastor. The more difficult our relationship became, the greater the difficulty to continue in ministry. That which I'd held dear all my life—salvation as a young boy, surrendering to preach as a young man—began to crush me. I knew there was no escape—that I would have to continue bearing this and somehow do the best I could."

We had periods of trying everything we knew to work at our marriage, and when we saw no real progress, we'd hit a long spell of discouragement and drift into a pattern of indifference. We'd work at our marriage for a while, and then give up. When things reached a desperate point, we'd try again. This cycle was repeated over and over for several years.

The spiritual struggle that resulted from our estranged relationship eventually resulted in a drastic decision. Let me provide some background information. At the early age of thirteen, LeRoy surrendered to preach and, although he was young, he was given a surprising number of opportunities to preach. At eighteen he began pastoring a small rural church right out of high school while going to college. LeRoy knew pastoring was his calling, but eventually our marital stress brought him to a breaking point. Ten years into our marriage, LeRoy resigned his position as the senior pastor of a large and growing church. We had a toddler and a five-year-old, and he walked away not knowing if, or when, he'd ever be able to return to the pastorate.

I was shocked and devastated. I knew he was leaving what he was created to do. But he knew he couldn't continue to serve his congregation with integrity. He worked in a difficult secular job for three years before returning to the pastorate. During those years, we had a friend and fellow pastor who met with us, hoping to help us work through some of our conflicts. We also attended various marriage conferences. And I'm sure all those things were contributing factors to speak truth into our lives along the way, but we never saw lasting change until we both came to a point of humility and brokenness.

TRUE LOVE COMES CRASHING IN

We had crossed our first turbulent decade and were heading toward the second when love captured my heart. Oh, I don't mean the love I was looking for on that honeymoon night when I cried myself to sleep from (perceived) neglect. Not the love I'd been searching and grasping for. No, true love was about to come crashing in with a shattering force.

The children and I were heading out the door for their piano lessons. I was loaded down with the heavy, music-book bags draped across both shoulders, with my workbag and purse on my arm. We were running late and I was in a rush. I don't know if it was our schnauzer under my feet, or the metal storm door handle grabbing one of the tote bag handles, but somehow, I careened down the steps, and tumbled off our five-foot-high porch, landing in an awkward pile of books, totes, dog, and purse.

We made it to piano class, but I could tell something was happening in my neck, shoulders, and arm—and it wasn't pleasant. When I started to lose feeling in my fingers and hand, it was time to get things checked out. An MRI captured the lovely pictures. Three herniated discs. I spent months in physical therapy and on bed rest, trying to ward off the surgery the neurosurgeon had scheduled.

There's nothing quite like a prolonged illness to put further strain on an already fractured marriage. I wanted to be pampered and cared for. My husband was struggling under his own load and was not accustomed to me being a needy invalid. He wasn't sure what to do with me. Added to this, he had to be out of the country for a few weeks while I was still bedridden. I felt completely abandoned and unloved.

A few weeks after he returned, when my neck pain became manageable enough to get back to a more normal life, I was so thoroughly disgusted with our marital relationship that I decided to take some time to get away and think. I used the excuse that I needed to work on a study I was writing. I took off to a cabin.

> I KNEW THE WORD, BUT I WAS FAILING TO APPLY ITS TRUTHS TO MY HEART IN THE AREA THAT MATTERED MOST. I WAS FAILING TO LOVE MY HUSBAND.

It is ironic to me now (not really ironic but providential), and I shake my head when I think of the absurdity of it all . . . in my spiritually pathetic condition, here I was, heading off to write a study for women based on 1 Peter (check out 1 Peter 3:1–6 and laugh with me). What a joke. I certainly was *not* the poster child for the "meek and quiet woman" or a wife who honored her husband as this text describes.

It's interesting that 1 Peter 3 links the wife's conduct to the disobedient husband's heart being captured. More often, I've seen the opposite effect. I've seen women who've driven their lost husbands away from any interest in the gospel because of the way the wife treats them. I've been the woman who drove her Christian husband away from a passionate walk with Christ as his faith was shaken by the duplicity of my life as a believer.

I loved Jesus. I loved His Word. I never missed my daily "devotional time." But I was blind to my need. I knew the Word, but I was failing to apply its truths to my heart in the area that mattered most. I was failing to love my husband. But thankfully, God was about to give me my wake-up call.

Although I had much head knowledge, it wasn't until God opened my eyes to my heart's condition in that little cabin in the woods, that I began to get a true picture of my great need and the role my attitudes and actions played in LeRoy's depression and his lack of desire to be the spiritual leader in our home.

Shortly after settling in at the cabin, I opened my Bible to discover a little booklet written by Nancy Leigh DeMoss.[2] The diagnostic questions interspersed with snippets of Scripture cut through my hardened heart.

Questions like:

In the way I talk to and about men, do I show their God-created worth and value?

Do I make it easy for men to fulfill their God-given calling to lead in the home, the church, and the society?

Do I respond to men in ways that communicate appropriate respect and affirmation of their manhood?

Hmmm . . . honestly, no. I enjoyed intimidating men. I admired men who demonstrated capable strengths, but I had little or no compassion for what I viewed as weakness or incompetence.

Do others see in me an inner radiance and beauty that are the result of a grateful, yielded, trusting spirit?

Do I bless my family, friends, and acquaintances by speaking words that are kind and wise?

Do I seek to influence others by means of gentle words, rather than controlling or intimidating them with harsh words?

Ugh . . . (sigh) guilty. I'm the one who was confronted by the lady telling me that I walk on people, remember?

Do I receive instruction with a meek, obedient spirit?

Do I motivate my husband to grow spiritually . . . ?

I was nailed. When I opened this little booklet, I really had no idea what was waiting for me. I thought I'd breeze through it and then jump into 1 Peter.

As I started reading it, I jotted a few questions on a brand-new, yellow, eight-and-a-half by eleven notepad (which I completely filled during my stay at the cabin). I'm looking at it now. The first sentences are written in large, angry swipes with a bold, black pen:

Am I boastful?

Arrogant?

Do I try to lift myself up?

Do I feel superior to others around me?

Am I always trying to present myself in the best light?

I was trying to process what I was reading in the little booklet by asking myself some heart questions that came to mind while looking up the related Scriptures.

Remember what I said earlier? *True love was about to come crashing in with a shattering force . . .*

This is when the shattering started.

As I slowly (*slowly!*) worked my way through the questions and

Scripture, I saw how far I was from the beauty described in the verses I was reading. The verses weren't new to me—I'd taught through many of these passages. The truths weren't strange or unfamiliar. But when I slowly held up the truth of the Word, like a mirror, and put these questions honestly to my heart, my hardened exterior began splintering.

God was introducing me to a season of brokenness unlike anything I'd ever experienced.

Remember the "Deadly Three" from chapter 4? You know, those components that make up the destructive fierce woman?

Ingratitude: The Demand for "MORE!"

Pride: It's All about Me!

Fear: False Evidence Appearing Real

In contrast to those destructive tendencies, in this chapter, I want to share with you the life-giving components that God used to revive my heart and our marriage.

Humility: The Response of a True View of God

Grace: God's Empowering Response to Humility

Love: The Fruit Born from Dying-to-Self

The shattering work of love that week was brutally sweet. God opened my eyes to an ugly sight: my heart. And when I looked at myself from His vantage point, it broke me. The process of humility had begun.

HUMILITY: THE RESPONSE
OF A RIGHT VIEW OF GOD

When I blog on the topic of humility, a common response I hear is concern that I'm proposing women become "doormats." (My husband chuckles when he reads one of these comments, because he knows I'm no doormat!) Being a doormat seems to be the world's definition of humility—viewing yourself as having no worth or value and laying down for others to walk over you or take advantage of you. But that is not biblical humility.

It's obvious that humility is not a character quality many admire today. Sherry Argov, a *New York Times* bestselling author, comedian, and radio show host, offers the following advice to women:

"Humility? Don't worry. It's a treatable affliction, a mental glitch. If you catch yourself being modest or humble or any of that non-sense, correct the problem immediately . . . If someone else doesn't like your confidence, that's their problem. *Why? You always come before they do, that's why*"[3] (emphasis hers).

Her counsel flies in the face of our calling as Christ-followers. It's the flip side of God's instruction in how to treat others. Her advice echoes the attitude of our culture, which gets hung up on the idea of humility and views it from a negative perspective. This necessary virtue gets a bad rap today. Perhaps people have confused humility with unhealthy debasement.

Humility is *not* beating up yourself or submitting to abusive behavior. Humility is *not* having a negative self-image. No, not at all, in fact . . . humility's view of self is eclipsed by a right view of God. In reality, humility has little to do with how I see myself but has everything to do with how I see God. Humility is the true response to a proper view of God.

Humility opens the door for God's presence to be at home in our hearts (Isaiah 57:15) and His grace to move in to the situation at hand (James 4:6; 1 Peter 5:5). Jesus compared this condition to that of a little child. It's the recognition that we are helpless; completely dependent on Him. Humility doesn't grasp for, or demand control, but it gladly surrenders to the Master's control. When we maintain a steady gaze on God, childlike humility permeates our thoughts, attitudes, and actions.

How Humility Affects a Fierce Woman:

* She recognizes God is God and she's not, so she can release control to Him.
* She recognizes she's not always right; therefore she doesn't demand others see things her way.
* She's teachable and open to input/correction for spiritual growth from others. She's willing to be held accountable after being confronted with blind spots.
* Because she recognizes God's worth and value, her submission to Him motivates her to treat others with kindness and respect.
* She's a "soft" warrior. Her strength is not diminished by humility but is refined and tempered by it. She is soft clay in the Potter's hands.

As I worked my way through the little booklet's diagnostic questions with the accompanying Scriptures and asked God for His honest assessment, a floodgate of memories opened. I recalled the many times I'd voiced an opposing opinion harshly or countered LeRoy's leadership decision with a "superior plan." I saw how my perfectionist bent had developed into a hypercritical spirit. I recognized that my tendency to "take charge" had stifled his passion.

IS IT EASIER TO THINK OF PRACTICING HUMILITY WITH FRIENDS OR COWORKERS THAN WITH YOUR HUSBAND?

I realized that my tone, facial expressions, and attitude were a source of painful emasculation in his life. I came to grips with the ugliness of my own heart.

More than just scribbling the statements on paper in that sunlit cabin, I internalized the truth that: my superior attitude offers a low view of God and a high view of myself. I began to glimpse the reality and hideousness of my pride. And as a result, I now find it a necessary discipline to maintain a steady gaze on God, truly seeing Him as He is—high and holy, in order to maintain an honest and accurate view of myself.

When I have this focus, I can clearly see that apart from His grace, I am sinful and needy and prone to wound and harm those around me.

I'm stripped bare.

Holding a superior attitude is not an option when I realize I'm looking up to Him from the same lowly ground all stand upon. He is God alone and I'm compelled to bow before Him in humility and worship.

"Do nothing from selfishness or empty conceit, but with humility of mind regard one another as more important than yourselves" (Philippians 2:3 NASB).

Does this verse give you an uncomfortable feeling? Or does it sound impossible to you, like it does to me? Do you find it a little offensive? Is it easier to think of practicing humility with friends or coworkers than with your husband? This verse is tucked into one of the New Testament's weightiest passages, where we find God humbling Himself by adorning skin for His mission to die on a cross.

And we are instructed to have this same mindset!

Mind blowing, isn't it?

There in that cabin, I slipped to my knees and poured it all out to my heavenly Father. I confessed. I had bellyaching crying jags. I ranted and wrestled with it all for hours at a time. I didn't surrender easily; I feared letting go of my position of control in our relationship. I was fearful of interacting with LeRoy in humility. My mind reeled with crazy thoughts: *If I let him know that I realize how wrong I've been and ask his forgiveness, he'll take advantage of me, he'll make me pay for the years of pain I've inflicted.*

But God didn't leave me in a despairing heap on the floor. He came with healing grace.

GRACE: GOD'S EMPOWERING
RESPONSE TO HUMILITY

God never requires us to obey Him without providing the power for obedience. As God began opening my eyes to my self-centeredness, my lack of love, my harsh and demanding spirit, I was flattened. I was undone. I remember being completely overwhelmed with the realization that I was responsible for much of our marital pain.

I told God I didn't know where to start or how to deal with the enormity of the mess I'd made. But that's the thing that's so amazing about God. He's all about extending His precious mercy to those who ask. His tender heart of compassion responds to our need. God delights to show up in our lives when we admit we can't do it on our own.

Humility opens the doorway for God to move in with grace that transforms, grace to overcome the temptation to sin, grace that brings rich growth and maturity. The thing we most desperately need in our marriages is God's grace. *What I most desperately need in my life is God's grace.* When I acknowledge that need and cry out to God for grace (His empowering help for that specific situation), He pours it out in full measure and creative ways.

"Clothe yourselves, all of you, with humility toward one another, for 'God opposes the proud but gives grace to the humble'" (1 Peter 5:5).

As I cried out to Him for wisdom and help in moving beyond my point of despair, He led me to a passage in 2 Chronicles 20. The chapter opens with messengers alerting the king of Judah to danger on the horizon. They would soon be surrounded by a multitude of enemies. Jehoshaphat was filled with fear. He was overwhelmed by a situation over which he had no control.

". . . we are powerless against this great horde that is coming against us. We do not know what to do, but our eyes are on you" (2 Chronicles 20:12).

The king was unprepared to face opposition of this magnitude and he knew that, humanly speaking, there was no possibility for victory. But he had a proper response. In his distress, King Jehoshaphat took his dilemma to God and appealed to Him for help. He was reminded that the battle (as well as each of our battles) did not belong to him, but "the battle . . . is God's" (v. 15).

A simple truth.

As I focused on this simple truth, it suddenly occurred to me how silly it was to grasp for control, to use my fierceness as a shield of protection, or to depend on my efforts to "make my marriage work" like I wanted it to.

I knew what I had to do. My eyes were finally opened to the role I played in our relational struggles, and I had to come clean with LeRoy and ask his forgiveness. I was filled with fear at the thought of fleshing out all God was showing me. I feared LeRoy's reaction. I feared that I wouldn't be able to change or respond differently, but I knew I had to follow what God was leading me to do.

I had to lay down control; I had to prostrate myself before God and let Him fight this battle.

I had to cry out for His grace to respond differently in my role as a wife.

I had to trust God.

Jehoshaphat bowed his head with his face to the ground, and all Judah and the inhabitants of Jerusalem fell down before the Lord, worshiping the Lord. The Levites, from the sons of the Kohathites and of the sons of the Korahites, stood up to praise the Lord God of Israel, with a very loud voice.

They rose early in the morning and went out to the wilderness of Tekoa; and when they went out, Jehoshaphat stood and said, "Listen to me, O Judah and inhabitants of Jerusalem, put your trust in the

Lord your God and you will be established. Put your trust in His prophets and succeed" (2 Chronicles 20:18–20 NASB).

I had spent five days seeking God alone at the cabin. When I arrived I was a haughty, hard-hearted, self-righteous wife, convinced that my husband was responsible for our misery. As my time away drew to a close, my heart had softened and turned completely. Now it was time to face my husband in repentance and seek his forgiveness. I needed God's grace in full measure for a conversation beyond my natural inclination or ability. I left the cabin a somewhat fearful, but still fierce, woman. I was starting down the road to becoming a soft warrior.

How Grace Affects a Fierce Woman:

* She recognizes that grace is the great leveling factor— leaving no room for a superior attitude.
* She keeps her gaze fixed on Christ, focusing on His position and character.
* She rests in the knowledge that God is sovereign and always at work; therefore she can trust Him to accomplish what is needed in her life.
* She cries out to Him for help rather than forging ahead in her own strength.
* As she learns to walk and respond consistently in grace, she is conformed to the image and beauty of Christ.

LIVING OUT LOVE

You may have reached a point similar to where I was before my stay at the cabin. You may have determined to harden your heart or erect walls to insulate yourself from the pain that love can bring. For me, I had to learn the hard way that "true love" is much different than the selfish version of love I'd seen promoted all my life. As C. S. Lewis says,

To love at all is to be vulnerable. Love anything, and your heart will certainly be wrung and possibly broken. If you want to make sure of keeping it intact, you must give your heart to no one, not even to an animal. Wrap it carefully round with hobbies and little luxuries; avoid all entanglements; lock it up safe in the casket or coffin of your selfishness. But in that casket—safe, dark, motionless, airless—it will change. It will not be broken; it will become unbreakable, impenetrable, irredeemable.[4]

I've learned that true love means "living out love," which is much different than the world's idea of "falling in love." I've learned that practicing true love does not promise a painless exchange. It doesn't guarantee the results you may be hoping for. In fact, living out this kind of love requires a painful release and even a type of death. But from that death, beautiful fruit is born.

I've shared with you that our first experience of true love originates at the cross. First John (NASB) gives a clear definition of love: "We know love by this, that He laid down His life for us . . ." This portion of the verse is where first He gives, then we receive love. We receive the benefit of our gracious God condescending to capture our hearts, bearing the full weight of our sin, removing our shame and guilt at the cross.

But the process of love doesn't end here.

Finish reading the verse in order to appreciate love's full obligation and beauty:

"We know love by this, that He laid down His life for us; and we ought to lay down our lives for the brethren" (1 John 3:16 NASB).

LOVE: THE FRUIT BORN FROM DYING TO SELF

Did you get that? Love is laying down our lives, our self-centered agendas, our "all about me" attitudes, our selfish selves. The death that love requires is . . . mine. Love is laying it all down in order to truly give rather than take. But this kind of love, true love, can only be birthed through the grace that is the fruit of humility.

THE PURSUIT OF LOVE CAN ONLY COME BY TRAVELING THE ROAD OF HUMILITY.

Marriage carries with it daily opportunities for expressing this kind of love in real-life-hard-against-the-grain situations. It can be the greatest sanctifying agent in your life, but in order for sanctification (growth in living out love) to occur, humility is the needed mindset.

Humility is the heart posture before God and your mate that provides fertile ground for bearing this vital fruit of the Spirit. Andrew Murray puts it bluntly:

"Our love to God will be found to be a delusion, except as its truth is proved in standing the test of daily life with our fellow-men . . . humility toward men will be the only sufficient proof that our humility before God is real . . . and there is no *love* without humility as its root"[5] (emphasis mine).

The pursuit of love can only come by traveling the road of humility. Love is not self-seeking, thus love must be birthed through humility. At the bowing of the head, the humbling of the heart, grace finds entrance. And grace empowers a fierce woman to truly love. Kristin expresses this idea in a note she wrote to me recently:

"I think it's *finally* all coming together for me. The first many years of my marriage, I thought things were all about me. Then I started learning what marriage was supposed to be and what love really is—something for me to *do*. Then after at least fifteen years or so, I started to see how everything changes when you really do concentrate on loving that other person—and how your emotions follow."

STEP INTO THE RIVER OF LOVE

True love flows in a reciprocal stream. It's a complementary dance of receiving and giving in kind. It's what Jesus was referring to when He startled the religious leaders with the simple call to love God and love others (Matthew 22:34–40). And this is the call Jesus extends to us as His disciples. But, don't miss this—the cost of this discipleship (living out love) is . . . *death*!

"And He was saying to them all, 'If anyone wishes to come after Me, he must deny himself, and take up his cross daily and follow Me. For whoever wishes to save his life will lose it, but whoever loses his life for My sake, he is the one who will save it'" (Luke 9:23–24 NASB).

Love is painful. Love is vulnerable. Love plunges into relationship knowing it will encounter pain and rejection. Love is what compelled God to create, even while knowing man would rebel, knowing separation would occur, knowing the fall would require redemption in order for reconciliation to take place. True love requires personal sacrifice and sometimes, even death.

Reading these words, you may be tempted to imagine that true love is being willing to step in and rescue someone who's in mortal danger by taking heroic measures, which may cost your life. That type of literally laying down our lives in physical death to rescue a loved one is rarely required. But in order to cultivate true love, a true death is required—the death to self. And the kind of self-death I'm describing is not a onetime occurrence. It will need to be repeated daily, even moment by moment. This death allows us to live the crucified life described by the apostle Paul: "I have been crucified with Christ; and it is no longer I who live, but Christ lives in me; and the life which I now live in the flesh I live by faith in the Son of God, who loved me and gave Himself up for me" (Galatians 2:20 NASB).

The crucified life enables you to bear the fruit of love, which only comes through the humility of dying. Letting go, laying down your life, in order to pick up the cross to die allows Christ to live and love through you. It allows you to experience intimate unity with Him as well as with your mate.

Putting to death self-centered agendas, selfish pursuits, self-motivated plans, self-pity, and self-absorption will require laying it all down. It may be a painful release, but from that death, the river of love will flow. From that death bursts precious fruit: "Truly, truly, I say to you, unless a grain of wheat falls into the earth and dies, it remains alone; but if it dies, it bears much fruit" (John 12:24).

Are you cringing each time I mention death and dying? Do you think I'm proposing a view of marriage that promotes spousal abuse or requires you to suffer under a demanding husband in silence? Trust me, I'm not advocating that type of model. True love will require dying to self, but unselfish love may involve humble confrontations as well (we'll cover that in chapter 10).

PLEASE HOLD ON TO HOPE. GOD IS AT WORK.

Because of the love we've been shown by Christ, we have the ability to love others. His love becomes an overflowing stream; a steady river working its way from the Source throughout creation. Love flows from the Savior, to you, then through you to your mate, your children, family, and friends, flowing from them back to you, and from you back to the Savior. True love delights in the widening of its banks to quench an ever-growing number of thirsty souls.

How Love Affects a Fierce Woman:
* She travels the road of humility and opens the doorway to grace.
* She embraces the call to follow Christ, knowing it requires a painful release—death to self.
* She lays down her life by plunging into the love of Christ.

* She steps into the river of love and becomes a reciprocal stream of receiving and giving love.
* She loves God and others with the abandon of the fierce but soft warrior who knows no retreat.

I'm so thankful that God is gracious. He knew my heart. He knew I loved Him, but with a young and naïve type of love that stopped short when it came to the hard choices of true love. In mercy, He opened my eyes to what true love is and how far from that I was. When I was festering with self-centered garbage and intense pain, He didn't leave me wallowing in the mess I'd made. He rescued me from myself.

What about you?

Is He opening your eyes to anything you need to see?

In the next four chapters, I'll be sharing with you the process of using your fierceness to take on the mantle of the soft warrior as you battle for your marriage. I'll be giving you practical suggestions for fleshing out love to your husband.

Please hold on to hope. God is at work.

Perhaps your marital struggles are far different from what LeRoy and I experienced. Maybe you're wishing your husband could retreat to a cabin so that God would open his eyes and deal with him! I've been there. I thought I'd never see changes, and although my husband is now the joy of my life, at one time he was so distant and swallowed up in dark depression, I thought he'd never recover. But God changed both of us.

God delights in transforming His children and their lives, and this includes your situation. I've been amazed by the life-changing power that occurs when God's grace enters through humility—but it has to begin in at least one partner. And when one starts down the road of humility, so often the other joins in.

No matter how severe the challenges or wide the divide, my husband has a great word that he offers to couples whenever we do marriage counseling:

"Humility is the key to overcoming every marital problem."

✳ HEART ISSUES ✑

1. How do you define humility? Is this one of the character traits that others would use to describe you? How would your approach to others and your response to difficulty look different if you were characterized by this virtue?

2. Humility is often confused with wimpiness. Humility is not a personality trait but rather a work of the Spirit. Consider how the men in these verses were fierce in their passion for Christ but humble in their approach: Acts 13:46; 2 Corinthians 3:12; 10:1–2; Ephesians 6:20; 1 Thessalonians 2:2.

3. First Peter is filled with instruction and encouragement for believers who are experiencing true suffering. Wedged in the middle of this book is a message to wives that challenges our approach to our husbands. I find it interesting that this message is followed in chapter 4 with the key to serving others.

   As a good steward of God's manifold grace, we serve with the strength He supplies (1 Peter 4:8–11). Keep this passage in mind as you read the instructions in 1 Peter 2:21–3:6.

4. Prayerfully read through 1 John 4 before answering the following questions:

   According to 1 John 4:7, where does love originate?

   How is His love manifested in and through us (1 John 4:9–11)?

Reread through 1 John 4:20–21, replacing the words he
with she, his with hers, and his brother with her
husband.

Where is your heart today? Is there anything God is asking
you to lay down or let go?

How are you demonstrating humility in your marriage
relationship?

Have you developed the practice of depending on God's
grace as you relate to your husband?

How are you demonstrating love to your husband?

CHAPTER 6

Love from the Inside Out

❧❧❧

"If I love to be loved more than to love, to be served more than to serve, then I know nothing of Calvary love."

— Amy Carmichael[1]

I think I was just eight or nine years old when I had my first lesson in manipulating men. I remember it vividly. I was watching an old movie. (I would love to find that movie today and view it with my husband!)

I don't know the title of the comedy and can't recall who played in it, but I remember being impressed with the power of manipulation as I watched. The plotline focused on a newlywed couple. The young bride's mother gave her daughter the "secret weapon" for marriage: a book on puppy training. Her mother told her to use the same principles of reward and punishment from the pet manual and apply them to her relationship with her new husband. The mom claimed she'd used this technique for years on her husband with great success! I don't remember much else about the movie; it seems the young husband finally figured out he was playing the role of "puppy-in-training," which caused a huge conflict, but I feel sure it finished with the typical "happily ever after" ending.

When women hear our story, they want to know how we reached the point where we are now. When I tell them that I never would have dreamed it could be this good, that we would be able to enjoy each other this much, and are experiencing a relationship that is better than any I could have imagined, women want to know—how?

First of all, this book is not a self-help manual intended to fix your husband. If you approach these next chapters as a behavior modification technique to use in manipulating your mate, you're missing the whole point. The only stories that truly end with the couple living "happily ever after" are marriages transformed by the power of the gospel—not by manipulative techniques.

In fact, if you've skipped the last chapter, I'm asking you to please return to it and soak in it for a while, because the practical suggestions I'll be sharing in the next four chapters need to flow from a heart that has been changed and beats for the purpose of glorifying God. These are not Twelve Easy Steps to Getting the Man of Your Dreams! When we reach the place where we are willing to die to our selfishness and walk in humility, and are seeking to love our husbands in the way I shared in the last chapter, we'll demonstrate that love in real-life situations. But this has to be a process that comes from the inside (heart change) and works its way out (practical demonstration).

Our "happily ever after" didn't start right away—it took time. When I went home from the cabin to ask LeRoy's forgiveness, he was reserved and watchful. There wasn't a big joyous celebration. He had long since given up on our relationship and was skeptical that anything would improve. The inner change God did in my heart needed to be lived out over the course of time.

Remember the Fierce Woman/Fearful Man cycle I mentioned earlier? Your marriage may be caught in that destructive cycle and appreciation is a key to breaking the cycle. Your husband may never admit this to you, but he may fear you. He may be terrified to make decisions because he feels he never does anything right, is unable to please you, or could never measure up to your expectations. Or he may be intimidated by your fierceness or passion. Years before, LeRoy had slipped into "self-preservation mode" because I had (unintentionally) established a home environment where he felt threatened:

> I'm very noncombative. Like a lot of men, I was passive when relating to my wife when I should've stood up to take leadership but I felt I was no match for her intensity. It seemed like I could never measure up to what she wanted, and would never be able to measure up. I felt like I was not the husband she wanted, not the husband she expected me to be, and not the husband she needed. I certainly wasn't turning out to be the husband I'd hoped to be.
>
> As a man, I hated to admit it, but fear gripped my soul. Fear paralyzed me. I was afraid of my wife—afraid of disappointing her again. I am introverted by nature, but I'm not by nature a fearful person. I was afraid of making decisions. I was afraid of failure. I began to retreat further and further into a protective mode.

If your man fears criticism, emotional conflict, or a demeaning response from you, that fear may manifest itself in a number of ways including: isolation, building walls of protection, angry retaliation, or simmering resentment, all of which will destroy your marital unity and intimacy.

In order for my husband to be willing to leave his cave and come out of hiding, I had to prepare a place where he felt safe. Perhaps your husband's occasional lack of communication, grumpy disposition, or lack of affection is the result of not getting a good night's sleep . . . but if this behavior is a pattern, it may be that he feels unsafe in your presence.

Appreciation provides a safe place for our men. Even if your husband seems indifferent to your opinion of him, if he's like most men, he craves your appreciation. In the next four chapters I want to share with you some of the ways I learned to live out my love for my husband by using the acronym APPRECIATION.

A desire for appreciation is a recurring theme that LeRoy and I hear when talking with men about their marital struggles. In her book *For Women Only*, Shaunti Feldhahn states that out of the more than one thousand men she surveyed, only "one man in four felt actively appreciated by his family." Perhaps the more eye-opening statistic is that "44 percent of men actually felt *unappreciated* at home."[2] The italicized word is her emphasis, but I'm emphasizing it with her!

Gary Neuman, a family counselor and bestselling author, performed a two-year study on why men have affairs. According to his research, the majority of men cheated on their wives—get this—not because of any sexual attraction to another woman *but because of an emotional disconnection to their wife.*

The men stated the number one reason for this disconnection was feeling underappreciated.

"What I found is that men are far more insecure than they let on, and they do want to please their wives and feel valued. They like to win and as long as they are winning with their wife then they stay in the game." According to Neuman: "Appreciation is what they first and foremost get from the mistress."[3]

I don't share that information as the reason we should show appreciation to our husbands, and I don't recommend this approach as a safeguard merely to "keep your man from wandering." Appreciation communicates to your husband that he matters to you. It lets him know that he's valuable. Demonstrating appreciation is the response of true love and that is why I'm committed to practicing it. Let's start with the first three letters.

APPRECIATION

A: ADMIRE AND AFFIRM

Several years ago I traveled with LeRoy to a church where he was the guest preacher. I made the typical stop in the ladies restroom before the morning service and struck up a conversation with a woman there. She was holding a book in her hand written by a popular Christian author, so I asked if she was enjoying it. "Oh yes. It's very good! Reading an inspirational book is the way I get fed during the Sunday morning service!" I was a little stunned by her reply and started to tell her that my husband would be preaching, and it was worth listening to, but I restrained myself. My shock over the incident only increased when after the service, my husband and I left the church to meet the pastor and his wife for lunch. When we reached the restaurant, the pastor introduced us to his wife—the woman I'd met in the restroom!

> **APPRECIATION**
> » **A**dmire and affirm

I can only imagine how her lack of encouragement and support affected him. I had never met the couple before, and there are always two sides to every marital story, but treating your husband in a manner that communicates he's insignificant or unimportant is poison in any marriage. You may feel as though you currently see nothing to admire in your man, but you can learn to cultivate admiration for him.

Start the process by looking at the basics and being grateful for him: Has your husband remained faithful to you? Would he protect you if you were in physical danger? Is he contributing by providing income for your family? Does he attempt to be a good father? Is he a good neighbor?

TAKE A WALK DOWN MEMORY LANE AND REVISIT WHAT DREW YOU TO YOUR MAN.

None of these may apply to your situation today, but when you married him, surely he had some qualities you admired. Try to see glimpses of those same characteristics that may be lying dormant and communicate your appreciation for those things. A heart change toward your husband begins by mentally taking captive the negatives and focusing on the positives (2 Corinthians 10:3–5; Philippians 4:4–9). Take a walk down memory lane and revisit what drew you to your man.

Recently I was on the university campus where LeRoy and I first met. Nothing had changed; the classrooms looked exactly the same as when I first arrived on campus. I was surprised by my reaction—I actually felt tingles as I walked down the halls of the building where we had our first class together. I started reliving those early days of young love and I couldn't wait to get home and cuddle with my man!

You may not be able to physically return to your courting grounds, and you may have many painful years and experiences wedged between then and now, but I encourage you to review the good times. Peruse through your mental memory card and linger over snapshots of your first conversations, first kiss, and the moment when you knew you wanted to spend the rest of your life with this man. And if possible, it's a great idea to take an afternoon to relive early encounters by visiting those places with him. Let him know how precious those memories are to you.

If you are struggling with loneliness and isolation in your marriage, please don't focus on where you are now. Find joy in recounting times of intimacy and oneness. Find hope in the fact that

God wants to restore your marital unity even more than you do. You've not yet seen the rest of the story.

Affirm Often!

Our husbands need our affirmation. This is at the heart of the "helper" role. Your man needs to hear your voice of approval. He needs to hear you say, "I believe in you!" We have daily opportunities to slip affirming words into our husband's ears, but too often a man's efforts go unnoticed, so be intentional in watching for them. Give at least one encouraging statement daily and watch your husband come out from hiding!

Mike was trying to justify his relationship with his live-in girlfriend by explaining to my husband how "marriage changes things"—and not for the better. "Living with my girlfriend who loves me is better than being married to someone who hates me!" According to statistics, Mike's statement probably reflects a lot of people's sentiments right now. The number of cohabiting couples has doubled since the 1990s, according to a recent report from the Pew Research Center.[4]

Before he moved in with his girlfriend, Mike was married to another woman. Throughout the conversation Mike referred to his ex-wife as "Ms. Lucifer" several times and summed up living together versus marriage this way: "When I come home to my girlfriend, she's waiting at the door for me with hugs and kisses. When I used to come home to Ms. Lucifer, all I got was (expletive) and drama!"

His impassioned pitch for the superiority of cohabitation over marriage got me thinking about how different a marriage might look if the wife determined to give her husband the same treatment (or better) than she did when she was "the girlfriend" rather than "the wife." I often hear women complain about inattentive and unromantic husbands, but I wonder if a husband might be more responsive to a wife who puts effort into giving him affirmation.

How are you doing in showing your husband that you're still crazy about him? Let's look at some simple ways you can admire and affirm.

Show Affection

Do you intentionally take time to stop what you're doing to greet your husband in a way that shows you've missed him and you're glad he's home? Do you share kisses and long hugs frequently? Do you surprise him with intimate advances? Do you tell him you love him—OFTEN?

Let Him Know He Matters

Do you look him in the eye when he's talking to you? Do you make time with him your first priority, or are you only giving him partial attention as you check Facebook, do email, make a shopping list, or chat on the phone with a friend?

Show Interest

Do you ask him about things that are important to him? Do you applaud his efforts at work and encourage him when he's feeling inadequate? Do you take time to engage in conversation about things he's interested in?

Flirt

Do you give him playful attention and treat him like he's the hottest guy ever? Do you leave him little mushy love notes that raise his blood pressure a bit? Surprise him with little gifts in unexpected places?

Thank Him

Do you demonstrate gratitude for things easily taken for granted? Do you thank him for chores he does around the house, for reading to the children, saying the blessing over a meal, opening a door for you, or for providing income? Is "thank you" a regular phrase you say to him?

Encourage

Do you brag on him to his face and to others in front of him? Do you let him know specific ways you are proud of him? Do you affirm him for making difficult choices? Do you remind him of things he's done well when he's struggling with fear of failure?

After my eye-opening experience at the cabin, but before seeing any measurable effect on LeRoy, I was in conversation with a friend. I was sharing with her some things I admire about him and she asked me a simple question. "Have you told him that?" The question stunned me at first because I realized that, although I'd often thought about these things, I rarely voiced my admiration to him.

VERBAL APPRECIATION IS LIKE FUEL FOR THEIR MOTOR.

I stammered and replied, "Well, he already knows he's good at that . . ." Internally I was thinking, *He's already cocky and prideful enough, I don't need to fuel it with a bunch of compliments that will make his head swell.*

She encouraged me to start voicing everything I could that would relay my admiration. As I began doing that, I was amazed to see how hungry he was for verbal affirmation. I hadn't realized how much men need the wife's positive reinforcement. It's like fuel for their motor.

My reaction back then was similar to some of the female readers who responded to a recent blog I posted. It contained a questionnaire for men asking them to share how women can encourage men. These women expressed surprise after reading the honest confessions from men about their need for our verbal encouragement and affirmation:

"Oh Wow! thank you so much to the men that have and will respond to this post, please keep them coming . . . it's a real eye opener to what I believe my husband must be thinking and has blessed me tremendously . . . Now I gotta get into action, Lord helping me."

"I never knew men were so fragile. These comments are helping me immensely and I have much to pray about now. I want to support and encourage my husband and had no idea how to do that. Thanks to all the men who have commented. I never realized what a lousy wife I've been until now. I'm motivated to change with this new insight. My dear husband is going to get a new woman starting today!"

Or you may be the woman reading this and thinking, *My husband is the one who needs to change—not me! I wish my husband would do something I could affirm! There's nothing admirable that I can see in him . . . I can't get him off the couch to do anything!*

If it's difficult for you to sincerely admire your husband, ask God to open your eyes to positive character traits you're missing and creative ways to affirm your man. I've seen men who've lost all desire for living revive and rise to the challenges of responsibility when they know a woman believes in them. If this sounds like a description of your situation, I'm not saying you're responsible for your husband's laziness or depression, but I'm asking you to consider whether your husband has received inspiration from you or condemnation. This isn't always the case—but I wonder how many men have turned to the couch for relief because they're paralyzed by a crushed spirit.

"A man's spirit will endure sickness, but a crushed spirit who can bear?" (Proverbs 18:14).

In order to genuinely admire and affirm someone, it helps to understand what kind of challenges they face and what makes them tick. It helps to climb into their skin.

P: PUT YOURSELF IN HIS SKIN

Several years ago I was asked to speak at a prayer conference that took place about two hours away from our home. My husband offered to be my escort and chauffeur. The conference ended on a Saturday evening and I was totally exhausted as I climbed into our ride—a *lovely* (very used), maroon 1985 full-size Ford van. My husband loaded our luggage in the pouring rain and jumped in to start home. About an hour into the winding mountain drive, we had a blowout.

APPRECIATION

Admire and affirm
» **P**ut yourself in his skin

He managed to pull off the road onto the very narrow shoulder that sloped off to a sharp, Ozark Mountain descent. He went to check things out. When he opened the van door to pull out some tools, he suggested that I lie down on the couch in the back and try to get some sleep. This was going to take awhile. The rain was still coming down in sheets.

An operation that he could normally perform in a matter of moments, took closer to two hours because of several

MY LACK OF APPRECIATION LEFT HIM FEELING PRETTY WHIPPED.

complications: the torrential downpour, a tire jack that kept sliding down the muddy incline, tire lug nuts that wouldn't cooperate with the tire tool thingy, traffic that sent road spray shooting into his face every few moments . . . it was a bad deal.

Completely soaked and physically spent, my faithful road warrior climbed back in the vehicle. In my groggy, half-conscious state, it seemed like I'd only been asleep a few minutes. I raised my head from the couch in the back to cheerily call out, "Well, that wasn't too bad!" He turned his mud-streaked face to look back in the darkness with a reply, but I'd already settled back into nap position.

He'll be reading this at some point—and thank you again for

extending grace, honey!—and amazingly, he laughs about this story now. But at the time, my lack of appreciation left him feeling pretty whipped. I missed the opportunity to loudly cheer and applaud his manly victory over the wild elements of nature and machinery! That was a prime opportunity to voice a *loud* affirmation and express admiration for tackling a difficult challenge—*and I missed it*!

I'm not justifying my thoughtless behavior, but one reason I failed to fully appreciate my husband's accomplishment that night was that I hadn't experienced all he'd been through. I hadn't dealt with the stubborn lug nuts or the road spray in my face. I hadn't struggled in knee-deep mud with a worn-out tire jack or had to work on a steep incline in blinding rain (no, because I was napping in the nice warm van!). In order to truly appreciate his service to me that night, I needed to practice the important process of empathy.

If someone could bottle and sell empathy, they'd probably win the Nobel Prize, find the solution to world peace, and put divorce lawyers out of business. When I empathize with others, I'm identifying with them through imagining what they're experiencing. I'm crawling into their skin to view the world through their eyes and I'm vicariously experiencing their joys and sorrows, pain and happiness, pressures and disappointments. When I put myself in their shoes, compassion and understanding are birthed.

To help us get a handle on what makes men feel appreciated, let's have a few men share their thoughts. I hope this will help us "climb into a man's skin" (um . . . vicariously). I've gathered several comments from various sources and compiled a list of answers from men that I've found helpful in giving me insight on what communicates appreciation to a husband.

* Say "Thank you" more frequently and mean it.
* LISTEN!!

* Watch for signals—men can't always put into words
  what they're feeling.
* Hand out compliments—men like to know they're
  doing a good job.
* Accept us—stop trying to change us!
* I'd love to hear my wife say, "You've got what it takes!"
* Let me know when you like something I've done.
* Remind me when I've done well previously.

After attempting a home improvement project, Dan said, "This week I picked out the type and color of new shingles for the roof. My wife said they looked terrific when she saw them applied . . . Phew!"

I can just imagine Dan's fear and trepidation as he entered the hardware store. "Will she say this color works? Are these shingles the ones she'd pick?" Then as he worked away on the roof, "What if she hates this? Maybe I should've gone with the grey color instead . . ."

I wonder how many husbands carry out their role of protector and provider hoping to hear "You are awesome!!" but instead are greeted with "Why did you do it that way?" or "Well, you sure messed that up, didn't you?"

James 2:8 describes love's royal law as an action of empathy. "Love your neighbor as yourself." Put yourself in his skin, consider how you would want to be treated and use that knowledge to demonstrate love to your husband. At least nine times this love law is repeated throughout Scripture, spanning both testaments. The same principle is reiterated in the golden rule as we are commanded to treat others in the way we'd want to be treated.

Empathy births compassion. Compassion is the necessary ingredient for loving the unlovable.

I've compiled some ways to help in the process of "crawling into your husband's skin," and I hope you'll add your own ideas as you consider the specifics of your situation.

* When he's irritable, remind yourself that "hurting people hurt others" and consider where his heart may be.
* Enter his world at every opportunity.
* Ask him about spending a day with him on the job to give you a better understanding of the pressures he faces.
* Become familiar with his background, family relationships and history, early childhood, and pivotal events of his life in order to gain a better understanding of how he views the world and what impact these experiences have on his responses to you and others.
* Become acquainted with his hobbies and interests; find out what his passions are and why.
* LISTEN!! Ask him to help you understand pressures he's facing by talking to you about them (without jumping in with unwanted advice!). Invite him to share with you his goals and dreams.

You may be thinking this is pretty one-sided and wondering why you have to be the one putting in all this effort. My response to that is: love is birthed through dying to self, remember? Rewards come from dying. We find freedom in Christ and in turn that freedom flows into your marriage. LeRoy and I have experienced that beautiful freedom. Here is how he describes our relationship now:

> Where at one point I was so paralyzed by fear that I wouldn't even make a decision because I knew there could be repercussions or negative consequences, now I don't fear a reprisal.

Now I have freedom to go to God, to pray, to lead, and even if it doesn't turn out to be the greatest decision, if I fumble or drop the ball in some way, I know that Kim will say, "Well, you're still my man, and we'll trust the Lord together." I know that she'll give encouragement. I once thought our marriage was going to crush us both, be the death of me, but now we experience freedom and joy in our relationship. It is a safe place.

P: PRAY LIKE YOU MEAN IT

I remember the days when I would pray, "God, get 'im" prayers, you know, prayers from a heart of offense and self-pity: "Do you see how

A P P R E C I A T I O N

Admire and affirm
Put yourself in his skin
» Pray like you mean it

he's treating me? Convict him . . . show him his hard heart . . . make him miserable!" Today my conversations with the Lord about my husband sound a lot different. If we're willing to practice empathy, we can pray with greater understanding of our husband's daily challenges and spiritual needs. If we pray for them in light of the grace we've been shown, prayers will take on a less self-centered tone and turn to humble and loving intercession.

I don't pray through these every day, but through the years some of the Scriptures I've prayed for my husband include praying for personal integrity (Psalm 15:1–2); for hope, peace, and joy (Romans 15:13); for wisdom and direction (Ephesians 1:17–19); for a marriage beyond our imagination (Ephesians 3:20–21); for fruitfulness through different stages of life (Psalm 92:12–15).

These are just a few examples of prayers for my mate. I've learned that praying effectively can *not* happen if I'm sinfully angry, filled with self-pity or self-centered motives, or holding on to known sin (James 1:20; Psalm 66:18).

Our husbands need us standing in the gap for them as prayer warriors on their behalf. The enemy would love nothing more than to see you spending your mental and emotional energy dismembering your husband rather than going to your knees to intercede for his spiritual growth or salvation.

If you are married to a nonbeliever, the challenges that come as a result of spiritual disunity probably puts more stress on the marital relationship than any other conflict. Many women in that situation express that they face a temptation to use loud and obnoxious pressure tactics with the hopes of waking up a husband to his need for Christ. In fact one woman recently admitted, "I didn't share my new faith with my husband; I pushed, forced, and shoved." But this situation is one where we need to pray more than we preach.

Edie chose to let her actions speak rather than her words. She held her tongue when she was tempted to clobber her man with the gospel. As a fierce woman, she chose the route of a soft warrior.

She invited the young women in her Bible study group to join her in praying for John's salvation. She told them she was convicted to literally follow the principle found in 1 Peter 3:1–2 and "win her husband without a word" by letting her behavior be her gospel message. She practiced self-control and patience as she waited.

A few short weeks after the group started praying for John's salvation, Edie discovered she was pregnant with their first child. Her prayer intensity increased as she cried out to God to give her child a Christian father. Weeks turned to months, then a year, but she saw no signs of spiritual life; if anything, his spiritual disinterest only increased.

Edie was tempted to resort to nagging, preaching, or begging John to turn to Christ, but her fierce determination never wavered. She believed Jesus could win him without a word from her. I believe her self-control and patient Christlike lifestyle prepared his heart for a most unusual encounter.

While coming home from a business trip, Edie's husband switched his airline reservations to an earlier flight. God was rerouting his day in order for him to spend the afternoon beside a certain seatmate. Little did John know, but this seatmate had started his day with a heavy burden to share the gospel with whoever sat beside him on the plane.

> YOU MAY BE IN SUCH A HARD PLACE THAT YOU HAVE NO DESIRE TO PRAY FOR YOUR HUSBAND AT ALL AND "GET 'IM" PRAYERS ARE LIGHT COMPARED TO WHAT YOU FEEL.

Moments after his plane landed, John interrupted Edie's day with a phone call announcing that he had just become a Christian. Later she described him as uncharacteristically emotional and passionate as he relayed his fresh salvation testimony.

Edie's determination to obey God's direction in "winning her husband without a word" is an example of a woman fiercely interceding for her man. She was one who grabbed on to the hem of God's will and didn't let go.

You may be in such a hard place that you have no desire to pray for your husband at all and "Get 'im" prayers are light compared to what you feel. You may be in deep waters without hope of rescue. I want to assure you, the Savior sees, knows, and cares. Micah encourages us to wait for the God of salvation—put no confidence even in the members of our own household—but look to the Lord for our help. "But as for me, I will look to the Lord; I will wait for the God of my salvation; my God will hear me" (Micah 7:7).

Pour out your heart to the Father and let Him know where you are; ask Him to give you His heart to intercede. The exciting and encouraging thing about praying for your husband is that *God is on your side* if you're praying for your husband to be all God created him to be. God wants that more than you do, so you can pray in full confidence that what you're asking is according to His will (1 John 5:14).

As his bedmate and life partner, you know your husband in a way no one else does, and you're able to pray for him in a more intimate and knowledgeable way than anyone else on earth can. Don't take that unique position lightly, but press into your responsibility to love your husband well by interceding in spiritual battle by praying for him. You may have prayed for your husband for years, but I want to encourage you to hang in there and continue praying earnestly for your man.[5]

⁂ HEART ISSUES ⌒

1. To appreciate something means we value or highly regard that object. I appreciate my car. It's old, but fairly dependable. It's not flashy, but it fits my style. Not many would go after it, but I value it. (My husband would say I'm describing him at this point.)

It's easy to place value on an inanimate object that doesn't inflict emotional pain or leave me reeling from feelings of rejection, but it's hard to value someone when they keep breaking my heart. If you've reached the point where you have no desire to even attempt to show appreciation to your husband, try to separate your *feelings* from the fact that your husband is one who is valuable. He is created in God's image and given life by Him for a purpose. He matters. And God desires for you to help him be the man God has created him to be.

He wants you to evoke the kind of motivation that one husband expressed to me: "I feel more of a call to be God's man when I'm with her."

Go back and review the ways you can "Admire and Affirm" your husband. If you have no desire to attempt these, ask God to renew your heart. Ask him to fill you with appreciation for your husband and the desire to show love to him.

2. Appreciation provides a safe place for our men. Does your husband feel safe with you? How do you know? Does he freely voice his opinions if they differ from yours? Have you ever asked him whether he fears discussions with you or your reaction to his decisions?

    Revive Our Hearts produced a video that shares our marriage testimony. Many couples have found this a helpful tool in addressing their relationship struggles. Consider viewing the video together and asking your husband if he can relate to the struggles LeRoy expressed: http://www.youtube.com/watch?v=x-CG47kBNOM.

3. Read through 1 John 5 and consider the implications of verses 1–4 in light of your marital relationship. Search for Scriptures that apply to the areas of need in your husband's life and record these for use in your prayer time for him. Hold to the truth of 1 John 5:14–15 as you pray.

Letting Go and Grabbing On

❧

"If I refuse to be a corn of wheat that falls into the ground
and dies . . . then I know nothing of Calvary Love."

— AMY CARMICHAEL[1]

It was a cute bungalow built in the forties. My daughter-in-law found it one day while she was crossing town to meet me at the mall. She and my son had worked hard, sacrificed and saved to purchase their first home, and after months of paperwork, negotiations, and elbow grease, they were finally moving in. She and I spent a day doing some cleaning before the furniture arrived.

So many quaint features define houses from that era, but the hardwood floors were one of my favorite details in this cottage. Their rich, brilliant shine gave the bungalow a homey glow. Although there were a few scratches and signs of wear and tear in a guest bedroom, through the main part of the house the wood looked well preserved. *Until some of the furniture arrived.*

I noticed it right away—a long scratch in the hardwood flooring, starting in the dining area and ending in the living room. Apparently the damage happened earlier that morning, because when I asked Lindsey about it, she'd already seen it. Her response both amazed and pleased me. "Oh yes. I saw it. I told Caleb not to feel bad about it. It's all right. Now we have our own mark. Everyone who's lived here left their mark and now we've left ours."

I've been there. I've had prized possessions broken, stolen, or lost, and when it's no fault of your own, there's a huge temptation to unload in anger. I've failed more times than I've had victory. I'm thankful my son's wife already understands the value of holding temporal things loosely and letting the "little stuff" go.

In marriage, as in life, there are many "die-to-self" moments along the way where you choose to let the little stuff go. Like when he keeps you awake with his loud snoring through the night and then slurps his coffee in the mornings; presents you with a skillet instead of jewelry for your anniversary; neglects your honey-do list (again); skips a Saturday of antiquing with you to play golf with his buddies instead.

These are the small, daily opportunities to practice the kind of dying we talked about that true love requires. It takes intentionality and discipline to say to yourself, *Okay, get in line here—this is a die-to-self moment!* And you'll fail if you try to do it in your own strength. You've got to invite God to pour His grace into the situation.

Getting victory in the small, daily die-to-self moments helps to prepare you for the biggies: the day he tells you he's fired because he lost an important account; the day you find the hidden stash of magazines; the day he leaves for work and doesn't return.

When our dreams come crashing down, when our song is over, when nothing works as we had planned, when all we hoped for is gone and we're left with bitter tears and a heart full of regret, we have a choice to make. We can imprison our offender, grasp for control, wallow in discontentment OR . . . let go and grab on to grace!

As we continue working our way through the APPRECIATION acronym, in this chapter we'll look at the important process of letting go of the little stuff and grabbing on to the important.

R: RELEASE YOUR PRISONER

LeRoy knocked on several doors at homes near our church. He was inviting people in the neighborhood to check us out. A sweet young family took him up on the offer and started attending our church. Soon God began to capture their hearts. Randy first came to salvation, then Patty, his wife.

APPRECIATION

Admire and affirm
Put yourself in his skin
Pray like you mean it
» Release your prisoner

Shortly after that, Randy stopped in one afternoon to see LeRoy in his study at the church. Randy was weeping uncontrollably and so broken that it was difficult at first for LeRoy to understand what he was saying. His conversion to Christ caused him to realize he needed to come clean on some sin issues in his life. He hoped giving a heartfelt confession to God (and to my husband) would give him some peace.

After listening to Randy's entire story, LeRoy gave him tender and compassionate counsel, but then leveled with him that he needed to share this with Patty as well. After several minutes, Randy agreed, but was terrified by the thought, knowing it would devastate her. He asked LeRoy to come with him to talk to her.

LeRoy agreed to go with him and called me to meet them at their home so I could take care of their toddler in a separate room while they spoke privately. I didn't know the details of the situation when I arrived but as soon as I saw Randy's ashen face, I knew it was serious.

Randy confessed to Patty that he'd been involved in an ongoing homosexual relationship that began when he was a teenager.

LET GO OF ANGER AND GRAB ON TO GRACE —OR—HOLD ON TO BITTERNESS AND LET GO OF PEACE.

Although Randy loved Patty, and hated himself for his addiction to the relationship, he just couldn't seem to let go of it. After coming to know Christ, he knew he couldn't continue this double life any longer, but didn't know how to get free. He poured it all out to Patty as LeRoy watched and prayed.

I was in the other room, so I wasn't an eyewitness to her reaction, but LeRoy said it was amazing. Her face was white with shock when she initially heard Randy confess his infidelity with a homosexual lover, but after processing and silently praying, the first words out of this baby believer's mouth were, "Randy, I forgive you." Patty had a choice when receiving this devastating news: let go of anger and grab on to grace—or—hold on to bitterness and let go of peace.

Patty's immediate reaction, followed by a life of loving forgiveness, was instructive for me. Over the next several years, I watched their marriage grow and deepen as honesty and humility defined their relationship. Patty's reaction probably saved their marriage. Her willingness to forgive had an impact not only on their lives, but as I've shared their story, countless other women have received encouragement to forgive their husbands as well. I've watched women first react in shock, then receive hope and courage to forge on, deciding that if she can forgive him for that, surely I can forgive my husband.

Jesus paints a graphic picture of the results of unforgiveness in His parable of the wicked servant in Matthew 18. In the story, there is a servant who owed the king (representing the heavenly Father) a debt that would take more than a lifetime to pay off. The servant begged for mercy, and the gracious king forgave him the entire debt.

The forgiven (but wicked) servant then turned to a fellow slave who owed him a small amount of money and demanded immediate payment. Although the fellow slave begged for mercy and patience for time to repay the debt, rather than forgiving him and releasing him from the debt, the cruel servant (the one who'd been released from the huge debt he owed to the king) had this fellow slave thrown into a debtor's prison (this is why he's referred to in the story as the *wicked* servant).

When the king heard about his unwillingness to forgive a small amount (especially since the king had released him from his enormous debt), the king had the wicked servant thrown into prison where he was turned over to the torturers. Jesus then closes the parable with a stern warning to those who are unwilling to forgive.

The biblical standard of forgiveness seems impossible to keep . . . it is unbelievably high:

"Be kind to one another, tenderhearted, forgiving one another, as God in Christ forgave you" (Ephesians 4:32). ". . . Forgiving each other; as the Lord has forgiven you, so you also must forgive" (Colossians 3:13).

Whenever I quote these verses to myself, whenever I share them with a woman who is holding on to hurt, unwilling to let go and forgive, the effect is always the same. First there is the shocking realization that God's standard requires me to respond in forgiveness to this person who has *so* wronged me with the *same forgiveness* Jesus has shown to me?! Then follows the reminder of how unworthy I am to *receive* forgiveness from a holy God, which brings me to the uncomfortable dilemma of whether I will place myself (figuratively and ironically, of course) above God by holding on to unforgiveness— or whether I, the undeserving, forgiven, wicked servant, will extend the same grace and forgiveness I've been shown.

Going through this exercise always
takes me back to the cross . . .
and there I must release what I'm holding on to . . .
in order to embrace the cross . . .
pick it up . . .
and follow Him.
To the Death. Again.

The most important lesson I've learned in letting go of hurt is that: I cannot keep the biblical standard of forgiveness . . . *without* returning to the cross and relying on His grace.

Going to the cross and focusing on the forgiveness I've been shown by a sinless Savior gives me the *only* perspective for understanding and offering forgiveness. Going to the cross reminds me of what really matters, so I can release the stuff that really doesn't.

A lot of our injuries and offenses will be avoided if we let go of certain ways of thinking *before* the disappointment happens. The forgiveness process is so much simpler if I've already adopted the lifestyle of letting things go that hold potential for offense. Sometimes it helps just to spell it out in black-and-white. How about doing that with me now? Can you identify some things you've been holding on to and be willing to let them go? Read the following paragraphs slowly, carefully considering each point.

Unrealistic Expectations: Do you place pressure on your husband to do the impossible? To read your mind, think like you think, or know what you want him to do or how you want him to treat you—*instinctively*? Do you expect him to act more like your girlfriend than a man? Do you expect him to relate to God or to spiritual things in the same way you do? Do you place greater demands on him than you do yourself? Do you expect him to have more self-control than you do? Be more understanding? Have thicker skin? Do no wrong?

If then you have been raised with Christ, seek the things that are above, where Christ is, seated at the right hand of God. Set your minds on things that are above, not on things that are on earth. For you have died, and your life is hidden with Christ in God. When Christ who is your life appears, then you also will appear with him in glory. (Colossians 3:1–4)

If Only: Do you daydream about how much better your life would be "if only". . . you'd married someone else? . . . could find someone else now? . . . your husband would be more like the incredible lover on the screen? In the novel? Or like the man who chats with you online? Or "if only" he were like that model Christian man at church? Does the "phantom Christian man" compete with your husband for your affections? Can you let go of these "if onlys"?

Put to death therefore what is earthly in you: sexual immorality, impurity, passion, evil desire, and covetousness, which is idolatry. On account of these the wrath of God is coming. In these you too once walked, when you were living in them. But now you must put them all away: anger, wrath, malice, slander, and obscene talk from your mouth. Do not lie to one another, seeing that you have put off the old self with its practices and have put on the new self, which is being renewed in knowledge after the image of its creator. (Colossians 3:5–10)

Fitting It All in My Little Box: Do you demand things be done your way? Do people fear bringing you an alternative plan? Do you think yours is the only way? The best way? Do you pressure others to adopt your way of thinking? Do you get upset if you have to try something new or do something differently than your preference? Does your husband have to defer to your way of operating to keep you happy?

Here there is not Greek and Jew, circumcised and uncircumcised, barbarian, Scythian, slave, free; but Christ is all, and in all.

Put on then, as God's chosen ones, holy and beloved, compassionate hearts, kindness, humility, meekness, and patience, bearing with one another and, if one has a complaint against another, forgiving each other; as the Lord has forgiven you, so you also must forgive. (Colossians 3:11–13)

Unfulfilled Dreams: Are there things you hoped for and goals you've set that are still unfulfilled? Is disappointment affecting your treatment of your husband? Do you blame him for your loss? Do you resent him for not bringing your dreams to pass? Are you placing a burden on him to perform a work that only God could do?

And above all these put on love, which binds everything together in perfect harmony. And let the peace of Christ rule in your hearts, to which indeed you were called in one body. And be thankful. (Colossians 3:14–15)

Empty Suspicions: Do you hold your husband hostage with your suspicions? Does he continually have to prove to you . . . his integrity? His fidelity? His feelings for you? Do you suspect the worst rather than thinking the best? Do you stand as judge over his motives?

Let the word of Christ dwell in you richly, teaching and admonishing one another in all wisdom, singing psalms and hymns and spiritual songs, with thankfulness in your hearts to God. And whatever you do, in word or deed, do everything in the name of the Lord Jesus, giving thanks to God the Father through him.

Wives, submit to your husbands, as is fitting in the Lord. (Colossians 3:16–18)

My husband was considering making a major decision that was going to affect my life dramatically. Daily. I felt strongly that it was the wrong decision. I voiced my concerns and thoughts. He listened, but it didn't change his mind. I was struggling with it all when a friend quietly reminded me of the fact that one day, when I stand before the Lord, He's not going to hold me accountable for straightening out my husband on all those earthly choices, God will hold LeRoy accountable for the decisions he makes . . . but God will also hold me accountable for loving my husband well.

My friend's statement challenged me to get my eyes off the temporary and put them on what matters—the eternal. Challenging myself with eternal-perspective questions helps me when I have trouble peeling my tightly gripped fingers open to let go of the temporary.

Questions to Loosen Your Grip:

* Is this temporary or eternal?
* Will this really matter a month from now, a year from now, in eternity?
* Who is benefitted by my hanging on to this?
* What is the worst that can happen if I let this go?
* Am I operating in fear or in faith by holding on to this?
* Will holding on to this be harmful to my walk with God? To our marriage?
* Is holding on to this worth the potential of crushing my husband's spirit?
* When I stand before God one day, will He commend me for keeping a death grip on this?

What if every woman would become as passionate about letting go of the little stuff as she is about clinging to her personal preferences or holding on to her power of control? What if every woman would apply her fierceness to cultivating self-discipline for the die-to-self moments? What if "letting go" and forgiveness became her way of life?

E: ENCOURAGE HIS LEADERSHIP

I was staring at the carpet when the marriage counselor asked me to state the one thing I most desired from LeRoy. Without hesitating or batting an eye, I replied, "To pray with me." The counselor, who was actually a close friend and pastor, seemed a bit surprised by my answer and challenged me with "Really? That's really the one thing you would name that you want most from LeRoy?"

> **APPRECIATION**
>
> **A**dmire and affirm
> **P**ut yourself in his skin
> **P**ray like you mean it
> **R**elease your prisoner
> » **E**ncourage his leadership

This conversation was held a few years before I went to the cabin. Our pastor friend knew we were struggling in our marriage and was trying to help us by offering some counseling. It seemed like neither he nor LeRoy realized the deep longing and need wives have for their husbands to lead. Although I voiced my desire that day and often pressured and pushed for LeRoy to take on spiritual leadership at home, it would be years before I saw that desire fulfilled.

At that time, I was filled with resentment toward a husband who could pray publicly or with people in counseling, but in our intimate moments together would rarely pray with me or even converse more than was necessary. That was before my eyes were opened to the fact that many men tend to feel intimidated by the idea of "leading" their wives spiritually, and most men don't respond well to a wife's pressure in this area.

Often couples are caught in a vicious cycle much like ours: the wife pressures her husband for leadership—and the more she pressures him—*the farther he runs*!

Our desire for a husband who will lead is a good desire. God created men to serve as spiritual leaders. But there is an art to motivating a man without pushing him. It's a fine line and walking it requires wisdom, patience, and grace. Walking that line begins by preparing a safe place as we're learning with the APPRECIATION acronym.

> MEN ARE SAYING—*IF YOU WANT YOUR HUSBAND TO LEAD, MOVE ASIDE AND LET HIM!*

I've asked a number of men the same question: "What can a wife do to encourage her husband to take the leadership role?" Again, climbing into their skin is enlightening. But just a word of warning . . . some of their answers may burn your ears!

"Easy; the idea of knowing she is standing by her man does exactly that. Kind, soft-spoken, and gentle words tell him you love him and support him no matter what, and he'll rise and stand tall for you." (Tim)

"Women can best encourage their husbands by stepping down themselves. This allows their man to step up to the plate. A man shouldn't have to compete for these positions, but the reality is, he does . . . husbands need a teammate, not an opponent." (Michael)

"My wife trusting in me raises the bar for me more than anything. No man who attempts to follow Christ wants to let down a woman who truly puts her trust in his leadership and protection." (Chuck)

"I hear this all the time—women want the man to take the lead but then step all over him with lack of patience. Many times men are slow to take that position out of fear and maybe lack of knowledge, but if a wife will encourage them with small steps first, he will gain confidence and likely rise in time to be the man you want. But he won't if you continually challenge and tear him down . . . Again, encouragement is helpful." (Andy)

And here is how LeRoy felt when I was pushing him to be the leader:

"The whole time Kim was expressing her concerns for me to be more of a spiritual leader, I was thinking, *What's the matter? I'm a great guy. I'm a Christian guy. I love the Lord. I'm committed to Him. What's the deal here?* There was this destructive process of her pressing with intensity, pushing me to be what she wanted me to be, her image of me, her expectations; and instead of reacting in a positive way or responding and being what she wanted me to be . . . I began to retreat further and further and further inward."

I was pushing LeRoy to be my spiritual leader, while at the same time putting myself in the position as the one in charge at home—controlling most of the decisions or at least "working the system" to get my agenda accomplished rather than having anything like a follower's heart.

Listening to these comments from husbands, it sounds like men are saying—*If you want your husband to lead, move aside and let him!* What I've found to be the most common factor underlying the high rate of male passivity is the wife's domineering control or demeaning attitude when her husband makes any attempt to lead in a direction she doesn't want to go.

We're friends with a couple who shared this humorous (but so true-to-life) story with us:

I come home and say to Mary Ann those three little words every woman loves to hear from her husband—Let's eat out. When I ask her what she's hungry for, her typical reply is, "I don't care. You choose."

So I say, "Okay, let's get Mexican food," and she says "Nah."

So I say, "Okay, how about Chinese?" and she says "Nah."

So I say, "What sounds good?" and she says "I don't know. You choose."

Mary Ann doesn't know what she wants, but what she wants is for me to figure out what she wants for her!

She really does want me to lead . . . As long as what I decide is exactly what she wanted me to do in the first place!

I've seen men take the lead once they are confident that we believe in their leadership. Many men mention the impact of a woman's support and make reference to a dramatic scene in the movie *The Natural*—

A struggling Roy Hobbs steps up to the plate in the ninth inning. After he makes two strikes, in a show of unsolicited response, a mysterious woman dressed in white takes a lone stand. Although he doesn't know who she is or why she rose from her seat in the stands, her silent support infuses Hobbs with fresh courage and confidence. On his final swing, he shatters the scoreboard with the game-winning home run hit. Hobbs's failing baseball career was turned around at the point when a woman stood to show she believed in him.

> **WHAT IF THE MAN YOU ARE REPULSED BY— IS A MAN OF YOUR OWN MAKING?**

You may be completely frustrated by your husband's lack of leadership at this point (as I once was) and have no desire at all to encourage him. You don't believe in him and you wouldn't take a lone stand to demonstrate it. In fact, you might feel like you're ready to walk out rather than stand up for him.

Let me challenge you with this question:

What if the man you are repulsed by—is a man of your own making?

I'm not blaming you for your husband's lack of leadership . . . really, I'm not. I'm just wondering whether your husband may be reacting to your disappointment in him in a way that's common for a lot of men. (Not that I'm excusing his reaction.)

Maybe your husband entered marriage thinking it would be easy. Maybe he'd never seen a man who modeled leadership. Some men start off the marriage thinking if they hold down a job and make the car payments, that should be all a wife would ever want! From his perspective he's a great guy . . . but then he gets hit with the news you need him to be more—to be some kind of "spiritual leader" fulfilling expectations he's never seen modeled or even considered . . . and the pressure to perform in a role he's clueless about has totally shut him down.

Maybe you've felt forced to step into the role of leader because of his passivity or irresponsibility. I encourage you to ask his forgiveness for stepping in to lead, and communicate to him your desire for him to fill that role. If you're willing to do that, here are a few suggestions as you take that lone stand as his most important encourager.

* Appeal to his God-given desire to serve as your protector.

* Encourage him through communicating your confidence in his abilities (even if that confidence is at an all-time low). If you have no confidence at all, recall an example from the past when he's shown leadership, and affirm him for it.

* Speak words that will inspire him to develop his manhood through stepping up to the plate: "I know you can do this!" "You are the best one for this job." "Your ideas are so creative." "Your leadership gives me security."

* Let him know how thankful you are for every tiny speck of godliness you see in him.

Make a Big Deal about Baby Steps

No matter how small the decision may be, commend your husband when he is decisive.

Some men carry a large load of responsibility and make multiple decisions throughout the day in their vocational role, but when entering the doors of their home feel inadequate and fearful to make the simplest choices. And sometimes he's tired from the day of making decisions and doesn't want to make any more! Look for opportunities to encourage your husband's role as the leader by asking his opinion or choice and then affirming his decisions—even if it is different than what you would have chosen.

If you've asked him to make the restaurant choice for the evening, don't complain when he takes you to a place you'd rather not eat—at least he was brave enough to choose! Your evening will be much more enjoyable when your eating preference gives way to the opportunity to encourage him.

I've found that when I encourage his leadership in the small things, he asks for my input in the big things.

Choose Your Battles Carefully

Most marital conflicts occur over issues much weightier than restaurant preferences, but some relationships are so fractured that daily trivialities become battlegrounds. I'm not saying we should never give input or share our thoughts.

I'm simply suggesting letting go of the little stuff. In the long run, your relationship will be better served if those trivial preferences can be left unvoiced.

Try Holding Your Tongue

"Whoever restrains his words has knowledge, and he who has a cool spirit is a man of understanding" (Proverbs 18:27).

Try holding your tongue and you might be surprised that your husband has a few good ideas of his own! You'll discover there is greater benefit in allowing your husband to take the lead than in you voicing all your opinions.

If he messes up, trust the Lord to use the consequences as a form of instruction in his life. At least he's starting to make choices!

Be Willing to Wait

If he doesn't pick up the mantle of leadership—wait. Give him time to step into the role. But in order for him to lead, you will need to release control (and stop telling him what to do!). Often women lament the fact that they desire a spiritual leader; they long for their husband to lead—but he won't.

It may not be that he won't lead but that he can't—because the wife is in his way!

I can plead "Guilty!" to being the wife who robbed her husband's leadership role in the past. But I can assure you, there is such freedom in operating God's way.

Before I leave this topic, let's hear what one more man has to say about this. Joshua Harris is a well-known author and pastor. Listen as he honestly shares from his heart:

> To affirm your husband's leadership is saying with your words and your behavior, "I support you. I believe you're called by God to play this role. I am committed to making your plan a success. I've got your back. I'm here to be your helper."
>
> Ladies, I don't know if you realize what a powerful thing this is. You will never nag your husband into godliness. You will never criticize your husband into being an amazing leader. You will never nitpick your man into being the man you want him to be.
>
> But your faith and encouragement and support will transform

him. Nothing stirs a man's heart to aspire to be a godly husband like the affirmation of his wife. Nothing.[2]

As I've released control, allowed my husband to make leadership decisions, and supported him (even when I wasn't sure his idea was the best route to take), he has grown into a godly leader who not only leads well but asks for my input all along the way. And God answered my heart's desire—LeRoy never lets a day pass without praying with me! (Check out more on this topic in the appendix: Challenging Your Husband to Robust Christianity.)

C: CONTENTMENT–GRAB ON
AND DON'T LET GO!

Earlier I shared that I asked input from my husband before meeting with my friend Anne to talk with her about rebuilding her relationship with her husband. I asked him to give me one word from a husband's perspective; one word of counsel that I might need to give to a woman who'd recently repented of a lesbian affair. The word he spoke was *gratitude*.

APPRECIATION

Admire and affirm
Put yourself in his skin
Pray like you mean it
Release your prisoner
Encourage his leadership
» Contentment

Although I knew gratitude played a vital role in building a strong marriage, until that moment I hadn't realized how significantly a wife's thankful disposition affects a man. I think there must be some kind of link between the man's role as provider that causes him to somehow feel responsible for a wife's unhappiness or dissatisfaction. A contented wife brings her husband a sense of fulfilled purpose and satisfaction.

In reality, a wife's contentment is not the husband's responsibility. Contentment flows from a heart that's settled the three most important truths of life:

- **God is God.** He is sovereign and working all things out according to His plan.
- **God is good.** I can trust His provision, His plans, and His personal work in my life because He is trustworthy.
- **God is worthy of all my worship.** He is my greatest treasure. He is where my heart is; all my deepest longings are fulfilled in Him. He is my complete sufficiency and who I most value.

When I sink deeply into those truths, I can be at rest and content with what He allows. I can cease striving. I can stop trying to control people and circumstances. I can stop manipulating and pressuring. I can find joy in the daily moments of my life, knowing each one is a gift from the Father and worthy of my gratitude.

I can rest in my love relationship with Him.

Yes, Lord

"I can't do this, Lord!" Tears fell, washing the worn and cracked linoleum. I was attempting to scrub my "new" kitchen floor. Every time I thought I'd found the bottom layer of grease and grime, another surfaced in muddy pools. I raced outside in disgust, only to be driven back inside the filthy kitchen by bitter February cold. "I can't do this—please help me!" was my constant cry.

During the three years that LeRoy stepped down from pastoring, we lived in a variety of interesting places, but this was the most challenging one yet. We were attempting to convert an abandoned diesel mechanic's shop into livable housing. We dubbed it the "flea house" due to an infestation that remained unfazed by the most powerful insecticides known to man—*they just would not die*!

Rodents in various sizes and stages of life, holes in the walls, the ceiling, and floors—all convinced me this was more than I could bear. The easiest thing was to blame LeRoy for our difficult living conditions, but in reality my lack of support and demeaning treatment contributed to the strain on our marriage that led him to step away from pastoring for a season—and that also put us in a difficult position financially and brought a lot of changes; one of the most challenging was our options for housing.

> **BECAUSE OF HIS FELLOWSHIP WITH ME THERE, THE PLACE I ONCE HATED AND THOUGHT I COULDN'T LIVE IN BECAME A PRECIOUS PLACE.**

Although I hadn't yet realized the need to change how I treated LeRoy, while living in the flea house I began to move from the demanding heart that yells, "I can't do this!" to a yielded response of, "Yes, Lord. I surrender to Your will. This is hard. I need Your grace. But I trust You."

It took a bit before I fully surrendered, but eventually that kitchen became my sanctuary. As I surrendered and began to say, "Yes, Lord . . ." Jesus' fellowship in that grime-covered room became more precious than what I'd ever experienced with Him. Again and again His glory filled the room as He met me there in the early dawn hours.

Because of His fellowship with me there, the place I once hated and thought I couldn't live in became a precious place. I remember the day I vowed to God that I never wanted to leave this house if it meant leaving His presence. After struggling and fighting for release, I had finally grabbed hold of Him and settled into contentment.

At this point I hadn't yet been to the cabin, but God took me through this process in preparation for the cabin experience—finding my contentment in Christ first, not in my relationship with LeRoy. In the flea house I was learning to rest in my love relationship with Christ.

Defining Marks of the Contented Fierce Woman:

* Christ is what her heart most highly values.
* The disposition of her heart is gratitude.
* She practices thankfulness rather than comparison.
* She lives with the attitude that everything she receives is more than she deserves.
* Confidence in God's character stabilizes her when everything seems to be against her and nothing is going as she'd hoped.
* Knowing God has all resources at His disposal—she asks largely but holds loosely.
* She doesn't fuel discontentment by focusing on what she wants but doesn't have.
* Her heart isn't clinging to the past or fretting for the future but is resting and worshiping in the moment.

Today I actually have fond memories of the flea house. What began as an "I can't do this nightmare" became one of my most treasured seasons of life. Not because the physical circumstances improved; they didn't really change much. No matter how much I scrubbed, I never found the bottom layer of "grime-less" linoleum. And although we patched the large hole in the floor and rid ourselves of most of the rodents, the fleas' continuous life cycle was a challenge till the day we finally moved out!

Although the house was basically the same when I left as when we moved in, my heart wasn't. My heart was changed. The flea house served as a refining tool to take me to a deeper level of surrender and eventually contentment.

Contentment is surrender's sweet spot. It's rooted in peace and its reward is joy. Contentment is gratitude's fuel. Contentment flows from a heart that says, "Yes, Lord."

Jesus, I am resting, resting.
In the joy of what Thou art;
I am finding out the greatness
Of Thy loving heart . . .
Simply trusting Thee, Lord Jesus,
I behold Thee as Thou art,
And Thy love, so pure, so changeless,
Satisfies my heart . . .

—Jean S. Pigott [3]

✳ HEART ISSUES ☙

1. The process of letting go of the temporal and grabbing on to the eternal begins with an understanding of who we are in Christ and appreciating the value of His work on the cross.

For the remainder of the book, we will be spending our "Heart Issues" time in Ephesians. Today, read through the first chapter and record what this chapter tells you about "who you are in Him." It's important to do this activity for the ground we'll cover in chapter 10.

Write out the spiritual blessings and benefits He's given to those who belong to Him; those who are in Christ.

2. Use Paul's prayer in Ephesians 1:17–20 and personalize the requests. Consider using this as a prayer for your husband as well.

3. In order to live a life of letting go and grabbing on and in order to practice the biblical standard of forgiveness, you will need the power that is described in verses 19–22. What is that power and what did it accomplish?

Every time you're tempted to give up, every time you want to hold on to your hurts, bitterness, and pain, recall this passage and ask for the power to let go and forgive.

Ask Him to display His resurrection power in your situation.

There's No One Else Like My Man!

*"We make men without chests and
expect of them virtue and enterprise.
We laugh at honor and are shocked to find traitors in our midst.
We castrate and bid the geldings be fruitful."*

— C. S. Lewis[1]

Last year a series of devastating tornadoes hit our area. Downed power lines and massive flooding cut off whole communities from the rest of the world. Large, uprooted trees lay across buildings, homes, and major roadways. Many in our state were without electricity for several weeks. I was trying to cook meals on a camp stove during the week we spent without lights or running water.

One evening, shortly after the worst of the storms passed through, a friend of mine stopped in at one of the few convenience stores still open for business. She struck up a conversation with some "real men" who were braving the elements. Several young men were in a caravan of heavy-duty pickup trucks that were fully supplied with chain saws and rescue equipment. They were pumped as they excitedly told her they were heading into the mountains to help out in a community where the storm had isolated several people. It was still pouring heavy rain, there was little visibility, and when most of us were tucked in our beds for the night, these guys couldn't wait to head off on a recovery mission adventure!

When she told me about it later, I replied, "Yep. That's what men live for—risking their lives on a rescue mission." Now, I don't know about you, but their adventure wasn't really a temptation for me. I mean, I am all about serving those truly in need . . . I'll fix a meal for a friend after surgery, care for a loved one who's ill, help you clean your house if necessary . . . but heading out in the middle of the night on roads with downed power lines to clear fallen trees (while in the pouring rain) is not something I'd be jumping with excitement to tackle. I would be willing, but I certainly wouldn't be high-fiving and getting an adrenaline rush as I took off to brave the wild elements.

Men and women are different—*and that's a good thing!* It's mind-boggling to me that we've reached a point in history where, if you state the fact that men and women *are different*, you can expect real backlash. Not too long ago, that observation was a no-brainer.

FORGETTING GENDER DIFFERENCES

I grew up surrounded by boys. I had two brothers but also lived in walking distance of my five cousins—all boys! When I was four years old and found out my mom was bringing home a new baby from the hospital, I begged for a girl! But seeing the "blue blankie" when they arrived home was a dead giveaway. Another boy.

By the time my brother was two, I had devised a plan. Why not outfit him in some of my old dresses, complete with a purse? We could call him Erica instead of Eric. Then we could let his hair grow long and no one would ever know the difference!

My mom, however, didn't buy it.

It's understandable that a young child might not realize there are intrinsic gender differences that go far beyond anatomy, hair length, and clothing styles, but sadly

YOUR HUSBAND'S MANHOOD IS GOD'S GIFT TO YOU.

it seems the world has forgotten that basic fact. We live in a culture struggling with gender issues: gender confusion, gender bending, unisex movements, and assaults on masculinity because of a perceived "patriarchal hierarchy." In all the noise, confusion, and gender rhetoric, perhaps you've forgotten that it is a beautiful thing to have gender differences.

Rather than trying to cram your man into a feminized "metro" mold in hopes of producing a more compatible mate, I hope this chapter will help you see the value of encouraging his manhood. I'm hoping you'll see the benefit of embracing gender differences. And if after reading this, you suspect you're guilty of quashing your husband's masculinity, then I can't wait for you to give your husband the freedom to live out his masculinity and experience what it's like to live with a real man!

In this chapter, we'll continue working our way through the APPRECIATION acronym. We'll investigate—and celebrate—the fact that your husband's manhood is God's gift to you. He's going to think, react, and live differently than you—because he's a man! Not only is he your complementary opposite in gender, in addition to that, he's unique; there's no one else like him! Appreciating him for who he is will bring spice and excitement to your marriage.

I: INVEST IN HIM

Most any typical Saturday in the fall, you won't find me on a mountain trail, hiking through colorful foliage, which I love doing; or scouring the antique shops, something else I thoroughly enjoy; or even—best of all —curled up in front of a crackling fire with a good book. No, you'll probably find me right next to my man, screaming to the top of my lungs, helping him cheer on our favorite college football team.

APPRECIATION

Admire and affirm
Put yourself in his skin
Pray like you mean it
Release your prisoner
Encourage his leadership
Contentment
» Invest in him

Come spring, you can check out my brackets during March Madness and later in the year, come along with us to a local baseball game. Why am I so into athletics you may wonder . . . Is it because I'm a huge sports fanatic? *No.* It wouldn't bother me at all if I never saw another athletic competition in my life (sorry to break that to those of you in our Razorback-watch-party group). I'm only all about sports because that's an easy and fun way to invest in my husband. It allows us to enjoy doing something together that's always been an important part of his life. You may discover that when you show interest and get involved in things your man finds enjoyable, that he's more willing to spend time on activities you choose. Last week my husband even attended a play with me, something he'd never do on his own initiative, but we've found we enjoy sharing time together no matter what we're doing.

See, I've learned that whatever I "invest in" pays off. Seven years after leaving the flea house, we had the opportunity to purchase a piece of property for our first home. When I put sweat equity into building the house by purchasing timber, having it logged, milled, and planed, hauling rock for the fireplace, sanding and finishing all the wood trim myself, laying the tile floors, working on almost every square inch of it—beginning to end—it paid off in huge dividends.

Because of the time I spent studying how to stain and finish wood, taking tile-laying classes, roaming the ends of the earth to find the best deals, I have a better understanding of our current home than anywhere else we've lived. I know this house intimately—its quirkiness, needs, unique character traits and flaws—better than anyone else. I also appreciate our home more than I would if it were a contractor's turnkey house.

I've also learned that investing in my husband brings the rich reward of intimately knowing, enjoying, and valuing him. By investing, I mean putting time and effort into getting into his heart and mind.

Studying him.

Becoming knowledgeable of his interests and passions.

Growing in my understanding of him.

Spending time getting to know him at broader and deeper levels.

Sadly, I've known (and at times been) the kind of woman who loves Jesus and loves to study His Word, but fails to demonstrate love to her husband by studying him. I remember when a husband in our congregation complained that his wife was so busy doing Bible study that he never had a hot meal and couldn't find clean laundry! That was a wake-up call for me. I'd stressed to the women in our church the need for studying the Word, but apparently failed in leading them to connect the dots when it came to applying the truth of the Word in practical ways like serving others, especially their families, in daily life. Remember that investing communicates that you value him. Here are some practical ways to invest in your man.

Prepare

Prepare yourself for time you'll spend with your husband. If you wake before he does, prepare your heart for the morning moments with him. Pray for him and for yourself before you even greet him.

Prepare to guard your tongue; and to speak encouraging, affirming words that will motivate and inspire him to tackle his day with courage (Proverbs 16:24; 18:21; 21:23; Ephesians 4:29).

Also, prepare for the "reentry" at the end of the day. Get ready physically, emotionally, and spiritually. By taking time with your appearance, as well as preparing your attitude, you are expressing to your husband that he is valuable to you.

Compromise

Often couples who come to us for marriage counseling admit their schedules and priorities need adjusting in order for them to build relational unity and develop companionship. When two people are running in opposite directions—compromise is needed to get them on the same road. Investing in this kind of compromise is essential.

Be intentional in planning mealtimes so you can spend these together—preferably at the dinner table, not in front of a computer or television screen.

If you're a night owl and your husband has an early morning work schedule, consider adjusting your sleep schedule, if possible, to match his. Going to bed together and having a nightly routine of ending the day together can add a lot to your relationship.

Do what you can to monitor your evening and weekend schedule to protect time together as a couple or a family. If you are spending more of your free time with girlfriends, church activities, social clubs, or the Internet than with your husband, it may be time to check your priorities. Ask your husband to help you evaluate the activities and responsibilities you have on your plate. Are any of these things pulling you apart? Can some of these things be let go, or can you compromise and find a solution that will allow you to be involved in the activity or responsibility together?

If you're in a busy season of life with children in multiple athletic, educational, or school activities, and you feel you're carrying the load by yourself, check to see if your husband is willing to be more involved. Perhaps he's unaware of the stress you're under. You may be surprised how responsive most husbands will be to a humble (not demanding) request for help. Appeal to their chivalrous spirit as a man.

Study

Become an avid fan and student of your husband. You should know him more intimately than anyone else does.

Are his coworkers or buddies better acquainted with his likes and dislikes, accomplishments and goals, struggles and disappointments? Do you spend more time unloading on him than listening to him? Are you intentional about getting to know his heart, his patterns, and preferences? Have you learned when he's most open to conversation and when he needs his space? Do you know how to make him laugh? Are you still on a quest to know him more?

In *The 5 Love Languages*, Gary Chapman explains that we each receive love in different ways, and that we each have a primary language in which we best express and interpret love: Words of Affirmation, Quality Time, Receiving Gifts, Acts of Service, and Physical Touch. If Words of Affirmation is your husband's primary love language, then he might not appreciate Acts of Service such as a drawer full of clean socks as much as a heartfelt "You did that so well!" (Visit 5lovelanguages.com for more on this very practical concept.)

Becoming a student of what communicates love to your husband provides the understanding to express love to him through his primary love language. Learning and applying these principles can revitalize a struggling marriage.

Honor

Public demonstrations of honor and loyalty are huge for a man. Invest in him by filling his ears with verbal encouragement that builds his confidence. Perhaps nothing demoralizes a man more than a wife publicly stripping him down through caustic comments or negative criticism (see Proverbs 12:4). Not only for our husband's sake but for the stability of our home, we need to set an example before our children of honoring their father. What are some ways a wife can make her husband less confident? Again, listen to what a few men have to say in answer to this question:

"The smallest little negative remarks can bite so deep. Even when the man has goofed up, don't jump on every opportunity to point out his faults. *Never* point out his faults publicly or to your friends. This can have devastating consequences to the marriage. Look for opportunities to do just the opposite and build him up. Husband and wife are one flesh. That means more than we know. When one tears down the other, they are literally tearing themselves and their children down." (Jeremy)

"How does a wife make a man less confident? When she is the opponent. She stands in the way of choices he is making. Another way is bashing her husband whether publicly or privately. Her words will eventually get back around." (Larry)

"Belittling him in front of his friends or talking poorly of him to her friends and family. Never ever run him down to others." (Cory)

Serve

"For you were called to freedom, brothers. Only do not use your freedom as an opportunity for the flesh, but through love serve one another" (Galatians 5:13).

Marriage can be the crucible for sanctification that only comes through serving without expectation of repayment. And marriage affords multiple daily opportunities to flesh out this sanctification through serving: laundry (thousands of loads—washed and folded), meals (preparation and cleanup), running errands, weekly (sometimes daily) grocery trips, home maintenance, and a myriad of other servant-type tasks.

Some might recoil from the idea of "serving" their husbands and think of it in terms of demeaning slave labor, and perhaps with good reason—some men have taken advantage of their wife's domestic service. This extreme is not what I'm promoting. In fact, I've rarely seen that extreme lived out. I have seen begrudging women fill a self-imposed role of "slave" in the home with a martyr mentality—a self-glorifying badge of honor. This is not the way of Christ.

What I'm encouraging is a Christlike attitude toward service—service that is performed with gentle kindness and a loving heart with no expectation of reciprocation.

Reconcile

Investing in developing good techniques for conflict resolution is necessary for building a healthy relationship. A good marriage is not one without conflict, but one where conflict is resolved through biblical means and results in spiritual growth for both parties. Invest time and effort in cultivating harmony in your relationship.

In any marriage there are multiple opportunities for conflict on a daily basis—issues with finances, employment, children, in-laws, church, or health problems. Understanding what areas have the potential to cause an argument to escalate or knowing the type of issue that can trigger an emotional outburst can help alleviate drama.

Ignoring conflict or stuffing feelings as an attempt to pacify and prevent confrontation is not a healthy way to resolve conflict. The wise couple will discuss how to tackle conflict before they are in the middle of an argument. For more on resolving conflict, see Guidelines When Confrontation Is Necessary in the appendix.

Investing in your relationship will bring a good return. You may not see it right away, but consistently practicing these actions will communicate to your husband that he matters and is valuable to you. "For where your treasure is, there will your heart be also" (Luke 12:34). Investing in your marriage indicates its value to you—which reveals your heart.

A: ACCEPT HIM

When we were first married, I viewed my husband through a romanticized imagination. In reality, the man I married couldn't quite meet those standards. The version of LeRoy I invented had many of his natural qualities, but I had an idealized version, which tacked a number of my personal expectations on to the real LeRoy.

> APPRECIATION
>
> Admire and affirm
> Put yourself in his skin
> Pray like you mean it
> Release your prisoner
> Encourage his leadership
> Contentment
> Invest in him
> » Accept him

Things like: hosting *lots* of social gatherings in our home (he's an introvert). Giving me long foot rubs (*not*). Instigating late-night spontaneous activities (he's asleep shortly after dark). Holding heart-to-heart talks into the late night hours (refer to prior sleep information). And cooking gourmet meals together in the kitchen (he didn't even know where the dinner plates were kept until more than a decade into our marriage—much less pots and pans!). Needless to say my dream version of LeRoy was not the one I ended up with on the honeymoon. I found out fairly quickly the two versions were incompatible.

So, I did what every self-respecting, self-centered, romance-hungry wife does; I determined to change him! My longing for the invented version of my man led me to push, plead, pressure, manipulate, demean, and bully him—hoping to conform him into my ideal. Not happenin'! The more energy I poured into pressuring him to change (as part of my "helper role," remember?), the farther apart we grew.

> **I DID WHAT EVERY SELF-RESPECTING, SELF-CENTERED, ROMANCE-HUNGRY WIFE DOES; I DETERMINED TO CHANGE HIM!**

But after my eye-opening experience at the cabin, I applied myself to the process of learning how to flesh out love to LeRoy and I came across a word that drastically changed my approach to him. I remember the day I was stunned by this passage:

> The one who eats is not to regard with contempt the one who does not eat, and the one who does not eat is not to judge the one who eats, for God has accepted him. Who are you to judge the servant of another? To his own master he stands or falls; and he will stand, for the Lord is able to make him stand. (Romans 14:3–4 NASB)

I realize this passage is specifically dealing with the issue of eating meat offered to idols, but while I was reading it, quite unexpectedly the words "God has accepted him . . ." stood out to me like a neon sign. The idea of acceptance with all the safety and comfort that action provides bore a hole into my heart.

Acceptance: favorable reception; approval.

Acceptance . . .

Acceptance . . .

The word kept running through my heart and mind. Acceptance. In the church at Rome, people were getting bent out of shape, puffed up in pride, and offended at fellow believers who weren't in line with their thinking. Their superior attitude was based on their own religious but not necessarily *scriptural* convictions.

But God had *accepted* this one who practiced something that others found questionable! My mouth fell open as I thought about my attitude toward my husband and his preferences that were so different than mine—his introverted personality and approach to ministry that I had scrutinized for years, what I considered his lack of affection for me, our diverse backgrounds—and realized I'd punished him for being different from me.

My own stubborn heart showed no acceptance for the true version of LeRoy; for years it clung to the idealized one who never appeared.

As I pondered this passage and its implications, a bittersweet feeling of compassion began to pour over me:

"What if I'd not been accepted by God? What if He'd been unwilling to offer 'favorable reception' to me when I cried out to Him for acceptance? And, who was I to withhold acceptance from my husband based on silly personal preferences?"

I was so ashamed.

As the idea began forming in my mind of letting go the imaginary version of LeRoy, and opening my arms to welcome the everyday, real-life version, with all his rough edges and dog-eared corners . . . a freeing release occurred. I realized I could stop all the effort I was expending. I could quit working at changing him! *Instead, I could accept him and learn to enjoy him for who he is.* He could have the freedom to be himself without fear of rejection or criticism. As I settled into the freedom of gracious acceptance, the dividing wall of "un-acceptance" no longer stood between us.

When I talk about "acceptance" of your husband, I'm not meaning ignoring or tolerating sin but acceptance of his individual quirkiness, his unique personality and preferences. I mean stepping down from the position of arbiter over his life. Learning to value differences in taste, interests, and personality traits.

Acceptance:

* Not pushing your social personality on him—pressuring an introvert into an extrovert mold or vice versa.
* Providing a safe and comfortable atmosphere for him to "be himself" around you because he knows you're good with his unique approach to life.
* Acknowledging and showing that you do not view your preferences as superior to his.
* Releasing him from the pressure of trying to live up to an "idealized version" of him.
* Communicating acceptance rather than verbally (or mentally) practicing sinful comparison: "Why can't you be more like . . . (so and so)?"
* Accepting his background and family's culture.
* Understanding that his walk with the Lord may not look like yours—because generally men and women relate to God and spiritual matters differently. And letting him know you're releasing that—God is in charge of his devotional life, not you!

We tend to slip into black-and-white thinking when it comes to how we think our mate "should" operate. Some men may wonder why we married them, when it seems what we really want is a Ken doll we can dress up and manipulate according to our whims. By having our preprogrammed expectations, we can miss out on the discovery and adventure of someone who isn't playing the role of "Ken" in the plotline of our imaginary drama.

You may not know what fun you're missing out on if you can't say *Vive la difference!* If one of you is an early bird and the other a night owl; if one likes vanilla, the other likes chocolate (I might argue this one!); passionate or reserved, talkative or quiet, predictable or spontaneous, tacos or pizza, cowboy boots or Italian loafers, ambitious or relaxed, attentive to detail or big picture visionary, slow responder or quickly decisive, social butterfly or basic loner, organized or messy (and loves it!)—consider acceptance as an opportunity for discovering new things and ways of living.

You may be a studious type with a master's degree who loves books and learning, married to an appliance repairman who loves tinkering but finds reading a chore. If you're trying to cram your blue-collar guy into a white-collar role—you're probably going to end up with one miserable man. There is nothing wrong with encouraging him to excel, but if for him "living the dream" means wearing a Maytag uniform, then determine to send him out to conquer his day with the assurance that you value him for who he is, not the uniform he wears.

I was told about one wife who woke her husband in the middle of the night to unload on him about his lack of affection and romance. She went so far as to have him read a portion from the latest romance novel she was reading and negatively compared him to the lead character by complaining, "Why can't you be more like him?"

I can't imagine how demoralizing it must've been for that husband to be compared to a fictional character in a romance novel . . . but her fixation on that character is no worse than inventing and pining for a version of the perfect husband.

He's a phantom.

He doesn't exist—other than in your own mind.

Put the phantom to death.

T: TREAT HIM LIKE A MAN!

Because of job layoffs in our area, a couple in our church moved across the country to a temporary job in the Northwest. When the job was finished and it was time for them to return home, they were struggling financially and needed help making such a costly move. Rather than send a hefty check to help pay for the cost or raise the money within our church family, my husband and a couple of other men saw this as an opportunity to initiate a "rescue mission."

APPRECIATION

Admire and affirm
Put yourself in his skin
Pray like you mean it
Release your prisoner
Encourage his leadership
Contentment
Invest in him
Accept him
» Treat him like a man!

LeRoy and one of the other men both have their CDL license, which allows them to drive a "Big Rig" across the country. By "Big Rig" I'm talking about a mean machine—a heavy-duty, tractor-trailer with eighteen wheels under five axles, able to carry forty tons; a diesel engine with ten gears and 500 horsepower. It's the kind of truck every little boy dreams of one day driving.

A church member offered the use of his tractor-trailer rig if they would deliver a load for his trucking company on the way to Oregon (transporting the load would cover the fuel cost for the trip). The three men worked out a plan to head out on a Monday night, driving the more than two thousand miles in alternating shifts and stopping to deliver the load of goods on the way to Oregon.

On Thursday they arrived at the family's home in the middle of the night and immediately started loading their furniture for the return trip. In order to make it back in time for LeRoy to preach Sunday morning, the men had no time for a rest break but had to start back home as soon as they finished loading the furniture and the couple's vehicle. After traveling across the country with little sleep or meals, they started the return trip as soon as the load was secure—at daybreak!

The trip appealed to the men on multiple levels. It gave them the opportunity to fulfill manly dreams: to live out the masculine spirit of adventure—the desire of exploring the unknown, pressing

MEN THRIVE ON CONQUEST AND CHALLENGE.

beyond the normal, pushing physical endurance to the limit and conquering. By surmounting the challenge of a cross-country drive—for the purpose of helping friends in need—they were living out manhood's commitment to responsibility and duty. By accomplishing the monumental task, it allowed them to excel as men by working out a real solution to a real problem. Conquering the challenge together bound them as a band of brothers.

Men thrive on conquest and challenge. They are fueled by tackling difficulty and successfully completing a mission. When my husband came home from that trip, you would've thought he'd won a war. And the icing on the cake for a man as he comes home from the battle is his woman's accolades: "Wow, honey! You're the man! I am so proud of you!" It's a man thing.

Today it's difficult to know how to treat a man "like a man" with all the gender blending and confusion. As I shared in chapter 3, men have been emasculated by our disrespectful treatment. Our culture isn't sure what a real man is, and men are confused themselves about how to live out manhood.

Once upon a time men knew that if a woman boarded the bus and there were no seats left, manhood required him to stand and give up his seat for her. Men knew they should hold the door open for a woman and defer to her—*Ladies, first!* These weren't begrudging acts of heroic service but men answering their inner call to fulfill their masculine role. But those days are long gone. The trickle-down effect of the women's liberation movement now guarantees us a place in the aisle of the bus and a swinging door in the face.

As important as those small tokens of respect for femininity are, God's plan for masculinity goes far beyond common etiquette and chivalrous acts. Men were designed to be leaders, protectors, and providers. True manhood runs deeper than the DNA, which produces a physique that is larger and stronger than their female counterpart.

God has placed within men a masculine heart that responds to danger by rising to the challenge as a warrior. Men thrive on serving others as rescuers. They experience the satisfaction of fulfilling their created purpose as they launch out in various leadership roles. Men are driven by their God-given responsibility of providing for their families.

You may be reading this and thinking "That's not happenin' at my house! I'd love for my husband to launch out and lead but he's stuck on the couch with a remote in his hand. The biggest challenge he's willing to face is the latest battle on his video game!"

You may be chiming in, echoing this sentiment. I hear where you're coming from, but I keep wondering whether the soldiers who seem to be MIA might actually be hiding behind a wall of rejection? I keep thinking about that husband who told me, "A man's gotta be winning. If he's getting no respect at home, if he can't be a winner there . . . he'll find someplace where he can."

From the earliest age, boys like to hear their mom cheer them on. My son told me many times how encouraging it was to hear me calling his name during his basketball games and shouting out "That's *my* son!" after he made a basket. Or how much it meant to him for me to reward him and his teammates with drinks and snacks at the end of a hard-fought victory.

We were with a group of friends recently when Parker, who is only six but already has the need to have his masculinity affirmed, stood in the middle of the room to loudly announce to everyone present, "Watch and be amazed!" His athletic feat was not quite as

HOW MANY HUSBANDS HAVE ABDICATED THEIR WARRIOR ROLE OUT OF FRUSTRATION AND FEAR?

impressive as his announcement, but we all cheered anyway. Men have a competitive drive to be a winner. Your husband needs you to "Watch and be amazed!" because if he's not winning at home, he'll find someplace where he can.

According to a recent CNN article, eighteen- to thirty-four-year-old men spend more time playing video games a day than twelve- to seventeen-year-old boys.[2] I wonder how many men are addicted to video games, golf, pornography, gambling, or have become workaholics, as a way to find release for the drive to excel as a "winner." Perhaps their warrior heart has shriveled. They no longer believe they've got what it takes to slay the dragon and so they comfort themselves with hours of soulless activity. They've become perpetual boys conquering the meaningless kingdoms of a virtual world.

I wonder how many wives, unintentionally, squelch their husband's desire to lead. How many husbands have abdicated their warrior role, as mine did, out of frustration and fear? I wonder how many men respond to a wife's intimidation by retreating into an adolescent role rather than believing they have the mojo to grab the helm of leadership and run with it.

Again, I'm not saying your husband is without blame or your marital problems are solely your fault. Not at all! Your husband's lack of leadership may be a result of not having the benefit of a good model of manhood, there may be health or emotional issues involved, but he is responsible for his behavior. This book isn't written to "fix the men" but it is written for women who are willing to battle for their marriage. I just hope you will evaluate your approach to your husband and consider what improvements you might need to make.

Seeing men adrift in a culture of perpetual boyhood, a few men have issued clarion calls to the brotherhood in hopes of countering this trend. William Bennett was interviewed about his latest book, *The Book of Man: Readings on the Path to Manhood*. He explained in an opinion piece for CNN why he wrote this guide to manhood: "For the first time in history, women are better educated, more ambitious, and arguably more successful than men . . . We celebrate the ascension of women but what will we do about what appears to be the very real decline of the other sex?"[3]

His observation reminds me of the question I was recently asked by a heartbroken wife. Professionally successful but maritally bankrupt, she cried in exasperation, "How do I encourage my husband to act like a man?" Before attempting an answer, we first need to clarify what we mean when we talk about husbands needing to man up.

What is true manhood?

How do we recognize it?

It's more than big trucks and sweaty gym shorts. True manhood shows up in daily choices that require character qualities like courage, integrity, perseverance, and self-sacrifice. It's being a man of honor—taking personal responsibility, fulfilling duties, demonstrating valor, and showing a willingness to sacrifice and lead for the greater good.

It is rock-solid strength that forges ahead with the determination to make it through the storm. True manhood stands guard over loved ones with protective eyes. It manifests the tenderness of a benevolent heart that seeks to provide for those in need. But most importantly, knowing his strength is not derived from himself, a true man walks in humble dependence on the One whose image he bears. He lives out the gospel by fleshing out the character of his Warrior-Savior.

How do we inspire our husbands to take up the mantle of true manhood? I don't have all the answers, but I'll share with you some of my observations from years of counseling with struggling couples:

Issue a Big Picture Invitation

Move aside if you're blocking the doorway, and encourage your husband to cross manhood's most critical threshold by inviting him to live out his masculinity in your home. Paint the big picture for him—not in terms of condemnation for how he's failed to live this out—but in statements expressing belief in him.

Consider sharing your heart (hint: over his favorite meal helps) with loving and gentle tones, which appeal to his inner drive to protect. Let him know you need him. Confess your own inadequacies as a good follower and encourager. Share with him how you've come to realize a husband's daunting role and the challenges men face in fulfilling this. If you've wronged him by demeaning his leadership efforts, ask his forgiveness.

Lay out an invitation he can respond positively to: "I believe in you, I need you as my leader—are you willing to help me learn how to encourage you in fulfilling your role? Will you teach me how to treat you like a man?"

Inspire

Stifling a man's dream takes the heart out of him. Give him freedom to go for his dreams. Don't squash him into your mold. Don't heckle his ideas that may seem far-fetched to you. Invest in his masculine drive to explore and conquer by cheering him on and inspiring him with your support.

Give him opportunities to live out his dream. Don't allow your selfishness or small-minded views to suck the life out of your adventurer.

Respect

You are not his mother or his teacher! You may feel like he expects you to serve him in those roles, and it may be easier to slip into that mode with him, but the reality is—it only makes the situation worse.

The tough thing about the issue of respecting your husband is that, according to Ephesians 5 and 1 Peter 3, respect is a nonnegotiable for the wife. We are required to respect our husbands—not based on their conduct or character—but based on the fact that they're our husbands.

> "IF A MAN KNOWS HIS WIFE BELIEVES IN HIM, HE'LL WALK ACROSS THE STATE OF TEXAS. IF HE DOESN'T, HE CAN'T WALK ACROSS THE ROOM!"

We are to respect our husbands . . . period. I am not saying that is an easy response to give, but respecting our husbands is our only choice if we want to obey Scripture.

Validate

Honor your husband by demonstrating genuine interest in his vocation. Ask questions that will give him the opportunity to let you in on his world, to share his accomplishments and victories—to give you the chance to "Watch and be amazed!"

Celebrate

Not enduring or merely tolerating his gender difference, but celebrating and relishing his masculinity. I don't mean encouraging the adolescent version of manhood we so often see elevated today—crude, rude, boorish behavior—but let him know you like when he exerts strength, you like him flexing his masculinity, and watching him perform as a "real man" turns you on!

I cannot overemphasize the need for women to encourage their husbands as men. I fear that the common tendency for wives is to emasculate rather than empower their husbands. When they need us to "Watch and be amazed!" we're rolling our eyes and making sure they see we are very much not amazed. Real men need real women who will fiercely prize and stimulate their masculinity. If we want our husbands to act like men, we need to treat them like men. I heard a man say once: "If a man knows his wife believes in him, he'll walk across the state of Texas. If he doesn't, he can't walk across the room!"

⚜ HEART ISSUES ☙

1. What if your husband saw himself as you view him—would he believe he could slay a dragon, or would he be ready to throw in the towel?

Paul closes his first letter to the Corinthian believers with a rousing charge, "Be watchful, stand firm in the faith, act like men, be strong" (1 Corinthians 16:13).

Act like men.

Paul was appealing to their inner drive of manhood. How can you make this same appeal without demeaning your husband in the process?

Ask God to teach you how to inspire your husband to "act like a man."

2. Are you guilty of treading on your husband's manhood by taking on his responsibilities?

Read through Ephesians 2. In verse 10 we find that God has prepared good works for your husband to be performing. He is God's workmanship. How have you encouraged him to fulfill all God has prepared for him?

3. In verses 11–22, Paul describes the alienation and division between those who were Gentiles and therefore outside the covenant of promise, and those who are from the commonwealth, that is, citizens of Israel. But because of Jesus Christ, the dividing wall is demolished. He is able to bring unity and peace. He is our peace.

If there is a dividing wall of unacceptance or resentment between you and your husband—seek the Peacemaker. If your husband is hiding behind a wall of rejection, appeal to the One who can bring peace and reconciliation to your home.

Ask your husband what things you could do to demonstrate your acceptance of him. Be prayerfully prepared for this conversation because, if he's resented your lack of acceptance or felt you've rejected his differences, he may unload more information than you expected.

4. Verse 22 describes our relationship as fellow believers as "being built together into a dwelling place for God."

If your husband has a relationship with Christ, then he is your spiritual brother. You are to stand, joined together, as a united and whole structure, housing God's glory. Does your relationship look like a unified and solid gospel structure?

Does your marriage showcase the glory of God?

The Biggies

"It was as if they were not making marriage, but being made by it,
and, while it held them, time and their lives flowed over them, like
swift water over stones, rubbing them together, grinding off their
edges, making them fit together, fit to be together, in the only way that
fragments can be rejoined."

— WENDELL BARRY[1]

In a day when the specter of divorce looms large over our nation,
Norma and Gordon's story shines as a light of encouragement.
Their romance could play as a Hallmark Classic. On the day
she graduated from high school, Norma accepted Gordon's marriage proposal. On May 26, 1939, they took the vow "till death do us
part . . . ," which they quite literally fulfilled. Their children claim the
couple's seventy-two-year long marriage was a "real-life love story."[2]

Over the course of seven decades, Norma, 90, and Gordon, 94,
had rarely been apart. According to their son, "They just loved being

together." On a mid-October morning, as they'd done for years, the couple headed into town together. On the way, they were involved in a car accident that placed them both in the intensive care unit of their local hospital in Marshalltown, Iowa. According to the news report, when they arrived at the hospital, the nurses knew not to separate the couple, and put them in the same room in ICU. Their beds were pushed together, and family members said they were holding hands but otherwise not really responsive.

With family surrounding them, Norma and Gordon spent their final hours as they'd lived their life—holding on to each other. When Gordon stopped breathing, rather than showing a flatline, the monitor was still recording a heartbeat. When the family asked how that was possible, the nurse explained that Norma's heartbeat was running through his body and being picked up by the monitor. Norma followed her husband's exit exactly one hour later. Literally united until death, they left this world holding hands.

Her heartbeat was running through his body. What a sweet picture of intimate connection. I rejoice at every report of a joy-filled marriage that pushes beyond the common; pressing into challenges and obstacles that threaten to tear it apart, in order to go the distance.

Every real-life love story echoes the ultimate love story that we see from the earliest pages of man's history. God initiated this love story. We hear Him use the language of love throughout Scripture as He calls to us as His bride, as He woos us with tender words of affection and promised sacrifice.

"I have loved you with an everlasting love; Therefore I have drawn you with lovingkindness" (Jeremiah 31:3 NASB).

In this chapter, I want us to finish our APPRECIATION acronym by looking at three of the "biggies": intimate connections, only a word, and never giving up. If these three are approached with the determination of a fierce woman who is committed to marriage, chances are the relationship will last the distance.

I: INTIMATE CONNECTIONS

In personal interviews with couples, as well as research through books and blog comments, I keep hearing one recurring theme: Husbands need more sexual intimacy with their wives! Obviously I'm not a man, and I don't pretend to be an expert in this area, but men assure me that this is more than just a desire, it is a legitimate need.

> APPRECIATION
>
> Admire and affirm
> Put yourself in his skin
> Pray like you mean it
> Release your prisoner
> Encourage his leadership
> Contentment
> Invest in him
> Accept him
> Treat him like a man!
> » Intimate connections

Jay posted this comment:

Sex: We can't leave that out can we? When our wives say yes to sex, especially when the wife initiates, we are hearing; "You are a real Man! You have what it takes to lead, provide for and protect me and I want to give all of myself to you." Every man desires to be a Man. Every woman desires to be a beautiful, desirable Woman. Sex is God's gift to marriage for the husband and wife both to affirm, bond to and build up one another. It is a holy act of love when done God's way."[3]

From the earliest days of creation and the first pages of Scripture, God places this beautiful gift within the sacred union. He lays out a plan for mankind to know and understand Him by designing a living metaphor to convey His grand mystery. Marriage is to serve as a picture of the gospel, and the language and passionate experience of sexuality give understanding to the intense excitement and reward of our union with God.

We'll look further into God's use of this amazing metaphor

in chapter 11, but for now, enter this section with the knowledge that your sexuality has more to do with glorifying God than it does your own enjoyment. With that said, God also intends for couples to experience holy sensual pleasure and delight through the sexual relationship and in that, the couple brings Him great glory.

Because your sexual delight in your husband glorifies God, it only stands to reason that the sexual relationship would be a primary target of the enemy. The physical act of oneness is not only a means of procreation (and the enemy hates *new* life), but also it's the pleasurable avenue through which the marital couple can experience the most intimate union possible (and the enemy hates marital unity). When a couple is united emotionally, spiritually, and physically—watch out, because there's real power there!

Please bear with me while I get a little personal with you. I've got some tough questions and I hope you'll receive this section as it's intended—I want you to fully enjoy all the good gifts God has for you—and one of the most enjoyable and sacred gifts He's given is sensual pleasure through sexual intimacy in the marital bed.

HOW WOULD YOUR HUSBAND DESCRIBE YOUR BEDROOM DISPOSITION? ARE YOU A WILDCAT OR A WET BLANKET?

Are you as committed to loving your husband well in the bedroom as you are committed to keeping your family well fed? How often do you tenderly seduce him? Intentionally arouse him through playful flirtation? Do you enjoy making love to your husband? Do you serve him well by giving him a pleasurable experience?

I wonder what would happen if women would expend as much effort in keeping their husband sexually satisfied as getting regular meals on the table. Do you think we'd see fewer roaming husbands? Maybe not. I'm not saying it's your fault if you have a roaming husband or that frequent sexual intimacy is the answer to your marriage problems. But what I am challenging you to consider is whether your approach and attitude to this important component of marriage is glorifying God.

I have an important announcement, girls. NEWS FLASH! Godly wives cultivate a sexy attitude toward their husbands. Taking a dutiful approach to sexuality—merely "servicing" your husband in docile resignation—is not a *godly* response to this sacred treasure of sexuality.

Sadly, a common complaint by men is: "She's a great wife and mom but sometimes I'd like to have more of a wildcat in the bedroom . . . I'd like to feel she actually enjoys when we have sex!" How would your husband describe your bedroom disposition?

Are you a wildcat or a wet blanket?

What does it communicate to your man if you're more passionate about shopping than sleeping with him? If you get more excited over trying out a new restaurant than catching an intimate moment on the couch, you may need to evaluate where your heart is and why your sexual enjoyment level is deficient.

Where's your passion level with your husband?

* Are you flirty and playfully sensual?
* Are you creative with your lovemaking?
* Do you plan for intimacy?
* Do you receive your husband as your lover?
* Do you tenderly initiate intimacy at times when he needs your attention?
* Are you fun and provocative in preparing for intimacy?
* Do you verbalize your enjoyment to him?
* Do you thank him for the experience?
* Do you mention the experience the next day with passionate gratitude?

* Do you let him know you're looking forward to the next time?

I'm fully aware that some women reading this are uncomfortable and frustrated at this point. I also understand that many of us have suffered from the abuse and perversion of childhood sexual violations. But sexual enjoyment within marriage is God's plan and He desires to redeem what the enemy has stolen.

If your attitude toward sexual intimacy is less than what God desires, this is a conversation you need to have with your mate. Often men are unaware that the sexual relationship can be challenging for women for a number of reasons. The wife may have a shame-based view of sexuality or distorted views of modesty. She may have painful memories of past sexual encounters, whether stemming from consensual though immoral relationships, or due to rape or incest. And many women simply are insecure about their body or appearance.

The husband may have a distorted view of the sexual aspect of marriage, or he could have an unhealthy approach to sexuality. Some men can start a quarrel with their wife in the den and fifteen minutes later be ready for lovemaking in the bedroom! They may not have a clue that it is difficult for women to warm up to the idea of sex after a painful conflict. Discussing these differences in an open and nonconfrontational manner is vitally important.

If you have difficulty with sexual intimacy, and have never had this conversation with your husband, please pray about how and when to share this with him. Don't allow the wounds in your life to rob you of this beautiful gift from God. I encourage you to talk with a mature woman who can help you navigate through your pain to a place of healing.

I well remember a conversation I had about sexual intimacy when

I was still a young bride. An older woman I had great respect for (she overflowed with love for Christ) was sharing with me the joy-filled physical relationship she and her husband had experienced for several decades. (At that time I wasn't even sure people that old still had energy or desire for that kind of thing!) She told me that not only was their time spent in passionate physical exchange but often prayers of thanksgiving would be intermingled in their lovemaking. It was a precious word to a share with a young, naïve bride.

And then there's the woman who struggles with the fact that her husband seems to be totally uninterested in her sexually. She's the one wanting more face time with him in the bedroom! I recall one young couple who were having relationship problems in their first year of marriage. She did everything she knew to stimulate sexual interest on his part—receiving only a cold response from him. Later she found out she was competing with his pornography addiction. Husbands who have allowed pornography to shape their sexual appetite generally develop a perverted view of physical intimacy and often lose interest in healthy, God-glorifying sexual encounters with their spouse.

However, if your husband seems to have a low sexual appetite, please don't jump to the conclusion that he's involved in some type of immorality. There could be several factors involved, such as poor self-image or embarrassment; resentment or anger toward his wife; low testosterone level; illness; low energy; fatigue; fear of inadequacy or underachievement. And some men simply are not as interested in sex as others.

If any of the extremes I've shared are descriptive of where you are, please have a conversation with your husband. I'll give more guidance on how to approach a husband who is caught in the addiction of pornography or an immoral lifestyle in chapter 10. Perhaps your husband isn't involved in immorality but is consistently inconsiderate or demeaning—this same approach can be taken by prayerfully, humbly confronting him with this sin. There is so much more to say on this topic than what this small section allows. I encourage you to check out some of the resources on this subject that I have listed in the appendix.

O: ONLY A WORD

It was Thanksgiving Day and the whole Wagner clan was spending the day at Granny's house. I noticed Papaw setting up his new video recorder in a corner of the dining area, but after a bit, it blended in with the rest of the furniture and I forgot it was there. After everyone filled themselves with turkey and dressing and downed the final cups of coffee and pie, we piled into the living room to visit. Papaw wasted no time popping the tape into the VCR (this was pre-DVD era!) so we could watch the events of the day unfold on the TV screen.

APPRECIATION

Admire and affirm
Put yourself in his skin
Pray like you mean it
Release your prisoner
Encourage his leadership
Contentment
Invest in him
Accept him
Treat him like a man!
Intimate connections
» Only a word

I was shocked as I watched myself interact with the family. Oh, there were no arguments or moments of drama—but until I watched that video recording I was completely unaware of how harsh my tone could be, how brusque my responses and how quick I handed out criticism. My cheeks were burning and I wanted to run from the room as I saw the ugliness of my fierceness in full color.

A common characteristic of fierce women is our ability to voice our opinions freely and speak with blunt honesty. When we deliver untempered verbiage to men, it can come across to them as a slam rather than just a strong opinion—and often we're completely unaware of how we sound. But to be honest . . . sometimes some of us actually want to slam.

What is it about "man-slammin"? Why does verbally slamming our husbands come so easily to some of us? Why does it feel good to put down a man we perceive isn't treating us right? I wonder if it might be that we, as women, have learned that our words and wit are the best defensive weapon we have.

> **WHEN WE DELIVER UNTEMPERED VERBIAGE TO MEN, IT CAN COME ACROSS TO THEM AS A SLAM RATHER THAN JUST A STRONG OPINION.**

Let's face it, most of us can't physically take down a man, but many of us have learned the art of emasculating with our words, tone, or body language. Why is that behavior enjoyable at times?

Power

It gives us a sense of power and control to watch our words cause a man to crumple in defeat. Some men don't crumple, some fight back, but even that reaction proves that we struck a nerve that causes him to lose control. I'm ashamed to admit, for too many years I enjoyed verbally assaulting, and I wonder if that may be the case with you.

If you're brave enough to try it, ask one of your children to set up a video recorder at random times through the week to be replayed to the family later. You may not have anything to be ashamed of and possibly even get a kick from the viewing, but I think many of you might be surprised by what you see. You might also appreciate getting a true (albeit painful) picture because, although some wives want to slam their man, I think *unintentional* harm is much more prevalent than intentional.

Often men can wrongly perceive a woman as criticizing a decision he made when the woman just meant to ask a question or get more information. You may not be intentionally man-slammin' but just trying to communicate. If the man seems to pay little attention to what she is voicing, a woman can become frustrated, and her speech can become louder, edgier, and more annoyed just because she feels she's not being heard. In a similar way as the mom who says to a toddler, "I can't hear you when you're whining," a man might react, "I can't hear you when you're criticizing me." A wise wife will learn to speak so her husband can hear what she's saying.

Words Are Powerful

The power of the tongue is amazing. No wonder Proverbs says, "Death and life are in the power of the tongue" (18:21). Sadly, I've often used my tongue and unintentionally crushed a loved one's spirit. James describes the tongue as a "restless evil" and full of deadly poison. He also uses the metaphor of a forest fire to describe the destructive consequences of an untamed tongue: "How great a forest is set ablaze by such a small fire!" (James 3:5).

Once when I was a young mom, I became so disgusted with my inability to control my harsh words that I determined to close my mouth for three whole days. I went on a "tongue fast." My children were old enough for me to explain why I was "holding my tongue," and thankfully my daughter was able to read my quickly scrawled notes when I had to communicate. I recently came across a journal entry written around that time that gives a glimpse into the process God was taking me through:

> I am now firmly convinced that in all my years of living with LeRoy, my mouth has done much damage and brought him great harm. I never intended to hurt him . . . what I thought was helpful insights, meaningful input, or words of counsel . . . actually made him feel totally inadequate. What I intend as a simple suggestion sounds to him like a "failure alarm" and replays the same song in his mind

repeatedly . . . "You'll never measure up . . . You'll never measure up . . . no matter how hard you try, you'll never measure up and you might as well give up . . . 'cause you'll never measure up."

This mental recording was leading LeRoy down a dead-end road. But at the time, he was stuck in a cycle that warped his perspective. Every word I said (no matter how well intentioned) was like a continual dripping . . . a slow and steady stream speaking failure. "A continual dripping on a rainy day and a quarrelsome wife are alike," Proverbs 27:15 asserts.

ULTIMATELY THERE MUST BE A HEART CHANGE THAT RESULTS IN A MOUTH CHANGE.

I wonder if the wife this verse refers to considered herself "quarrelsome" or if she was thinking she was "helping her husband improve" or perhaps that she needed to give continual input for his own good. By God's grace, I've grown some in the years since the "tongue fast," but there are still times when I find myself wishing I could tape my mouth shut!

An unguarded tongue easily runs out of control. A tongue can slander, gripe, complain, accuse, and annihilate, and all within a matter of minutes! Tongues have the ability to inspire the hardest heart but also crush a tender spirit. This is why Proverbs 21:23 warns us to "guard the tongue" in order to stay out of trouble.

But how do we do that?

Most of us would agree that guarding, or taming our tongues, is ultimately a deep-rooted heart issue. So, duct-taping the mouth is merely a topical solution—it only results in stopping the verbal flow of inner garbage. Ultimately there must be a heart change that results in a mouth change . . . but . . . could part of the heart purification process involve the difficult choice to *bridle* our tongues?

James warns us that we've nothing to boast about in our

Christianity if we're not actively working to "bridle our tongues." Just as a horse needs a bridle to direct its course, we need to put "bridles" or disciplines in place that will help in taming our tongues. This also trains us in the heart issue of needed self-control, a fruit of the Spirit.

While James states that no one in her own power can "tame the tongue," thankfully God provides all we need to discipline this unruly critter (2 Peter 1:3–8). As we cooperate with Him, yielding to the Spirit's control, the heart begins to respond and the tongue comes under the discipline of the "bridling" effort.

Here are some practical tips to help tame that unruly tongue:

Ask the Holy Spirit

Ask the Holy Spirit to reveal when your tongue does not glorify Christ, and for grace to speak life-giving words. When everyone in the household is having trouble taming their tongues, call for an "Ephesians 4:29 Day" when all agree that "no unwholesome word" will be spoken that day but only words that give encouragement, blessing, and grace—and invite the Holy Spirit to take charge of your tongues for the day!

Ask for Input from Family Members and Friends

This can be humbling but it allows those who know us best to uncover "blind spots." Please don't do this if you're prone to respond to their honesty with an offended spirit or hurt feelings. Also, don't unload your grievances or clobber them with their blind spots if they don't ask for your input. Before inviting inspection, be prepared with a receptive heart! (See Proverbs 27:5–6.)

Post and Plant Scriptures

Nothing is more effective than the Word when it comes to gaining victory over strongholds. Do a word study on the tongue and record specific Scriptures that apply to your personal struggle with the tongue. Proverbs and James are great places to dig out wisdom on this topic. Grab a few verses that personally apply and post them in prominent locations and begin planting these in your heart and mind.

Ask a Friend to Hold You Accountable

Share specific areas of need and pray together for victory and grace. If you don't have a friend willing to come alongside you in this project, consider using your journal to hold yourself accountable. Get honest and write down when you fail or when you get victory. After logging your journey for a period of weeks, see if you can trace common trigger points for both failure and victory.

Practice the Principle of Crying Out for HELP!

When tempted: Stop. Close your mouth. Take a deep breath and cry out for God's grace to overcome the temptation to spew poison (or start a forest fire) with your tongue!

Use Fewer Words

Practice the spiritual discipline of "quiet" (Proverbs 10:19). I really cannot overemphasize the beauty of restraint that comes from measuring your words. Much of what flows out of our mouths is better left unsaid.

When we were first married, my husband challenged me with the ideal of "only speaking when spoken through," i.e., "spoken through" by the Holy Spirit. I only know One who was able to fulfill that, but I still think it's a worthy standard to shoot for.

One thing I've learned since I've started guarding my tongue and no longer running my mouth with nonstop verbiage . . . my husband has more to say!

As Oliver Wendell Holmes put it, "It is the province of knowledge to speak and it is the privilege of wisdom to listen."

Learn to HALT!

I wish I'd known the HALT principle as a teen, and especially as a young bride. Practicing it would have saved me from countless conflicts, I'm sure. This principle is not for "sweeping things under the rug" or avoiding difficult conversations, but should be used as a protective device for times when it would be best to delay any conversation with heavy content, which could lead to conflict or emotional meltdowns.

Here's how it works in relation to the tongue. Restrain your words—or even just shut your mouth—and delay weighty conversations when you are:

H—Hungry
A—Angry
L—Lonely
T—Tired

You may be tempted to unload the frustrations of your day on your husband as soon as he walks in from a long day on the job.

Push pause.

Although you may be bursting at the seams to vent, be sensitive to the fact that your man may be tired. He may have faced many challenges through the course of his day, as well. Give him a break. Give him time and grace to relax, refuel, and recharge, before entering a conversation that will require much energy. Ask God to give you the grace to HALT before speaking.

Life-Giving Words

Guarding our tongues is more than protection against speaking "death-filled" words, but it is the means of being a verbal life-giver as well. Remember that woman from Proverbs 27:15 who's like a continual dripping? If she's pouring out ugly criticisms and harsh rebukes, she's dripping death words (Proverbs 18:21). What do we do if we enter a home or building with a leaky roof and a continual dripping? If the drip lands on our heads . . . we'll run for cover.

Women often complain to me that their husband doesn't seem to listen . . . or that he never wants her input or suggestions. It reminds me of the continual dripping. Perhaps after standing under the drip one too many times, he decides he needs to take shelter, to run for cover . . . and he's decided to stay put. He's closed his ears to the continual dripping because he doesn't want to be hit with it again.

APPRECIATION

Admire and affirm
Put yourself in his skin
Pray like you mean it
Release your prisoner
Encourage his leadership
Contentment
Invest in him
Accept him
Treat him like a man!
Intimate connections
Only a word
» **N**ever give up!

The husband who's run for cover will need to believe you're pouring out life-giving words rather than continually dripping death before he's willing to open his ears to listen. And that will take time.

It took a long time of pouring out life-giving words before my husband came out of hiding. But the foundation of consistent life-giving words has now given me a platform to speak truth, blessing, and yes, even counsel, into his life. He welcomes my input and invites my suggestions often.

N: NEVER GIVE UP!

I was searching for words to give hope and comfort to yet another woman dealing with her husband's infidelity. I've heard the same story so often, but every time it freshly breaks my heart. Cell phone records showed numerous texts and calls throughout the day and late night hours to a woman he worked with, a woman with the

reputation of involvement with several different men at his company. And this wasn't the first time he'd been unfaithful. I was
appealing to her to wait before doing anything hasty, to allow God
to work through her husband as he was confronted biblically by
godly men of the church.

"I can't do this again! I will not go through it another time!" Her
pain and anger were justified and understandable.

LeRoy's reaction to me privately was "Is he still seventeen, or
what?" His frustration stemmed from disappointment over yet
another man, in a long line of men, who so easily toss aside marital fidelity. The virtues of loyalty, honor, duty, and integrity seem to
hold no claim on their lives. A broken vow means nothing to them.

Another loss.

She texted me the next day that she'd moved out.

We've not yet seen how this will play out. We're praying, sharing truth, waiting expectantly, and hoping he'll respond to biblical
confrontation. But one thing is evident: once again, vows are only as
binding as the commitment level of the couple.

Carol and her husband shared a close friendship with John and
his wife. The two couples, along with their young children, developed a friendship that included spending family vacations and
holidays together. Both couples would have described their marriages as happy until Carol and John began to "fall in love." The
foursome then became a twosome. Carol and John cast aside their
vows with their first spouses to voice new vows to each other when
they wed.

They described their relationship as moving from friendship to
one where they couldn't help themselves because they had fallen in
love. John said he'd never believed in such a thing as a soul mate
before meeting Carol. The couple's infidelity was highly publicized
due to their visible social status—John was an executive at a large

company, while Carol, besides being a mother of two, was a reporter and anchor for a local television station.

In an interview with a newspaper columnist, John conceded he had concerns about the pain it would bring to their children and spouses if they acted on their feelings. In the end, feelings won out over the prior vows shared with first spouses. Carol explained that her children would know she wasn't perfect, but would one day understand her actions because of her love for John.

Sadly, this modern "romance" graphically depicts a prevalent notion of love. But this type of "love" leaves a wake of pain and devastation. Vows are lightly made and easily broken when self-centered feelings take priority.

Ask anyone who knows my husband well and they'll tell you he's pretty picky when it comes to performing a wedding ceremony. Oh, he doesn't get hung up on the cosmetic details of the event, what kind of wedding venue, indoor or outdoor, if the bride's wearing jeans or a formal . . . but he does get hung up on some other stuff. Stuff like the couple's commitment level and willingness to put in some tough marital prep time with us.

> WE FEEL LIKE WE'RE CONTINUALLY STANDING ON THE SIDELINES, YELLING, "HANG IN THERE! DON'T GIVE UP! THE LONG HAUL IS WORTH IT!"

He wants the couple to understand the seriousness of their vows. We cover those things in great detail in our lengthy season of required premarital counseling (which also prevents some couples from asking him to perform their wedding ceremony). He'd rather put in a ton of work on the front end of their marriage than find their marriage in shambles later.

The bulk of his pastoral counseling is marital. We feel like we're continually standing on the sidelines, yelling, "Hang in there! Don't give up! The long haul is worth it!" We've seen people create the most bizarre justifications for leaving their mate.

Several years ago a middle-aged man with a loving wife, two precious children, and a high amount of respect in our community and church came to my husband to tell him he was going to leave his wife. Over the course of several conversations, he used "spiritual" reasons to defend this as a righteous choice. He'd determined that since he had been "outside God's will" when he married his wife, he now needed to terminate the relationship. It seems that his meeting another woman suddenly made it all clear—and it was now "God's will" for him to marry her.

Typically when a couple agrees to wed, they enter marriage believing they've found the one person who will satisfy their desire for companionship, but within five years too many couples' dream of marital bliss ends in divorce. So it's time to move on to find the "right one," the one who'll be what they hoped to find the first time. Messed-up thinking like that not only litters the landscape of our nation, but it seems to characterize many in positions of leadership in our churches. But Jesus has a different take on this issue.

When a group of people asked Jesus about the issue of divorce, He used the first couple to illustrate His answer. He stressed the joining of two, and used a very powerful and descriptive word—"joined." In the original language, this word carries the sense of an indissoluble union.[4]

"And He answered and said, 'Have you not read that He who created them from the beginning made them male and female, and said, "For this reason a man shall leave his father and mother and be joined to his wife, and the two shall become one flesh"'?" (Matthew 19:4–5 NASB).

What couples desperately need today is staying power when the going gets tough. We need right thinking and the network of loved ones willing to hold struggling couples accountable to their marital vows. We need pastors and churches who promote covenant marriages—no-turning-back marriages—and not only promote them but help build them through biblical modeling and training. We need couples who understand and embrace the big picture and God's plan for marriage.

Staying power:

* Take the word *divorce* out of your vocabulary.
* Rather than running to friends who'll "dis" your husband with you, surround yourself with truth-speaking friends who will help you stay committed to your marriage.
* Cut off every source of temptation for extramarital relationships.
* Be intentional in applying every effort to cultivate unity.
* KEEP DATING!!! (Each other, of course—and this one's huge.)
* When tempted to give up—revisit God's big picture for marriage.
* Keep your heart closely tied to the cross and yielded to the gospel.

Understanding and embracing the gospel gives couples the staying power needed to flesh out true love in marriage. Usually the biggest shock for a new bride is the amount of serving, hard work, and die-to-self moments that marriage requires. More than domestic duties, beyond daily responsibilities and piles of laundry, just the gritty challenge of "serving" can come as quite a blow to someone accustomed to living primarily for herself.

Knowing how unprepared I was as a newlywed, I've taken many young women to meet my parents in order to prepare them for living out the hard places of their vows—the "for better or for worse" part; the "in sickness and in health" part. I want them to see more than what the glitzy bridal magazines are showing them.

For the last four years of my father's life, my mom was his primary caregiver. He valiantly fought a ten-year battle with lymphoma, but after it reached his brain he began a slow descent that eventually took all his mental abilities. When my mom vowed at age eighteen to care for him in sickness and in health, she wasn't much more than a child. She surely couldn't see what the final years of their more than five-decades-long romance held.

Clasping hands with the six-foot-four, muscular young man at the wedding altar, she would never have guessed that the brilliant love of her life would one day lose the ability to drive, walk, frame sentences correctly, bathe, toilet, or feed himself. This highly intelligent man who could do calculus in his head, recall names, historical events, dates, and insignificant details with clarity and precision . . . in his final years never knew the day of the week, the season, or current year, and couldn't recall the simplest of facts. Thankfully, he knew our names to the end.

The giant of a man who brought a room to life with just his smile and never met a stranger settled into a silent existence in his final months. The days were long and lonely. But my mom served him faithfully, daily, until the once blazing fire of his life slowly ebbed into a smoldering wick; then he was gone.

If you ask my mom why she continued caring for my dad, when eventually her own health began to significantly deteriorate, her simple reply is—she loved him.

The idea of abandoning her vows was never a thought. She loved him. She loved him with the kind of love that has staying power. This is the kind of love I want women to embrace. A love that goes beyond feelings. A love fleshed out in a commitment that stands the test of time and hardship. A love tied to a vow that's settled in the heart as a lifetime commitment to God first and then to her mate.

This is the kind of love I'm talking about. This is the kind of love I invite you to give to your husband.

⚘ HEART ISSUES ↵

1. We've covered a lot of territory in this chapter as we've looked at "three biggies." Where does this chapter find you?

    What are the biggies you struggle with?

    How committed are you to satisfying your husband sexually (and enjoying it)?

    How committed are you to guarding your tongue and pouring out life-giving words to your husband?

    How committed are you to living out your vow "till death do you part"?

    How are you displaying your commitment in these areas?

2. Prayerfully read through Ephesians 3.

    Four times (depending on your translation) Paul uses the word "mystery" in referring to the hidden work of the gospel that God is now revealing. According to verse 10, God is putting this amazing mystery on display for the angels to see what He's hidden for ages. They've longed to see and discover this mystery (1 Peter 1:12).

    What does verse 10 say He's going to use as His vehicle or agent to display this mystery?

    How long has He had this plan (v. 11)?

3. Let the description in verses 16–19 become your prayer in order to carry out the level of commitment I'm inviting you to in this chapter. I pray for you to experience (as I have/am) the beautiful reward

that verse 20 describes. Ask God to restore your marriage. Ask Him to give you and your husband a unity and love beyond what you can even imagine.

Remember, the happiness and reward that mature love brings will never be known by those who give up early. Use verse 21 to pour out your heart in praise to our glorious Savior as we conclude this chapter.

CHAPTER 10

What If He's Not Listening?

"I require all things that are grand and true,

All things that a man should be;

If you give all this, I would stake my life

To be all you demand of me."

— MARY LATHRAP[1]

I laid the receiver in the cradle. Hot tears slid and dripped off my chin. Failed again. Another wasted phone call. Why wouldn't he listen? How could I make him understand? We'd be celebrating our two-year anniversary in the fall—only eighteen months into this marriage and I was lonely, frustrated, and miserable. Why wouldn't he just come home?

My mom's diagnosis of breast cancer earlier in the year brought changes to all our lives. She was recovering from a massive double mastectomy, but she still had a long way to go. She needed me to come home during our summer break to care for her, so when LeRoy and I finished final exams, we packed up our lives and made the move from Dallas.

My father offered him a temporary job in his business for the interim period. A job in the office I hoped? Nope. Not quite. What I'd always feared . . . LeRoy climbed into one of those big trucks and took off over the road. Remember the kind of truck I described in chapter 8? You know—the kind that every little boy dreams of driving one day? Eighteen wheels pulling forty tons?

Yep. That kind of truck.

It was one long, desolate summer. I was absolutely opposed to him taking off for weeks at a time for this kind of job. Now, before you think my husband was totally insensitive, from his perspective this was the best option for taking care of our financial needs before returning to school in the fall. But at the time, I was too immature to look beyond today and trust that God had this all under control. I was also too selfish to see that this was the best way, for now, for him to take care of us financially. All I could think of was my pain. I was consumed by loneliness. I was miserable with the long solitary nights and angry that he didn't seem bothered by the situation. I didn't see him suffering any—*in fact he seemed to actually be having fun!*

Being on a tight delivery schedule as a truck driver made it difficult for LeRoy to squeeze in time for phone calls, plus back in the day calling wasn't so easy. There were phone booths (google it if you're under thirty) at public locations for motorists to use when needing a phone while in transit. Not having cell phones, iPhones, or any kind of mobile communication device meant you couldn't talk to your hubby anytime you wanted. No texting. No email. No immediate access. I seemed to be continually hoping and waiting for the phone to ring because I certainly couldn't call him whenever I wanted to talk to him—no cell phone for him to answer!

Whenever LeRoy could find time to make a call, it was a major hassle to find an area large enough for his Big Rig to pull into and park so he could use a public phone booth. If I happened to be at the grocery store or out running errands when he called, forget it. At least we had an answering machine. If he called while I was out, he'd leave me a brief message saying he would try to call again and reach me in a day or two (sigh). Our calls were few and far between, and when we did connect, the call was short.

I gave you that long explanation to let you know—I had little contact with my almost brand-new husband that summer.

And I hated it.

Now, you would think that when we finally had a chance to talk, I'd be jumping up and down with excitement and bubbling over with sweetness.

Nope.

In my twisted way of thinking, I decided he needed to know how miserable I was. He needed to hear my pain. I was one wretched woman dripping my death words into his ears: "Death and life are in the power of the tongue . . ." (Proverbs 18:21).

Do you think he looked forward to those phone calls?

Nope.

Do you think he looked forward to coming home?

Nope.

As I look back now, I'm actually surprised he didn't just keep heading to California and never return! I certainly wasn't influencing him to come home and snuggle—who would want to wrap their arms around a grouchy porcupine?

I really did miss him, I really wanted to talk and laugh with him—and sometimes that would happen, but most of our calls and brief visits were spoiled by my complaining about how unhappy I was with his job, our life, and griping about his willingness to spend so much time on the road.

I appealed for him to get off the road, to come home, to find a different type of short-term job, to do anything for us to be together! My appeal fell on deaf ears.

I was a puppy. I was very green and immature . . . should have been further along in what we call the sanctification process, but I wasn't. I didn't realize how self-centered I was, and I didn't know how to handle adversity. I had a lot to learn. But I also needed a voice.

I was making appeals for change, but no one was listening. I needed to learn how to prepare a place to stand so that my request would be heard.

BUILDING A PLATFORM OF INFLUENCE

Can you relate to the frustration of talking, but feeling like your husband isn't listening? Are you irritated thinking he's really not measuring up as a husband? After walking through the APPRECIATION acronym, you may feel as though I'm saying all the responsibility for improving your marriage relationship lies with you.

YOU NEED TO PREPARE A SOLID FOUNDATION TO SPEAK FROM BEFORE YOUR APPEALS WILL BE HEARD.

Far from it.

But keep it in mind that love is a powerful change agent and as you apply yourself to following the way of the cross, you'll find that even if you see no change in your husband, a beautiful change will begin within you.

Remember, *you* can't fix your husband—neither can you fix your marriage. You may have shown love and appreciation but nothing's changed. In this chapter, I'm going to give you several practical steps to aid you in becoming a woman of influence in your husband's life.

I'll also include in the appendix guidelines for confrontation that's necessary when physical or mental abuse or other blatantly sinful situations are present. You need to prepare a solid foundation to speak from before your appeals will be heard.

Let's work our way through Ephesians 4 and find components to use in building a platform of influence. This chapter will be more meaningful if you read through the verses referenced in each section. Pull out your Bible, and let's do some digging so we can lay the foundation for your platform!

POWERFULLY POSITIONED (EPHESIANS 4:1–10)

In the Heart Issues section at the end of chapter 7, I asked you to compile a list as a record of "who you are in *Christ.*" If you haven't done that, I encourage you to go back and do that activity or review Ephesians 1. This will give you a better understanding of your position in Christ.

In Ephesians 4:1 Paul makes an important designation when he labels himself the "prisoner of the Lord." Paul's heart was fully captured by Christ. He'd settled the issue of ownership long before his imprisonment. He was Christ's bondslave, and in this position of slave—because he was submitted entirely to God's authority—Paul was actually in the greatest position of influence possible. When we're letting God call the shots, we become influential for His purposes—God is all about influence.

God wants to use our position as bondslaves to Him as a means of influencing those around us to know and love Christ.

It's all about bringing Him glory.

Paul's influence wasn't limited by his location (prison). You and I are reading what he penned while in prison—*almost two thousand years ago!* I'd say that's pretty influential. He trusted God with his future, with the outcome of his trial in Rome—literally with his life.

From his dark prison cell, Paul couldn't look forward through the millennia to see the impact of his sacrificial service on the church and the world, but you and I now know how powerfully he was used.

You may feel as though you're pretty insignificant. You may have lost any sense of purpose and believe you're stuck in a rut of meaningless activity. You may feel your role as a wife has no bearing on God's kingdom being advanced. But I want to remind you, if you are Christ's bondslave, if you're plugged into God's plan—He will accomplish more through you than you can imagine! Trust me; His purpose for you is on a *huge* scale.

The most important aspect of a woman of influence is her position: who she is in Christ.

Has He fully captured your heart?

Have you settled the issue of ownership?

Do you live as one who belongs to the living God? Are you seeking your satisfaction in Him or are you looking in other places? Are you looking to other people to fulfill your deepest needs? Your husband can't be your all in all. A hazy fog from prescription drugs may take the edge off—but it won't satisfy . . . a Facebook affair may give you tingles, but that's an empty fix. Nothing. *Nothing* can compare with Christ. There is no buzz, no high, no relationship that comes near. The Beautifully Fierce Woman's identity and value are rooted in her relationship with Christ rather than in a relationship with a man.

If you only get one thing from reading this book—please get this:

MAKE SURE JESUS IS YOUR ALL IN ALL. HE ALONE DESERVES TO FILL THAT PLACE OF LONGING, TO BE THE ETERNAL LOVER OF YOUR SOUL, TO BE THE SEAT OF YOUR AFFECTIONS. HE IS THE LIVING GOD. LET YOUR HEART FIND ITS JOY IN THE ONE WHO IS "OVER ALL AND THROUGH ALL AND IN ALL."

When you settle the issue of ownership and sink your heart and desires deeply into all that entails, a lot of the peripheral stuff that keeps bogging you down—bitterness, anger, unforgiveness, discontentment—will be settled. When that's taken care of, you may find that your voice no longer needs to be heard on a few issues. It may be that a "platform to speak from" is not your greatest need—perhaps your greatest need is a heart change.

A lot of my misery that summer as a trucker widow could have been alleviated if I'd focused on Jesus as my all in all. I loved Him, spent time in His Word (randomly, not devotedly), and I belonged to Him. Naturally, I missed LeRoy, and it was right that I did. But my heart kept drifting, as I spent more time pining to be with my husband rather than passionately pursuing Christ and finding joy in *His* presence (Psalm 16:11); He who was always with me and not out on the road! I was a long way from what Paul describes as "walking worthy."

WALKING WORTHY

Do you find it a little humbling, as I do, that Paul is imploring his readers to "walk worthy" of their calling to follow Christ—while he's writing from a prison? I mean, if there's anybody who's got the credibility to challenge his readers on their commitment level, it's the apostle Paul! "I therefore, a prisoner for the Lord, urge you to walk in a manner worthy of the calling to which you have been called" (Ephesians 4:1).

I've spent—no, wasted—too many years wandering around in self-pity. And whenever I hear Paul speaking from a prison, I have to duck my head and admit that I've never endured the amount of opposition he faced (check out 2 Corinthians 11). So no matter how hard, lonely, or difficult—no matter where you are right now in your marriage—I hope you'll listen to this faithful warrior, as he goes on to spell out what walking worthy looks like. He makes it pretty clear: "With all humility and gentleness, with patience, bearing with one another in love, eager to maintain the unity of the Spirit in the bond of peace" (Ephesians 4:2–3).

NONE OF THIS COMES NATURALLY; IT COMES AS A RESULT OF THE POTTER CONFORMING US TO THE IMAGE OF CHRIST AS WE SURRENDER TO HIM.

Hmmm . . . if this is what a "worthy" soldier of Christ looks like . . . if this is the conduct that conveys my position in Christ . . . how am I doing?

Are these identifying characteristics shaping my relationship with my husband?

Do I respond to him in humility and gentleness and regularly exercise patience?

Do I show him the kind of love Christ shows me?

Am I eager to maintain one-souled unity with him? (Philippians 2:2).

None of this comes naturally. And none of this comes immediately at the point of conversion to Christ. It comes as a result of the Potter conforming us to the image of Christ as we surrender to Him (Jeremiah 18:1–4; Romans 8:28–29). It comes from being pliable, soft, moldable clay in His hands. His grace then brings growth and maturity. And this kind of growth comes from personal pursuit of Him, but also from being plugged into the body—His church.

Plugged In and Benefitting from the Body of Christ (vv. 11–13)

God has provided a network to aid believers in growing up to look like Christ. It's called the church. He's put into place shepherds, older believers, mature saints, teachers, and exhorters who will instruct, model, confront, and hold us accountable in our walk. The best place to grow young plants is in a greenhouse, and the best place to grow young believers is within a healthy church.

A church that follows the Titus 2 model of older training younger allows the young mom to glean from the years of experience of an older mom. It provides newlyweds with the resources of wisdom from golden-agers. It places single women, the needy, and lonely within a family, a home of loving fellowship and protection. The church (as we'll see later in this chapter) provides the means of recourse for wives who are suffering under abusive treatment by their husbands.

You may be wondering why you're not seeing this happening within your church, or perhaps you've been burned by a church experience. I appeal to you to seek God and ask Him to plant you and your family in a Christ-centered, Word-driven, God-glorifying, healthy church body where sound doctrine is taught and lived out. I believe one of the reasons I struggled so much that summer is that I wasn't plugged into a church that held me accountable or supplied teaching that challenged me to grow.

Growing Spiritually (vv. 14–16)

Personal spiritual growth isn't as easy as you might think. You may have known Christ since childhood, and now be connected with the type of healthy church I've described, but if you've only plopped into the pew and are waiting for the miracle of maturity to descend, I can tell you that it won't be happenin'.

I remember being a young woman with a passion for Christ, so wanting to be conformed to His image, to look like Christ, yet continually discouraged by my consistent failure. My harsh tones, angry outbursts, petty immaturity, selfishness, self-pity, and general all-around ugliness toward my husband indicated I was not growing into the beautiful warrior for Christ I so desired to be.

It took awhile, but eventually I learned that sincere desire alone was not enough. I didn't yet understand that being a "living sacrifice"

(Romans 12:1) means just that. It requires more than just dying to my old self-centered desires, but it also requires loving Christ more than self, and that means applying His truth to the hard choices of daily life. My goal—or the destination I had in mind—was spiritual maturity. My desire was to grow up to look like Christ (Ephesians 4:15). But I wasn't going to reach that destination by being an inactive participant in the living sacrifice process. Becoming a woman of influence in your husband's life will require spiritual maturity.

To think we can reach spiritual maturity by just waiting for it to take place is about as silly as wanting to travel from Arkansas to Michigan by sitting in a parked car. If I get in the car (salvation/ conversion) and just wait—I am in the driver's seat, have my map (and a GPS!), full tank of gas, I'm really excited, lots of desire—but I never turn the key or back out of my driveway, i.e., the hard work of actually driving the car toward my destination, I will never make it to Michigan or even to the end of the block!

Building a platform of influence comes at great cost. The personal cost for growth to take place is making the hard choices that result in conformity to Christ. If I truly want to see change take place in my life (and in my marriage), it means I must climb up on the Potter's wheel, with love for Christ as my motive. I must view the hard places of my life as my altar, and lie down as a living sacrifice—and from that death, love for others will flow (Ephesians 4:16). Remember, one characteristic of a Beautifully Fierce Woman is that her life is lived all out for God's glory rather than the smallness of self.

Pouring Out Life-Giving Words (vv. 15, 29)

A platform of influence is built on conversations of grace. Conversations of grace are not empty words without meaning, or comfy, feel-good talks where sin is ignored, but grace talks are filled with honesty and delivered in humility. When the heart is Christ-centered rather than self-centered, and when the mind is governed by truth and love for others is the motive for speaking, gracious conversation flows freely (Luke 6:45).

That summer, I wasn't holding any grace talks. Instead I was a continual, annoying dripping (Proverbs 27:15), and my husband ran for cover. He wasn't listening. Instead of dripping death words, I needed to learn how to pour out life-giving words.

What do I mean by life-giving words?

I like how these verses describe them: "A word fitly spoken is like apples of gold in a setting of silver" (Proverbs 25:11). And, "Let no unwholesome word proceed from your mouth, but only such a word as is good for edification according to the need of the moment, so that it will give grace to those who hear" (Ephesians 4:29 NASB).

> A WORD ACCORDING TO THE NEED OF THE MOMENT IS SOLID TRUTH AIMED AT FILLING HIS HEART WITH HOPE AND CONFIDENCE IN GOD.

It is pouring out life rather than dripping death with statements that fit the need of the moment such as when your husband calls home to say he's just been fired. Or when your eyes are on the unattended-to house repairs while his are on the Internet. Or the times when he's running late yet again, or he's determined to stay in a vocation you hate, or when he's bought into the lie that he'll never be able to do anything right.

Every day brings opportunity to choose to speak life, to give a word that's "according to the need of the moment, so that it will give grace to those who hear." More than words of affirmation (chapter 6) or assurances of your support—a word according to the need of the moment is solid truth aimed at filling his heart with hope and confidence in God. A Beautifully Fierce Woman, remember, is one who is known as a sincere encourager.

Using Words That Fit the Need of the Moment

"It's going to be all right." Whether we feel like it or not, the truth is that, because of God's sovereignty and goodness . . . even if the worst scenario possible plays itself out . . . if we believe God . . . then it is going to be all right in the end. Perhaps not in our lifetime—but it will be all right. At a time when doubt is assaulting and fear is reigning, this simple word of truth helps to put steel in your husband's spine.

"We've not yet seen the rest of the story." I love this truth! I love the fact that I'm old enough now to truly appreciate and believe it. I often open old journals to encourage myself with the knowledge gained on this side of the trial I've recorded there. When I read where I was broken, suffering, and crying out for help—and now see what God was doing and how He's used that in my life—it provides courage for today.

"This is an opportunity for us to be conformed to Christ's image." You don't have to preach a message on God's sovereignty or spell out Romans 8:28–29 to your husband at a moment of crisis. Simply make this truth statement with a smile and a hug to let him know you're confident of God's work and assure him there's grace to make it through! The Fierce Woman courageously faces her fears, and she can encourage her man as he does the same.

Practicing Purity of Heart, Mind, and Body (vv. 17–25)

In order to build a platform of influence, you need the dignity of spiritual maturity, you need love for Christ and others, you need to be pouring out life-giving words . . .

And you need purity.

Purity is developed by continually bathing in the Word (Ephesians 5:26), being refreshed by the Word, instructed by the Word, and feeding on the Word (Psalm 119:9, 24, 38, 130–31).

Truthful thinking, speaking, and living come from Word-saturation. When my thoughts begin to conform to God's thoughts, it will affect my perspective and eventually my behavior. I won't be able to respond to a Facebook flirtation or spend hours in romance fantasies. I won't be at ease maintaining a secret lifestyle.

I won't be satisfied living like my "old self" if I'm actively applying myself to the pursuit of godliness. In Scripture, it's called being trained in righteousness (Titus 2:12–14). A Word-saturated woman won't be comfortable vegging out in front of a garbage-filled screen or neglecting the spiritual disciplines that nourish a needy soul.

The regular practice of spiritual disciplines purifies the heart, mind, and body and include reading, meditating on and memorizing Scripture, fasting and prayer, bodily exercise, inspirational and solid doctrinal reading, godly fellowship, singing, and contemplative worship. The purification process strips me of self-serving, impure motives, and refines my perspective—which is necessary in building a platform of influence. This is the kind of behavior that can influence your husband without you even opening your mouth:

". . . They may be won without a word by the conduct of their wives, when they see your respectful and pure conduct" (1 Peter 3:1–2).

Removing the Devil's Opportunity and Preserving Unity (vv. 26–32)

One piece of counsel my husband and I repeatedly stress in premarital sessions is: once you're married, do not go to bed with unfinished business. Don't end your day with unresolved conflict (but also don't stay up till 3:00 a.m. trying to get your point across!).

The enemy uses every opportunity to find an open doorway in your relationship—and once there, he starts taking vital ground in order to build a stronghold for his influence in your life. When I'm holding on to bitterness and hurt, I'm grieving the Holy Spirit. I've "lost contact" with Him in a sense. When I'm in unrepentant sin, I go off kilter fast. We all do. That's why stuffing our problems leads to more problems. We must be diligent to work at unity by keeping lines of communication open.

Late one night, in our first year of marriage, I was put to the test on preserving the fellowship with LeRoy. We'd spent our first Christmas as a married couple at my parents' house and came home loaded down with leftovers from the meal. The entire three-hour trip home, I couldn't stop craving the meringue pies that I had carefully placed on top of our luggage in the rear hatchback compartment of our little Toyota before leaving Mom's house.

We were living in a rental home at the time and had inherited a herd of wild roaming cats (really; thirteen to be exact). They hid out in a barn on the property but would show up anytime food was on the premises. I'd learned the hard way that I had to close the car doors and hatchback while unloading groceries or they'd plunder any packaged meat or food items left in the open vehicle.

Our normal routine when unloading from a trip is that on arrival we each grab as much as we can and head into the house with the first load. Then as LeRoy brings in the rest, I put things away inside. As I was grabbing my things, I stressed to LeRoy to bring in the pies first before the cats could get them. He assured me he had this under control and asked me to go inside and start getting ready for bed. I was happy to comply—*we were wiped.*

I WAS GETTING READY TO BLOW WHEN HE HELD UP ONE HAND AND SAID, "WAIT."

I knew something was wrong when I heard him quietly say, "Honey, can you come in here, please?" He was standing at the kitchen doorway with two pie plates, one in each hand, and a sick look on his face. I came closer to see. Little ugly paw prints tracked all through both meringues and one pie was thoroughly demolished. I took one of the plates from him and started fuming. My blood began to boil (mainly at the cats—but I was pretty mad at him as well). In an almost trembling voice he explained, "I'm sorry, but by the time I went back outside to get these, they'd already swarmed the pies."

He could tell from the look on my face that this wasn't going to be pretty. I was getting ready to blow when he held up one hand and said, "Wait . . . before you say anything . . . I just want to remind you that angels are watching. And the spirit realm is waiting to see how you'll react to this. The enemy would love for this to get to you!"

Oh, great. How could I say anything after that? His little impromptu speech about the spiritual realm (whether entirely theologically accurate or not) had shut me down before I had the chance to let a word spew. It took a lot to swallow what I wanted to say, but out of respect for "watching angels" (hate to admit it but—it certainly wasn't out of respect for my husband), I kept quiet. I've told him in the years since that incident that I wish he would've pulled "the spiritual realm is listening" card more often to get me to hold my tongue!

Remember the HALT principle from the last chapter?

This is a perfect example of when that principle needs to be put into action. I was hungry and tired by the time we made it home that night . . . a prime target for the enemy. If I would've let my anger boil over and unleashed my tongue on my husband, we both would've probably gone to bed in a stew—mad and not wanting to reconcile. And that is the most fertile ground for the enemy to plant his venomous lies. This is why Ephesians 4:26 gives the warning to not let the sun go down on your anger.

The answer isn't to stuff your anger or vent it—but let it go by grabbing on to the forgiveness and grace that builds the protection of unity.

PROTECTION FOR RELATIONSHIPS

The Beautifully Fierce Woman has the power to influence and inspire because she lives under the Spirit's control. It is important to remind ourselves that we're in a spiritual battle, and it is imperative to guard unity in our marriage. When we're divided by a wall of unforgiveness, the Spirit is grieved (Ephesians 4:30), and that leaves us vulnerable to the enemy's attacks. But thankfully Ephesians 4:32 gives us the cross-centered way of operating that brings protection for our relationships: "Be kind to one another, tender-hearted, forgiving each other, just as God in Christ also has forgiven you" (Ephesians 4:32 NASB).

And here we reach the heart of living out the gospel: forgiving each other just as we've been forgiven. The way of the cross prevents the enemy from capitalizing on opportunities to divide a couple and plant his poison in vulnerable minds. The way of the cross provides the power of influence for the soft warrior's battle for her marriage.

The only hope for two sinners to survive and thrive in a marriage is by adopting this as our criteria for relating to one another: the gospel saturated lifestyle of kindness, tenderhearted care, and cross-centered forgiveness in the good times and in the tough times. This is our protection.

No matter how you may be feeling about your relationship with your husband, one thing is certain: God's heart is one of reconciliation. None of us deserve God's forgiveness, mercy, or blessing—yet He gives it. None of us deserve His commitment of fidelity—yet He is unrelenting in it. None of us deserve second chances or His patience—yet He is long-suffering with each of us.

As you make progress in the areas we've looked at in Ephesians 4, your influence with your husband will have more opportunities to grow. This allows you to speak to your husband about concerns and make appeals to him for change; to voice your opinion and be heard.

But if your husband is unaffected by the work God is doing in your life, or if he's caught in a sinful lifestyle or web of destruction, it may be time for a confrontational grace talk.

WHAT ABOUT MY HUSBAND'S SIN?

God has called us to display His character. He's called us to demonstrate His mercy, grace, truth, forbearance, patience, endurance, and even joy in suffering (Colossians 3:12–19; Philippians 3:7–10). With that in mind, however, we should never pretend that sinful choices are "no big deal" or ignore our husband's sinful behavior. "Better is open rebuke than love that is concealed. Faithful are the wounds of a friend" (Proverbs 27:5–6 NASB).

As I've mentioned throughout this book, it is extremely important to give out words of encouragement and affirmation to our husbands. But it is equally important to be salty speakers (Colossians 4:6) and the voice of truth in their ears. The Beautifully Fierce Woman faithfully confronts by speaking truth in love rather than enabling sin by keeping silent.

Usually when I sit down to visit with a woman about her marital struggles, I give her two words that need to be implemented in the relationship: honesty with humility. When there's been a lot of strife, blame shifting, isolation, and injury, there needs to be changes in how the couple communicates. Often words are vented that should be left unspoken and words are withheld that need to be voiced. Usually by the time a wife comes to talk with me about their problems, things are starting to pile up, and issues that she and her husband need to discuss lie buried beneath a silent shroud of pain.

Some would say a wife should remain silent, never opening her mouth based on 1 Peter 3:1–6 (like Edie, when she prayed for her husband's salvation) and in some instances, especially for the wife married to a nonbeliever, a silent but godly disposition is the best witness. But Scripture doesn't present a model for marriage that encourages the wife to stuff issues that need to be discussed or to sit idly by watching her husband caught in a destructive addiction. We're instructed to humbly and lovingly confront the sin of a fellow believer—even if that believer is your husband—he is still a brother in Christ (Galatians 6:1–2; Matthew 18:15–18). If this is your situation, look over the Guidelines for Confrontation in the appendix.

Don't give in to despair; there is hope. God has not left you without biblical recourse. We are responsible to walk in love and grace—but that can include confronting a husband in sin or making an appeal to a stubborn mate. Your husband may not be practicing sin that rises to the level of intervention by church elders. Perhaps he's rude, inconsiderate, or selfish in behavior but oblivious to these tendencies. Adapt the Guidelines for Confrontation to your situation. Inconsiderate behavior is grounds for a salty grace talk with your man. But remember to build your platform for influence before starting this conversation or he may not have ears to hear you.

CHRIST MUST BE THE CENTER OF YOUR DEVOTION AND AFFECTIONS.

If you are alone in your desire to work on your marriage, it may take years for your husband to respond—and perhaps he never will. The reality is—you may go through the process of building a platform of influence, you may change your approach to him, you may show appreciation and apply yourself to demonstrating Christlike love, you may appeal to him and even confront him—and your husband may never change.

If you will release expectations and find your joy in your relationship with Christ, you will reach a level of surrender that provides contentment no matter what your husband chooses. To reach that level of surrender, however, Christ must be the center of your devotion and affections. Look to Him to fill your deepest needs and allow the Potter to mold you into His image.

You may feel like the weary wife who once said to me, "I know you're right, Jesus needs to fill my deepest needs . . . but I just want someone with skin on to give me a hug." I remember that deep place of loneliness. I silently voiced those same words many times. Just a quick word of warning: as you are waiting for God to work in your marriage, realize that you are in a vulnerable position and be alert to the danger of turning to inappropriate or sinful sources of emotional affirmation or affection.

Plug into a healthy church body for fellowship and accountability. Godly women and a spiritually mature couple can be a valuable resource for counsel and friendship. If possible, plan double-date nights with an older couple who can serve as a good marriage model.

I wanted to close this chapter with a warm, fuzzy story. But instead I'm going to tell you about a wife who's in a very hard place—even after faithfully applying these principles—because you may be in a similar season of pain. I want you to see her example.

Out of respect for her privacy, my dear friend will remain nameless in this chapter. But even as I type these words, I'm lifting her name to the Father—knowing He sees, cares, and is at work—even though we can't tell what He's doing or how long her nightmare will last. We continue to cry out to Him and to trust Him.

One of the things I love most about my friend is how much she loves our Savior. Her glow when she describes Him indicates she knows Him well; she displays beauty developed in the school of suffering. She's been praying for you as I write this book, knowing some of you are in desperate places.

Thankfully she's in a church that believes in living the truth of Scripture. For decades she was silent, never rocking the boat—but in the four years since biblically confronting her husband, she's lived day to day not knowing whether he might leave her unexpectedly or carry out his many other emotional threats. For years he had the outward appearance of the model Christian husband and father, but now she sees only brief and occasional glimpses of that man.

Her home is in foreclosure. Her children have physical needs she cannot meet. Her health is deteriorating under the daily stress she bears. But she radiates love for Christ and her trust is in Him.

As I write these words she's packing to leave. Her husband doesn't know she's leaving; it would be too dangerous. She's entrusted herself to God's care by following the counsel of the elders at her church who have walked her through this since the early stages. At times her husband responded to their counsel; at times he rejected it. She would see progress for a brief period but then be stunned by another disappointing blow. Recently he let her know he was through meeting with the elders for marital counsel and he's unwilling to take responsibility for his sinful actions.

She never thought her husband would harm her or her children —until this weekend. The serious threat of violence has led the elders to counsel her and the children to spend some time with family in another state. That will not be the end of the story. The elders will continue to pursue him—following the dictate of Galatians 6:1 —hoping to restore him spiritually and secure help for his mental and emotional condition.

My friend is not running.

She is not seeking divorce.

She is not abandoning him.

But she is entrusting him to God and waiting.

She is pressing deeply into the sufferings of Christ and learning the weight of the cross. She is bearing the fruit of the Spirit as she goes further into the walk of obedience day by day. She knows this isn't the end of the story. She knows the truth:

But we have this treasure in jars of clay, to show that the surpassing power belongs to God and not to us. We are afflicted in every way, but not crushed; perplexed, but not driven to despair; persecuted, but not forsaken; struck down, but not destroyed; always carrying in the body the death of Jesus, so that the life of Jesus may also be manifested in our bodies.

For this light momentary affliction is preparing for us an eternal weight of glory beyond all comparison, as we look not to the things that are seen but to the things that are unseen. For the things that are seen are transient, but the things that are unseen are eternal. (2 Corinthians 4:7–10, 17–18)

She hasn't given in to despair. She's not grown shriveled and cold through self-centered absorption. She's not wallowing in pity parties or airing dirty laundry to gain sympathy. She's relying on the Father's character and walking in the truth of His Word.

She's a Fierce Woman who's submitted fully to the Potter's hand. Through adversity, she's grown into a soft warrior who's waiting for her Master's next command.

⚜ HEART ISSUES ⚜

1. Review the process of building a platform of influence while reading the related Scripture references. Consider your normal approach when making appeals to your husband.

   How can you improve your platform of influence?

2. Can you relate to the opening illustration of wanting your husband to listen to your pain, but getting no results?

   How might God be using your situation to conform you to the image of Christ?

   How are you responding to the Potter?

3. If you recognize ways you've tried to manipulate your husband to change through guilt, tears, whining, the silent treatment, angry lectures, etc., rather than building a platform of influence to speak from, consider asking his forgiveness for your approach and let him know you understand why it may have been difficult to listen to your appeals.

Before going to your husband, go to God and ask His forgiveness first. Work at preserving unity in your marriage. Start this process by asking your husband how he would prefer you approach him when you have concerns or desire to give input. Ask him what improvements you can make in order to be heard and understood.

What's the Big Deal about Marriage Anyway?

"In a man-centered view, we will maintain our marriage as long as our earthly comforts, desires, and expectations are met. In a God-centered view, we preserve our marriage because it brings glory to God and points a sinful world to a reconciling Creator."

— GARY THOMAS[1]

Leslie, a striking beauty in her early twenties, was finishing her college degree while living with her boyfriend. She was raised in a loving home, and her parents were still married and living in the same community. Shortly after Leslie and her boyfriend started visiting our church, she came to me for counsel. She was confused about why she and her boyfriend had so many struggles, why so much in her life seemed out of control and messed up. She was seeking answers.

When I shared the gospel with her and described marriage as a picture of Christ's love for us, she listened intently. I let her know that problems like she was describing are usually the result of people doing things out of order, not being in a relationship with God, and not doing things His way. Then I gently told her she was being disobedient to God by living with her boyfriend. Her response was wide-eyed shock. Dumbfounded, she replied, "I am?"

Leslie's reaction and ignorance of God's views on marriage are probably the norm today. I have a burden for women like Leslie and others who've never heard the Great Story—God's divine mystery. I desire for women to see God's vision for marriage, and cannot write a book on marriage without including a chapter to fuel your passion as a Fierce Woman. I hope you will become a champion for marriage—not only your own but also marriages around you.

Because of that, this chapter will be a little different from the others, as we'll step back a bit to look at culture's perspective on marriage in contrast with God's plan for marriage. We'll see that He created marriage as a model for revealing something of Himself to us. And that, above all else, is reason to value marriage.

The God-given institution of marriage is being devalued and scorned in our culture, while rates of cohabitation and same-sex relationships are growing. Dr. Keith Ablow, a high-profile psychiatrist and member of the Fox News Medical A-Team, publicly recommends that we chuck the "dying institution of marriage." In a Fox news article Ablow claimed marriage is "one of the leading causes of major depression in the nation."[2]

In the years since God rescued our marriage, I've come to the conclusion that we are in desperate need of a biblical marital revolution —not just in our country—but one starting within the church.

Dr. Ablow's observation reinforces my concern:

From what I hear in my psychiatry office, and from what I hear from other psychiatrists and psychologists, and from what my friends and relatives tell me and show me through their behavior, and from the fact that most marriages end either in divorce or acrimony, marriage is (as it has been for decades now) a source of real suffering for the vast majority of married people.

To go further, I would venture that 90 percent of the married patients I speak with would rank their marriages in the top two stressors in their lives, while only 10 percent would rank their marriages as one of the top two sources of strength in their lives.[3]

Wow. What a tragic portrayal of marriage. Based on my years of experience counseling women, I would have to concur with his observation (not his solution, just his observation). I've been open with you that our own marriage was once a "source of real suffering" for my husband and me, and we've been amazed by the number of couples who have shared with us how that portion of our story is a description of where they are exactly.

The November 29, 2010 edition of TIME magazine asks the question, "Who Needs Marriage?" Belinda Luscombe explains the motive behind the magazine's cover story. "When an institution so central to human experience suddenly changes shape in the space of a generation or two, it's worth trying to figure out why."[4]

She cites chilling statistics: In 1960 "nearly 70% of American adults were married; now only about half are. Eight times as many children are born out of wedlock. Back then, two-thirds of 20-somethings were married; in 2008 just 26% were." She notes this stat from the 2010 Pew Research Pew poll: 44% of Americans under thirty believe marriage is "heading for extinction."[5]

While heterosexual marriage is rumored to be outdated and obsolete, the demand for homosexual marriage is on the rise. We may rant and rave over the loss of traditional marriage, but I understand why this generation sees marriage as no longer relevant. I even, in some ways, understand the growing number of same-sex relationships.[6]

My generation has done a poor job of presenting marriage as desirable. But also, when we understand the big picture, when we realize the role marriage was designed to play in elevating the gospel, it makes sense that it would be under attack. Pastor Scotty Smith relays similar concerns in his blog article where he prays for marriages:

> Lord Jesus, we come before your throne of grace today bringing marriages with us—our own and those of our friend's. Everywhere we look, there seems to be a growing number of friends who are discouraged, disconnected, despairing—even dying in their marriages. This makes us sad, but it doesn't really shock us, for a couple of reasons.
>
> It makes complete sense that the powers of darkness would assault the one relationship meant to tell the story of your great love for your bride. Of course marriage is going to be a war zone—the front lines of spiritual warfare until the day you return. Satan hates you, he hates the gospel, and therefore he hates your bride and he hates marriage. Of course marriage is going to be difficult—for there is no other relationship on the face of the earth which has more power to expose us and make us vulnerable, and arouse our longings and desires. Of course marriage is going to require your daily mercies and your steadfast love.[7]

Not only because of spiritual attack, but Pastor Smith goes on to offer an additional reason for the number of couples struggling—their cluelessness when entering marriage. He admits, "Like so many of us, I came into marriage with a little gospel and big naïveté. I had no clue about the depths of my brokenness, the degree of my selfishness, or the devices of my sinfulness. I had no clue about what it would take to love one person well the rest of my life (or even in the next hour)—a person who needs the gospel just as much as I do."[8]

You may be reading this while planning for a divorce.

> **GOD'S PURPOSE IN MARRIAGE GOES FAR BEYOND TEMPORAL THINGS.**

You may have decided you can't take the pain any longer and you've given up—walked out—you're done.

Or you may be the woman who's in the vulnerable position of maintaining a marital façade while flirting with an Internet affair.

You may be Anne, whom we met in chapter 4—locked into a heterosexual marriage while secretly involved in a same-sex relationship. Wherever you are, it's crucial to have a biblical understanding of God's purpose and plan in marriage.

Although my husband and I were unhappy, the answer to our pain wasn't divorce. The answer was allowing the power of the gospel to transform our hearts and our relationship. I'm extremely grateful for every moment of happiness we experience now, but there is a much bigger reason for protecting the institution of marriage than the stability of our nation or couples experiencing marital happiness, as important as those things are. God's purpose in marriage goes far beyond those temporal things.

WHY MARRIAGE?

"i need some godly advice i have a boyfriend who i live with. i know it is sin but i hoped i could help him to change ,but i know that i cant do it any longer . i have given my life to the lord and made a lot of changes thank god he took the life stlyle i was living . i thank him for it every day but my question is should i stay in the relationship or do i just need to let god do whats needing to be done?" (unedited blog comment)

What is the big deal about getting married?

Isn't marriage just signing a legal piece of paper?

Can't we just say we love each other and let that be enough? Why get married?

The blog comment and questions above are coming from a confused generation. When it comes to cohabitation or same-sex marriage, we're bombarded with messages like, "It's no big deal!" The culture is voicing opposition to God's model for marriage. It's screaming that Scripture's boundaries are archaic and too narrow.

Let me assure you, He is no narrow God. His immensity is mind-boggling, and when He lays out a design for life, He's delighting in giving us the best. He desires for us to experience joy beyond our imagination, and that only comes from doing things His way. He doesn't want us to forfeit His exciting plan for marriage.

A lack of clear teaching in the church, combined with a skewed cultural perspective of marriage, has resulted in a loss of appreciation for purity in premarital relationships, confusion over the traditional gender model for marriage, and a shameful divorce rate. Speaking of marriage as a lifelong commitment between one man and one woman or referring to the relationship as a sacred covenant sounds like a foreign language.

In a conversation recently I used the word "sacred" in relation to marriage and the teen girls I was talking to looked shocked. They seemed startled by the idea. Then one said, "Sacred—what a cool word. But I never would've thought to put that word together with marriage."

Here's some of God's thoughts on this issue:

"Let marriage be held in honor among all, and let the marriage bed be undefiled . . ." (Hebrews 13:4).

"But sexual immorality and all impurity or covetousness must not even be named among you, as is proper among saints . . . Walk as children of light (for the fruit of light is found in all that is good and right and true) . . . Take no part in the unfruitful works of darkness . . ." (Ephesians 5:3, 8–9, 11).

"So they are no longer two but one flesh. What therefore God has joined together, let not man separate" (Matthew 19:6).

I find it interesting and enlightening that in Jesus' conversation with the woman at the well in John 4, He didn't skirt the issue of her past relationships but zeroed

> **GOD'S INTENTION FOR THE MARRIAGE RELATIONSHIP IS PURITY AND LIFELONG FIDELITY.**

in on them. He made the clear distinction between her string of marriages in contrast to her current relationship: "You are right in saying, 'I have no husband'; for you have had five husbands, and the one you now have is not your husband" (John 4:17–18). If she was shacking up with number six, Jesus made it clear that He didn't view this relationship as a marriage or her current lover as her husband.

God's intention for the marriage relationship is purity and lifelong fidelity. His purpose in marriage is to use it as a physical picture to display to the world the beauty and holy character of His relationship with His bride, the church. When we choose to engage in immoral sexual activity, when we carelessly toss aside sacred vows or invent a new form of "marriage," it holds destructive consequences for the individuals involved, but more significantly, it results in the marring of His beautiful purpose for marriage.

ONLY TWO?

Today there is a lot of confusion and debate over same-sex marriage. We hear questions like:

Why do some people think marriage is such a big deal— isn't the real issue whether two people just "love each other"?

What does it matter if the union is between one gender or two?

I enjoy spending time with girlfriends much more than hanging out with my husband . . . women understand each other better . . . no wonder people are turning to same-sex marriage—*what's wrong with that?*

My answer is: Marriage is a big deal. It does matter if it is a heterosexual union, and no, the real issue is not whether people just "love each other."

Have you ever wondered why God created only two genders? Why only two? Why not three or even four?

Why not male, female, "unisex," and "other"?

Being God, we know He never wastes His efforts. He had a good reason. It wasn't a random choice but intentional on His part. (Okay, that's a no-brainer.)

But what is the significance of two?

I think the answer has more to do with God's explanation of Himself than it has to do with gender. God is the only truly unique being. God is a spiritual being and is totally "other" in the sense that there is "none like Him."

"To whom then will you liken God,
    or what likeness compare with him?
Do you not know?
Do you not hear?
Has it not been told you from the beginning?
Have you not understood from the foundations of the earth?
It is he who sits above the circle of the earth, and its
      inhabitants are like grasshoppers;
      who stretches out the heavens like a curtain,
      and spreads them like a tent to dwell in . . .
Have you not known?

Have you not heard?
The Lord is the everlasting God,
    the Creator of the ends of the earth.
He does not faint or grow weary;
    his understanding is unsearchable.
He gives power to the faint,
    and to him who has no might he increases strength."
    (Isaiah 40:18, 21–22, 28–29)

"Before the mountains were brought forth,
    or ever you had formed the earth and the world,
    from everlasting to everlasting you are God." (Psalm 90:2)

"Turn to me and be saved, all the ends of the earth!
For I am God, and there is no other." (Isaiah 45:22)

Did you hear that? God is making a statement about Himself that He repeats throughout the eons. A statement that reverberates across the span of universes yet unknown to us . . . He alone is God. There is *no other* . . . beside Him. He is the only "Other." He alone is the unique, transcendent God, the alone Other. There is no other like Him. Nothing or no one can boast being the same essence as God or on equal footing with Him.

WHY A HETEROSEXUAL UNION?

When we understand that God created marriage to serve as a model to portray His relationship with mankind, and we recognize there is a basic difference between infinite God and finite man, then we can see that same-sex marriage is a marriage model that presents a perversion: the uniting of two of the same rather than the model uniting finite and infinite (man and God).

Hang in here with me. Remember, we're looking at why God created two genders and placed these opposite genders in a marriage relationship rather than having two of the same sex in the marriage relationship. We're investigating why it's necessary when viewing marriage as a representative model to have two genders.

And trust me, God made marriage to serve as a representative model—representing the most significant work in the universe.

God's design of marriage is the physical model He created to display His great mystery: the relationship between Jesus (the divine Bridegroom) and the church (His bride) as seen in Ephesians 5:22–33. We'll look at that model later in this chapter, but first let's see how homosexuality reflects the exchange of God as deity—which is why we must reject same-sex marriage as a God-honoring option.

In order to see that, let's look at three "exchanges" that take place as recorded in Romans 1.

Exchanging: the glory of immortal God for images resembling mortal man (vv. 22–23): "Claiming to be wise, they became fools, and exchanged the glory of the immortal God for images resembling mortal man and birds and animals and creeping things."

Exchanging: the truth about God for a lie (v. 25): "They exchanged the truth about God for a lie and worshiped and served the creature rather than the Creator, who is blessed forever!"

Exchanging: natural sexual relations for unnatural sexual relations (vv. 26–27): "For their women exchanged natural relations for those that are contrary to nature; and the men likewise gave up natural relations with women and were consumed with passion for one another."

Do you see what is happening here?

The exchanges eventually result in homosexuality ("homo" originally borrowed from the Greek *homos*, meaning: same). The first exchange denies God's "otherness" and degrades Him by placing God on man's plane of existence, bringing Him into a "homogeneous" relationship to man (as though God is of the same corruptible nature or essence as man).

HOMOGENIZING GOD

When I say that God is totally "other," I mean He's not common with humans but is unique, a distinct Being different from mankind; immortal as opposed to mortal; Creator in contrast to the created. However, in the first exchange, God is stripped of deity—He's removed from His transcendent position of other and dragged into our realm as nothing more than a mere mortal, same as us.

It is an attempt to homogenize God, which denigrates Him. He's no longer above, beyond, and greater but is homogenous (the same as us).

The second exchange twists the truth about God (namely, that He's divine) into a lie. Putting God in the same category as man leads to the last exchange, which results in homosexuality.

But don't miss the point. I'm not railing against people who struggle with same-sex attraction, and I'm not even focusing on sexual immorality. What I'm talking about is much more serious than homosexual activity; homosexuality simply mirrors the spiritual dynamic that's occurring. I'm talking about placing God in the same category as humans or other created things. That sameness presents a model of God that is degrading. And that God-model—God stripped of His divinity—is what homosexual unions reflect.

CELEBRATING THE TRANSCENDENT

When partners unite in a model where there are two of the same rather than opposite genders, the picture of the "Transcendent Other" (infinite uniting with finite man) is missing. When we have a heterosexual marriage model, it is a celebration of the fact that the transcendent God, the One who is like no other, chose to initiate a relationship with finite man. Although we are in a relationship together, it is a relating of two very un-homogenous natures. God will never become "one" with mankind in the sense that He loses His divine nature or is no longer "other" (the transcendent deity). The marriage model with two opposite genders reflects two different natures in relationship.

What is the big deal about preserving the idea of traditional marriage?

What is all the fuss about?

When heterosexual marriages are exchanged for same-sex relationships, marriage's ability to serve as a model or visible portrayal of infinite God uniting with mortal, finite man is destroyed. The command to be fruitful cannot be fulfilled.

The model for the gospel is obliterated.

Please don't miss the importance of this—this is why heterosexual marriage matters.

I KNEW IT WAS WRONG

When Sandy phoned from across the country, I was happy but surprised to hear her voice. We hadn't spoken since she headed to college. She asked if she could come for an extended visit and spend some time with us.

When Sandy arrived, she was no longer the bubbly, fiery young woman who wanted to win the world to Jesus. Not only was she older, she was weary and looked strained under a weight of sin. She came to us for help. She wanted out. She wanted out of the destructive relationship that had held her captive for years.

She said she knew it was wrong.

When she left for college she planned to be a missionary. In her second semester she entered a secret life as a lesbian. For eighteen long years she ran. She told us that during those years, she still knew she belonged to the Lord; that knowledge never left her. She knew He loved her and she wanted to return to Him, but the pull of her lover was always too strong.

Sandy said she even tried to attend the large church that catered to homosexuals. She hoped to find relief, hoped to find God's acceptance there. She wanted Him to give her the freedom to redefine marriage to fit with her desires.

THE REDEEMER WAS PATIENT AND KIND AS HE WOOED HER BACK TO THE LOVE RELATIONSHIP WITH HIM SHE ONCE KNEW.

She listened week after week as the pastors did some creative reinventions with the texts that condemn homosexuality. She tried to believe all the justifications and buy into the spin they gave.

But it didn't help; she still knew it was wrong.

She tried to find satisfaction in her partner and drown the voice of truth in her head. But it would never leave her—the knowledge that she belonged to Christ and the knowledge that what she was doing was wrong (Romans 1:32).

Sandy came to us because she was tired of running. She wanted to return to Him, but she needed help—she'd been gone so long. We led her gently and it took time, but the Redeemer was patient and kind as He wooed her back to the love relationship with Him she once knew. He called her to repent and she heard Him through His Word, through the truth, through the reality of the gospel. And slowly she returned.

You may be like Sandy or Anne, or the growing number of women today who are trying to find justification for entering a same-sex union. You may be in a heterosexual marriage, but flirting with a lesbian affair. Please understand that God's purpose for marriage is much bigger than you.

We've seen that God created two genders for a heterosexual

model that would reflect the transcendent God in relationship with finite man. Now let's consider another marriage model He's placed within the Old Testament.

HESED

It was a few years before my cabin experience; we were still in the desolate place of isolation and loneliness. LeRoy had settled deep into his cave of silence and depression.

I was searching. I felt alone. Confused. I didn't know where to turn.

That's when I discovered what I claim as my favorite Hebrew word. When I first read the word with its definition, a reassuring sense of comfort and belonging came over me. Still today, just reading, saying, or hearing the word brings a secure calm and the reality of God's faithfulness resonates deeply in my soul—every time.

The Hebrew word חֶסֶד—*hesed* or *chesed*—is difficult to translate into English, because, according to language scholars, no English word has an exact correspondent to it. I discovered the word when I was reading Hosea and a footnote grabbed my attention. I've never recovered from the impact of the words I read that day. The footnote was in reference to Hosea 2:19–20 (NASB):

> I will betroth you to Me forever;
>> Yes, I will betroth you to Me in righteousness and in justice,
>> In lovingkindness and in compassion,
> And I will betroth you to Me in faithfulness.
>> Then you will know the Lord.

The footnote described *hesed* as "loyal, steadfast, or faithful love and stresses the idea of a belonging together of those involved in the love relationship." In this particular verse the word is translated "lovingkindness" (NASB) and refers to "God's faithful love for His unfaithful people."[9] Thus began my journey in a lifelong study and appreciation of this word and the truth it conveys.

I wish I could describe the arresting beauty of *hesed* and how its reality has affected me, but words fail. Anything I put in print is far too weak, too small, dull, and restrictive. When I attempt to describe *hesed*, words like loyal, steadfast, committed, kindly love come to mind—but these are pale. Our context for these words is contaminated by a fallen world and a history of broken promises.

I like this description of *hesed* by Old Testament scholar Norman H. Snaith:

> God's loving-kindness is that sure love which will not let Israel go. Not all Israel's persistent waywardness could ever destroy it. Though Israel be faithless, yet God remains faithful still. This steady, persistent refusal of God to wash his hands of wayward Israel is the essential meaning of the Hebrew word which is translated loving-kindness.[10]

Often we see *hesed* used in close relationship to God's covenant nature and action. I love how God takes *hesed* and applies it in His personal commitment to Israel to give us the context for understanding our relationship with Him by using marriage as a metaphor.

God's passionate pursuit of Israel is a marital parallel. He exhibits the characteristics of a tender suitor in His initiation of the relationship. In the record of the Exodus, YWHW is seen as an ardent lover and strong warrior delivering Israel from her captors. In the wilderness He is her protection and guide and repeatedly extends patience toward an immature, irreverent, and fickle bride (Psalm 78:12–41). In Deuteronomy He gives her spiritual leadership and instruction calling her His treasured possession. In Ezekiel He spreads the corner of His garment over her to cover her nakedness and lavishes His faithless bride with costly gifts.

"When I passed by you again and saw you, behold, you were at the age for love, and I spread the corner of my garment over you and covered your nakedness; I made my vow to you and entered into a covenant with you, declares the Lord God, and you became mine" (Ezekiel 16:8).

Of all the metaphors God employs in describing His love relationship with us, the marriage metaphor seems to be His favorite; it flows freely throughout all of Scripture. The fact that marital love is the narrative arc of three Old Testament books (Ruth, The Song of Songs, and Hosea) indicates the significance of this metaphor. In each of these beautiful portrayals, the picture of God's devoted and redemptive love is seen.

COVENANT

We can see telling parallels in God's devotion to Israel and His purpose in the institution of marriage, but the most significant is the nature of the relationship; its nature is one of covenant. He is a covenant-keeping God, and this knowledge in itself brings comfort and the sense of belonging I felt when I first came across the word *hesed*. But it also has huge implications when we apply it to the marriage relationship.

Throughout the Old Testament the magnitude of God's faithfulness stands in stark contrast to His bride's unfaithfulness. The book of Hosea in particular exposes the reader to the pain and anguish of the Almighty (through Hosea, the faithful husband), while at the same time showcasing God's unrelenting love and pursuit of His people (represented by Hosea's immoral wife, Gomer). Within this small book, the descriptive *hesed* is used six times.

The frequent use of the word, not only in Hosea but throughout Scripture, is significant. *Hesed* occurs 245 times in the Old Testament.[11] Perhaps no other word in all of Scripture so beautifully describes God's nature or vividly portrays His character. We see His heart most clearly when His actions demonstrate *hesed* through His covenant relationship with man.

The obligations and rights acquired through a covenant are translated into corresponding actions through *hesed*. *Hesed* is the real essence of *berith* (Hebrew for covenant), and it can almost be said that it is its very content. The possibility of the origin and existence of a covenant was based on the existence of *hesed* . . . they are not to be understood as being entirely synonymous but as being mutually contingent upon one another.[12]

> THE COVENANT RELATIONSHIP IS NOT DRY LEGALISM; GOD IS PASSIONATE IN HIS COMMITMENT TO HIS BRIDE.

Covenant. It's more than halfhearted promises or good intentions. For God, it is a sacrificial commitment sealed by His own blood. It is sacred faithfulness forging through every obstacle to pursue His bride. It is Hosea going to the slave block to purchase his wayward wife out of prostitution.

That's you and me.

And God not letting us go—no matter how far we've run.

This marital covenant is graphically portrayed in Scripture as an intimate and personal love affair between God and His people. Although it's seen as a binding, legal agreement, the covenant relationship is not dry legalism. God is passionate in His commitment to His bride. His deep emotion is clearly seen in the prophet's passages where God is lamenting the loss of the original love relationship.

Hesed is what drives and seals God's covenant. In the New Testament, it is the essence of the gospel: An unrelenting God pursuing an undeserving sinner and paying an unbelievable ransom to purchase an unworthy and unfaithful bride. He spills valuable blood to secure our redemption and wraps us in His rich robes of righteousness, speaking words of safety, "You are Mine now. All is well."

THE BRIDEGROOM

God designed the most intimate of all earthly relationships to serve as a real-life parable to depict His commitment to His bride. Marriage is God's platform that displays to the watching world a physical picture of a spiritual reality. Marriage is God's personal symbol and signature.

On the sixth day of creation, God created man "in his own image." Adam was designed to serve as a type—a limited representation of the Almighty (Romans 5:14). The role of husband was designed to portray the eternal Bridegroom—who will return for His bride, the church—as typified by the wife.

> Husbands, love your wives, as Christ loved the church and gave himself up for her, that he might sanctify her, having cleansed her by the washing of water with the word, so that he might present the church to himself in splendor, without spot or wrinkle or any such thing, that she might be holy and without blemish. In the same way husbands should love their wives as their own bodies. (Ephesians 5:25–28)

According to N. H. Snaith, Martin Luther, and others, the nearest New Testament equivalent to *hesed* is grace. As I read the footnote from Hosea 2:19 that day, perhaps that's what my weary heart was responding to—Old Testament foreshadows of the grace that secures me in the new covenant.

Whispers of a Bridegroom who would lay down His life to purchase me.

Hesed: unfathomable grace providing the way to an uncommon communion—the redeemed sinner in fellowship with Holy God.

Again, a model of God as the "transcendent other" in relationship with mortal man.

Infinite wed to finite.

The beauty of *hesed* is seen in its most glorious form on a bloody cross as my Bridegroom pours out the atoning price to redeem His bride. But it is also seen in the final pages that record our future uniting with Him. When He'll come for His bride as a returning Warrior-King wearing a robe dipped in blood.

> Then I saw heaven opened, and behold, a white horse! The one sitting on it is called Faithful and True, and in righteousness he judges and makes war. His eyes are like a flame of fire, and on his head are many diadems, and he has a name written that no one knows but himself. He is clothed in a robe dipped in blood, and the name by which he is called is The Word of God. (Revelation 19:11–13)

When the world bombards you with messages such as:

"You can do better—leave him and move on . . ."

"What does it matter if it's a same-sex marriage—you love each other—that's all that matters . . ."

"The heterosexual view of marriage is so outdated . . ."

"Living together before marriage? It's no big deal!"

When you hear those messages—I hope you'll be reminded of the cross. I hope you'll look long at your Bridegroom as He pours out His lifeblood to redeem you and live worthy of your betrothal to Him. As Fierce Women, strong but tender warriors, I pray you will make a visible stand for the beauty and value of marriage.

⚜ HEART ISSUES ☙

1. Read Ephesians 5 and hear this as a personal message written to you. What does verse 3 say about keeping yourself for your

husband only? How would Facebook flirtations or using romance novels as a form of fantasy to fuel your sexual appetite fit in with the message of this verse?

You may not see these forms of impurity spelled out—but they are there. Get honest. Apply this passage to your heart and consider its implications.

2. In verses 6–14 we see the principle of light opposing the darkness. How should you apply this passage to the culture's view of sexual morality? Of marriage? How will you apply this personally?

3. What does verses 22–33 say about the role of the husband? What are the parallels for the husband and the wife, and how do they operate with each other according to these verses? What is the great mystery? How are you displaying that great mystery?

CHAPTER 12

Dream with Me

❧❧❧

"Send them out 'fair as the moon, clear as the sun, and terrible as an army with banners' to revive a sick church and shake a sin-soddened world! A blazing bush drew Moses; a blazing Church will attract the world, so that from its midst they will hear the voice of the living God."

— LEONARD RAVENHILL[1]

When I went to the cabin in the woods to prepare a study on 1 Peter, it was really just an excuse to escape. I needed to get away. I needed to think. Living in the desert places of our marriage was taking a toll on my heart, and I decided I couldn't go on like this any longer.

I thought it was my plan to get away, but little did I know it was God who was actually leading me to that cabin on the river. He was preparing to open my eyes to the great mystery; to instruct me on the most profound love story ever lived.

The day I arrived at the cabin, if you had asked my theological stance on gender issues, I would have given the typical conservative answers. Whenever I taught on passages promoting roles for men and women, I gave lip service to the view that men and women are created with equal worth and value but are distinct in their roles and function.

I didn't shy away from instruction on the dreaded "s" word but addressed submission obligingly. I was far from understanding the meaning or implications of that word. To put it in theological terms— I was a professing complementarian but a practicing egalitarian.[2]

I think I went to the cabin hoping for some "comfort time" from the Father. I thought surely He was sympathetic to the suffering I was experiencing in my marriage. But instead of sympathy, I received a much-needed rebuke and wake-up call. In addition to the booklet I told you about in chapter 5, there were three passages from Scripture that God used specifically to break through my hardened exterior. In this chapter I'll tell you what I learned from those passages, as well as open the deepest places of my heart to share the great hope I'm living for.

Three passages took me beyond a mere cognitive understanding of the marriage model to a heart full of fire and passion for God's glory to be seen in my role in this profound mystery. Before that point, I think I merely tolerated the idea of submission, giving it a token nod of approval—living just inside its parameters—submitting in name only. What I mean by that is, if you had asked me whether I submitted to my husband's leadership, I would have replied with an emphatic "Yes, of course!" I wasn't an outright *rebel* . . . but the reality of it was—I knew how to work the system.

If LeRoy gave direction or made a decision I wasn't happy with, I wouldn't immediately turn and go the opposite way, because I knew I could eventually change his mind or manipulate the situation to my liking. I hate to admit this, but I followed in a long line of strong women who proudly described their role of "submission" to their husbands this way: "He's the head, but I'm the neck that turns him any direction I want." Today, putting those words in print and knowing how much I harmed my husband by adopting that model makes me feel sick.

I wasn't thrilled with the idea of submission back in those days because I didn't really understand its purpose. I accepted it because I couldn't help but see it in Scripture—plain as day—but I really didn't like it. I'd seen enough loud-mouthed, arrogant men who treated their wives like doormats, and even though I knew that wasn't what Scripture promoted, I think I had an underlying fear that if I really lived out submission all the way, I'd become some kind of mousy, weak-willed ninny. I'd undergo some sort of alien-type personality transplant. And LeRoy would rise up as this Monster-Macho-Rambo-Man to keep me cramped in that pitiful role. It was a scary thought.

In the Same Way . . .

What really started opening my heart to the possibility of embracing the idea of submission came with four little words in 1 Peter 3:1: *In the same way . . .* (NASB). Another version has this phrase condensed into one word: *likewise* (ESV). This phrase introduces the passage on the wives' role of submission: *In the same way, you wives, be submissive to your own husbands . . .* To be faithful in teaching, I needed to check out what the phrase "in the same way" was pointing back to. What was the wife's *example* for submission?

My eyes skimmed up to 1 Peter 2:13: "Submit yourselves for the Lord's sake to every human institution . . ." Okay, check . . . done that. I'm submitted to the law, the government, to LeRoy, no problem . . . but what does "in the same way" mean? I continued reading . . . "For you have been called for this purpose since Christ also suffered for you, leaving you an *example* to follow in His steps . . . while suffering, He uttered no threats, but kept entrusting Himself to Him who judges righteously; and He Himself bore our sins in His body on the cross . . ." (1 Peter 2:21–24 NASB, emphasis mine).

Had I been sleeping through Sunday school, or what? Why had I never linked chapter 2 with chapter 3 before? Why had I never thought about the implication of "in the same way . . ." when reading this passage on submission?

I had completely missed the heart of submission. I had disconnected Gethsemane, the cross, the surrender behind Jesus' cry *not My will but Yours* . . . from my call to submission. I had deleted the primary factor from the whole equation. What was I thinking? I've had this all wrong . . .

Now, if you read my Guidelines for Confrontation in the appendix, you know I'm not condoning spousal abuse; I'm not talking about a woman taking blows to her body from an irate husband, thinking she must "literally" follow Christ's example. But what I am talking about is an inward disposition of submission that was different from anything I'd ever given way to before. A yielding of my will, my way—for *His*—not LeRoy's way but *God's* way.

What I mean by that is, just as Christ was fully God, fully equal to the Father but submitted Himself to the plan of the cross, was *sent* by the Father to embrace the cross . . . in this same way, I needed to submit to the Father's plan for submission.

Oh, my.

I realized, I've been way off track . . . I'd never regarded submission this way.

This is huge.

It wasn't until I looked long and hard at the face of true humility —my fierce and mighty Warrior who submitted to the cross—that I began to understand the true heart of submission.

So Also Wives . . .

When I focused on the surrender of Christ and started getting a glimpse of what submission truly looks like . . . it took me a bit to recover from the encounter. I was a broken mess. When I could see clearly enough to read again, I started scrambling through Scripture to find other passages that would help bring meaning to this concept. I came to the marriage model in Ephesians 5 and saw a clear parallel there. I ate up this part: "Husbands, love your wives, as Christ loved the church and gave himself up for her, that he might sanctify her . . . In the same way husbands should love their wives as their own bodies . . . ." (Ephesians 5:25–28).

Yes. I'm all about this. This is what I'm talking about. LeRoy should love me like Christ . . . he's *so not there . . .*

But again, I had to grapple with the entire passage. The chapter starts like this: "Therefore be imitators of God, as beloved children. And walk in love, as Christ loved us and gave himself up for us, a fragrant offering and sacrifice to God" (Ephesians 5:1–2).

There it is again (sigh). Imitate Christ's example . . . in the same way . . . walk in love *as Christ* . . . then I worked my way through the chapter and settled here: "Wives, submit to your own husbands, as to the Lord. For the husband is the head of the wife even as Christ is the head of the church, his body, and is himself its Savior. Now as the church submits to Christ, so also wives should submit in everything to their husbands" (Ephesians 5:22–24).

I'd read this passage many times since salvation, but only then did the reality begin settling deep in my heart as I kept looking at the words . . . as the church submits to Christ, so also wives should submit . . . to their husbands . . . I kept repeating and examining that phrase. I couldn't escape the magnitude of these words. The "so also" instruction to wives here in Ephesians 5 matched the imperative tone of the *in the same way* instruction to wives in 1 Peter 3.

In 1 Peter I saw that I was to entrust myself to the Father's care and live in submission to God's plan in the same way Christ submitted to the Father's plan of the cross. In Ephesians I saw the parallel —the wife's role in serving as a representative of the church—just as the husband represents Christ. The passage communicated the clear message to me that just as the church responds in submission to Christ, *so also* I was to walk in submission to LeRoy.

I felt a little sick . . .

My pulse was racing, my mind conjuring up painful memories and fears . . . would I trust God? Could I trust His way of operating in marriage? Could I follow Christ's example . . . was I willing to be a faithful representation of the church—the bride?

So That . . .

I kept tearing through pages of Scripture, scribbling notes, jotting questions . . . pausing to weep . . . resisting what I was reading . . . then weeping again. Finally I came to the passage in Titus 2. Little did I know it would be my death knell. The passage contains some instructions for older women; practical teaching they are to pass on to the younger women in the church community. Things like not being malicious gossips, teaching good things, encouraging them to love their husbands and children . . . the submission part just seemed to be kind of tacked on to the end of that list.

"Older women likewise are to be reverent in their behavior, not malicious gossips nor enslaved to much wine, teaching what is good, so that they may encourage the young women to love their husbands, to love their children, to be sensible, pure, workers at home, kind, being subject to their own husbands, so that . . ." (Titus 2:3–5 NASB).

I was skimming through, about to turn to another passage, when these words stopped me . . . so that . . . I had been running through the "biblical womanhood" checklist of Titus 2 when these two words connected all the dots for me: *so that*.

So that . . . these two words let me know I needed to stop and see what preceded them . . . they are conditional words. Letting me know I would need to apply myself to the instructions right before this conditional statement (the womanhood checklist) . . . *so that* this next part doesn't happen.

What I saw next took my breath away.

Are you sure you want to know what followed the *so that* of the checklist?

The King James Version reads a little stronger and more in your face. It says we need to do all the good stuff in the checklist (the not gossiping, teaching younger women, loving your children and husband stuff) . . .

so that . . .

the Word of God will not be . . . *blasphemed*.

Blasphemed.

Did you read that? Did you get that . . .? Blasphemed.

That's serious.

The NASB is a little gentler ". . . encourage the young women to love their husbands . . . to be subject to their own husbands, so that the word of God will not be *dishonored*" (emphasis mine). The ESV charges wives to be submissive "*so that* the word of God will not be *reviled*."

That was it. I came undone and have never recovered.

I clearly saw what I'd been doing for years. I had been blaspheming, reviling, bringing dishonor to the Word of God. By professing to love God, claiming to have the indwelling power of the Spirit, upholding Scripture as God's revealed Word to others . . . while living like a shrew at home . . . I was making God's Word of no effect in my witness for Christ. By dishonoring my husband, I was bringing dishonor to God's Word and the power of the gospel.

What a serious indictment.

From a little girl I've lived with one driving passion. I've lived wanting others to know my Savior. I believe all of creation is to participate in filling God's earth with His glory. The rocks will cry out His praise if our lives fail to reflect His glory. I live and breathe to let others know how much He's done, how worthy He is, how much I love Him. I want all to know that He alone is God—there is no other like Him.

And at that moment, while reading Titus 2:5, the reality came crashing in that rather than filling the earth with His glory—in my marriage—I had *blasphemed* the Word of God.

I finally got it.

My treatment of my husband is directly linked to bringing God glory.

My world was rocked.

I was broken. Completely humbled. I cried out for days in repentance. I felt so totally undeserving of a glimpse, a look of forgiveness from the Holy God whose name I had impugned with my hypocritical actions.

How could I claim there was power in the gospel to transform lives—when I treated my husband in such an *un*transformed and ugly manner? How could I testify to grace, receive and revel in grace—when I withheld it from him? How could I cry out to God to purify His bride—the church at large—when I was such a corrupt example of the bride?

After five long agonizing days of walking through repentance and seeking God for grace to move forward, I asked LeRoy to meet with me at the cabin. I poured out my heart to him and slowly, we started the process I've shared in this book.

THE GREATEST LOVE STORY EVER LIVED

But that is not the end of the story. The work God did in my heart and the transformation that took place in our marriage is but a small glimpse of what He desires to do in His church—the bride that Christ is returning for. That's the big picture. That is the great mystery. The greatest love story ever lived—Christ paying the purchase price—His blood on the cross—for His undeserving bride.

And He's returning for her.

How often do you consider that thought? You and I are preparing for our eternal Bridegroom's return. That is the great marriage—the eternal sacred union—that awaits the church.

Are you preparing for *that* wedding?

Marriage isn't so popular in our culture today but weddings are still a big hit. Most every little girl dreams and plans for that special day when she'll float down the long aisle in her beautiful white gown toward her waiting bridegroom. Why is the bride wearing white? Again it's another symbolic picture.

I was stunned as I read an article that highlighted a previously unheard-of trend for wedding gowns. Designer Vera Wang, one of the "biggest names in the wedding world," introduced her Fall 2012 collection with a provocative new look: black wedding dresses. According to the article,

> WHAT ARE THE FABRICS THE BRIDE OF CHRIST HAS SLIPPED INTO TODAY? HOW DOES HER GOWN APPEAR BEFORE THE NATIONS?

Wang's gowns are designed with the idea in mind that "some traditions are meant to be broken" and then the reporter challenges the reader with this question: "What kind of statement would a black wedding dress make?"[3]

Good question.

What statement would a black gown make in contrast to the traditional white?

I think it provides a telling picture. The color stands in stark contrast to the gown worn by the bride of Christ. Her gown is woven of rare cloth—the finest linen—refined by the suffering of saints. Bright and pure white fabric, an eternal gown constructed by righteousness; enrobing her as a grace gift by her Bridegroom.

> I will greatly rejoice in the Lord; my soul shall exult in my God, for he has clothed me with the garments of salvation; he has covered me with the robe of righteousness, as a bridegroom decks himself like a priest with a beautiful headdress, and as a bride adorns herself with her jewels. (Isaiah 61:10)

The beauty of this bride is compelling. Her gown glows with the clear reflection of her Bridegroom's attentive care. Her splendor speaks of His wonder. At the sight of this bride—this pure and holy reflection—praise and righteousness will spread and grow.

> For as the earth brings forth its sprouts, and as a garden causes what is sown in it to sprout up, so the Lord God will cause righteousness and praise to sprout up before all the nations. (Isaiah 61:11)

What are the nations seeing today?

What are the fabrics the bride of Christ has slipped into today? How does her gown appear before the nations? Has she chosen dark colors of greed, malicious gossip, lust for power, hypocrisy in ministry? Are her embroideries woven with threads of pompous pride and self-seeking?

Surely some of her pearls have been harvested from distant lands, from wombs of oppression and suffering. But the gown that is most visible, the one seen by the nations—what is this gown revealing to watchful eyes?

To the eyes of the next generation?

To those of every walk of life who need to see Christ?

How is the bride's gown a reflection of her Bridegroom?

Christ loved the church and gave himself up for her, that he might sanctify her, having cleansed her by the washing of water with the word, so that he might present the church to himself in splendor, without spot or wrinkle or any such thing, that she might be holy and without blemish. (Ephesians 5:25–27)

Your purpose—the reason you were created—is to glorify God. Within the marriage model, you are representing the church in submission to Christ. Today—now—your marriage is to serve as a beautiful reflection to the world of the ultimate love relationship, that sacred marriage of the church and the Lamb. The choices you make on a daily basis—walking in humility, honoring your husband's position, gently motivating his spiritual hunger, affirming his masculinity, appreciating him as your husband—these choices are making up the bride's apparel.

What does your marriage look like to the watching world? To your children? Your friends? Are others drawn to Christ by seeing His power displayed in your marriage relationship?

Is the gospel message flowing through your marriage and touching others in life-changing ways?

Dream with me for a moment . . . We're standing alone in the middle of a green wheat field as a small stirring begins, almost imperceptible at first. Blowing so lightly, only enough to cause me to wonder whether there is a slight breeze or just my imagination . . .

Several years ago I experienced this vivid dream . . . not a dream in the night hours but in the afternoon. I was fully awake looking out my back door. It was such a personal moment with the Lord that I've never actually shared it with anyone but LeRoy. I certainly don't rank it as a "prophetic vision from God." I'm not sure what category to place this in, so I'll just say it was a real and vivid impression—and at that impression, a hope rushed over me that I've never lost.

Hope for what God might do.

Hope for revival.

Hope for the movement of His Spirit across His church—His bride—like the blowing of a gentle wind.

Faintly brushing at first, giving only slight movement to the tall grasses in a field, and then blowing fully—bending each stalk until every portion of the field is responding and swaying in dance— receiving the wind, turning to its pressure and bowing, then rising wavelike to receive more, until the entire field is swaying under the wind's control—like the Spirit blowing throughout His church.

Dream with me . . .

What if every woman who knows Christ began to live passion- ately for Him? What if she placed her affection and devotion on Him to such a degree that she was willing to obey the hard truths of His Word? And what if those women began to rely on God's grace to truly flesh out the Word in their daily lives—with their husbands, their children, friends, extended family, coworkers?

Imagine what could happen if Fierce Women grew into soft war- riors, pliable in the Potter's hands, recognizing their role as a clay container, clay invaded by a glorious treasure.

> But we have this treasure in jars of clay, to show that the surpassing power belongs to God and not to us. We are afflicted in every way, but not crushed; perplexed, but not driven to despair; persecuted, but not forsaken; struck down, but not destroyed; always carrying in the body the death of Jesus, so that the life of Jesus may also be manifested in our bodies. (2 Corinthians 4:7–10)

What if these warriors chose the way of the cross—dying to their selfishness in order for the glorious beauty of Christ to be seen? What if their obedience to the Word began to have an effect on those they encounter? Might husbands become inspired to take up the mantle of leadership in their homes, to live courageously as a visible representation of Christ to the watching world?

Imagine if families, affected by these transformed marriages, began living radically for Christ, loving Him and others. Shining as lights in a dark world. Living out the dream of spreading the gospel as a family unit.

What if churches were affected by these men and women, these gospel-saturated families? What if the church began to wake from a long slumber? What if the bride rose to her feet to prepare for the return of her Bridegroom?

> And from the throne came a voice saying,
> "Praise our God,
>> all you his servants,
>> you who fear him,
>> small and great."
> Then I heard what seemed to be the voice of a great multitude,
>> like the roar of many waters and like the sound of mighty
>> peals of thunder, crying out,
> "Hallelujah!
> For the Lord our God
>> the Almighty reigns.
> Let us rejoice and exult
>> and give him the glory,
>> for the marriage of the Lamb has come,
>> and his Bride has made herself ready . . ."
> (Revelation 19:5–7)

What if passion for God's glory became contagious; growing and spreading beyond one humble woman's sphere of influence—a destructively fierce woman who grew into a beautiful source of strength? What if that woman is you? And what if your passion and obedience became infectious?

MY PRAYER FOR YOU IS FOR YOU TO FULLY EMBRACE GOD'S CALLING ON YOUR LIFE AS A SOFT WARRIOR IN THE SPIRITUAL BATTLE.

Imagine what could happen if God raised up a great host of Fierce Women who would put on the whole armor of God—determined to stand against the schemes of the devil, each taking up the shield of faith—knowing they are warriors in a mighty spiritual battle. Warriors with hearts softened to the Potter's hand, refined by grace and each one battling with the power His Spirit provides.

In the introduction, I mentioned Lucy—a good and gentle warrior. Her adventures are recorded in The Chronicles of Narnia by C. S. Lewis. Through the years, LeRoy and I have often read this children's series together. At points, we both end up in tears as we envision battle scenes where the great Aslan (representing Christ) comes to rescue his children in danger. At the close of the final book, *The Last Battle*, Narnia is passing away as all who have served Aslan begin their new lives in his country.

As I leave you with these final words, my prayer for you is for you to fully embrace God's calling on your life as a soft warrior in the spiritual battle, that you would love your husband well, and live all out for God's glory as you begin the next chapter in the Great Story God has written for you.

But for them it was only the beginning of the real story. All their life in this world and all their adventures in Narnia had only been the cover and the title page: now at last they were beginning Chapter One of the Great story, which no one on earth has read: which goes on forever: in which every chapter is better than the one before.[4]

❀ HEART ISSUES ❧

1. If you didn't follow in Scripture as we walked through the three passages in this chapter, do that now and spend some time considering each phrase highlighted.

   In 1 Peter 2:13–3:6 focus on the description of Christ's attitude and actions. Consider His example. How are you reflecting that attitude in your approach to submission and your husband's headship?

   First Peter 3:6 instructs us to "do what is right without being frightened" (NASB). Are you fearful of submission? Are you afraid of what might happen if you fully yielded to this concept?

   What is the key to overcoming that fear? Christ, our example, entrusted Himself to . . . (1 Peter 2:23)? How could you apply this same principle in your situation?

2. The marriage parallel in Ephesians 5:22–33 is preceded by these instructions and warnings: Ephesians 5:1–2, 6, 15–18. How could these be helpful in fulfilling your role as a wife? How are you reflecting the church's submission in your marital relationship? What does that look like in your daily life? What are some things you need to do differently?

3. How are you fulfilling the instructions in Titus 2:3–5? Have you connected the dots of this passage? Is your treatment of your husband resulting in God's glory being seen or could it be said that His Word is being blasphemed? Does your marriage display the power of the gospel? If so, how?

4. Read Ephesians 6:10–23 in light of what we've seen in this chapter. The schemes of the devil are focused on the dismantling of God's glory in your marriage. How will you respond? What

weapons are provided in this chapter? How will you proceed in the battle for your marriage? For God's glory?

I am praying for you as you enter the next chapter in your marriage and I hope you'll consider what you've read here. I leave you with Paul's closing words, dear one: "Peace be to (you) and love with faith, from God the Father and the Lord Jesus Christ. Grace be with all who love our Lord Jesus Christ with love incorruptible" (Ephesians 6:23–24).

Notes

Getting Started: Fierce and Soft

1. C. S. Lewis, *The Horse and His Boy* (New York: Harper Collins, 2000), 176.

Chapter 1: The Beauty of Fierceness

1. "These Boots Are Made for Walking," © 1966 by Lee Hazlewood.

2. "I Am Woman," ©1971 by Helen Reddy and Ray Burton.

3. Christ employed a word here that speaks of a family pet. Matthew 15:26 footnote, *The MacArthur Study Bible* (Nashville: Thomas Nelson, 2006), 1390.

Chapter 2: And Then There's the Scary Side

1. Mary T. Lathrap, *The Poems and Written Addresses of Mary T. Lathrap,* ed. Julia R. Parish, The Woman's Christian Temperance Union of Michigan, 1895.

Chapter 3: Where Is the Man I Married?

1. Kathleen Parker, "A woman on men: What feminists don't seem to get," November 03, 2005, http://www.chron.com/opinion/outlook/article/Parker-A-woman-on-men-What-feminists-don-t-seem-1498983.php.

2. http://dictionary.reference.com/.

3. John MacArthur, *The MacArthur Study Bible* (Nashville: Thomas Nelson, 2006), 1791.

4. Maureen Dowd, *Are Men Necessary?: When Sexes Collide* (New York: The Berkeley Publishing Group, 2005).

5. Kathleen Parker, "A woman on men: What feminists don't seem to get."

6. Ibid.

7. Ibid.

8. Amy Chozick, "A New Generation of TV Wimps," June 10, 2011, http://online.wsj.com/article/SB1000142405270230443230457637155368201700.html.

9. http://shine.yahoo.com/channel/beauty/six-weird-fashion-trends-that-prove-men-are-the-new-women-2245141.

10. Ibid.

11. Hanna Rosin, "The End of Men," *The Atlantic*, October 10, 2005, http://www.theatlantic.com/magazine/archive/2010/05/the-end-of-men/8135/s.

12. John Piper, "Lionhearted and Lamblike: the Christian Husband as Head Part 1" http://www.desiringgod.org/resource-library/sermons/lionhearted-and-lamblike-the-christian-husband-as-head-part-1

Chapter 4: The Deadly Three

1. Nancy Leigh DeMoss, *Choosing Gratitude: Your Journey to Joy* (Chicago: Moody, 2009), 84.

2. C. S. Lewis, *The Abolition of Man* (New York: MacMillan, paperback ed., 1955), 35.

3. http://www.nytimes.com/2011/12/15/health/nearly-1-in-5-women-in-us-survey-report-sexual-assault.html?_r=1.

Chapter 5: The Life-Giving Trio

1. Jonathan Edwards, *Religious Affections* (Uhrichsville, OH: Barbour, 1999), 33.

2. Nancy Leigh DeMoss, *Biblical Portrait of Womanhood* (Niles, MI: Life Action Ministries, 1999).

3. Sherry Argov, *Why Men Love Bitches: From Doormat to Dreamgirl* (Avon: Adams Media, 2009), 13.

4. C. S. Lewis, The Four Loves as Found in The Inspirational Writings of C. S. Lewis (Nashville: Thomas Nelson, 2004), 278–79.

5. Andrew Murray, *Humility* (New Kensington, PA: Whitaker House, 1982), 43–44.

Chapter 6: Love from the Inside Out

1. Amy Carmichael, *If* (Grand Rapids: Zondervan, 1969), unnumbered.

2. Shaunti Feldhahn, *For Women Only* (Sisters, OR: Multnomah, 2004), 68.

3. Jessica Ramirez, "How to Keep Him from Cheating," *Newsweek*, September 24, 2008, as archived on http://www.thedailybeast.com/newsweek/2008/09/24/how-to-keep-him-from-cheating.html.

4. http://pewsocialtrends.org/2010/11/18/the-decline-of-marriage-and-rise-of-new-families/2/.

5. If you struggle in this area, two resources that many women have found helpful are Stormie Omartian's book *The Power of a Praying Wife* and Evelyn Christenson's *What Happens When Women Pray*.

Chapter 7: Letting Go and Grabbing On

1. Amy Carmichael, *If* (Grand Rapids: Zondervan, 1969), unnumbered.

2. Joshua Harris, "A Word to Husbands," The Council on Biblical Manhood and Womanhood, http://www.cbmw.org/Journal/Vol-16-No-1/A-Word-to-Husbands-And-a-few-More-for-Wives-1-Peter-3-1-7.

3. Jean S. Pigott, "Jesus, I Am Resting, Resting," *Hymns of Consecration and Faith*, 1876.

Chapter 8: There's No One Else Like My Man!

1. C. S. Lewis, *The Abolition of Man* (New York: Macmillan, 1955), 35.

2. http://www.cnn.com/2011/10/04/opinion/bennett-men-in-trouble/index.html.

3. Ibid.

Chapter 9: The Biggies

1. Wendell Berry, *Remembering*, as quoted from *Touchstone* magazine archives: http://www.touchstonemag.com/archives/article.php?id=24-01-034-f#ixzz1fhKXvj7S.

2. "Couple Married 72 Years Dies Holding Hands," *Des Moines News*, October 19, 2011, http://www.kcci.com/news/29528191/detail.html#ixzz1bHPH1bN2.

3. Kimberly Wagner, "Looking for a Few Brave Men," The True Woman Blog, July 28, 2011, http://www.truewoman.com/?id=1765.

4. John MacArthur, *The MacArthur Study Bible* (Nashville: Thomas Nelson, 2006), 19.

Chapter 10: What If He's not Listening?

1. Mary T. Lathrap, *The Poems and Written Addresses of Mary T. Lathrap*, ed. Julia R. Parish, The Woman's Christian Temperance Union of Michigan, 1895.

Chapter 11: What's the Big Deal about Marriage Anyway?

1. Gary Thomas, *Sacred Marriage* (Grand Rapids: Zondervan, 2000), 32.

2. http://www.foxnews.com/opinion/2011/05/06/dr-keith-ablow-cameron-diaz-right-4-reasons-marriage-dying-institution/.

3. Ibid.

4. Belinda Luscombe, "Who Needs Marriage?" *Time Magazine*, November 29, 2010.

5. Ibid.

6. See Albert Mohler, http://www.albertmohler.com/2011/02/28/how-did-this-happen-why-same-sex-marriage-makes-sense-to-so-many/.

7. http://thegospelcoalition.org/blogs/scottysmith/2011/12/01/a-prayer-for-marriages-ours-and-friends/.

8. Ibid.

9. Charles Caldwell Ryrie, *Ryrie Study Bible* (Chicago: Moody, 1995), 1378.

10. Norman H. Snaith, *A Theological Word Book of the Bible*, ed. Alan Richardson (New York: MacMillan, 1951), 136–37.

11. H. J. Zobel, Griefswald, *Theological Dictionary of the Old Testament*, vol. 5, ed. G. Johannes Botterweck and Helmer Ringgren, 5:44–64.

12. Nelson Glueck, *Hesed in The Bible* (Cincinnati: The Hebrew Union College Press, 1967), 47.

Chapter 12: Dream with Me

1. Leonard Ravenhill, *Why Revival Tarries* (Minneapolis: Bethany House, 1959), 102, 106.

2. Complementarianism affirms that both men and women are created with equal worth and value but recognizes gender role distinctions. The egalitarian view does not recognize role distinctions. This is my simplistic explanation; for further research see: *Recovering Biblical Manhood and Womanhood: A Response to Evangelical Feminism*, ed. John Piper and Wayne Grudem (Wheaton: Crossway Books, 1991). Also: http://www.cbmw.org/resources/articles/the-danvers-statement.

3. http://shine.yahoo.com/channel/beauty/vera-wang-s-black-wedding-dresses-unique-or-creepy-2589217/#photoViewer=1.

4. C. S. Lewis, *The Last Battle* (New York: Macmillan, 1956), 184.

Guidelines When Confrontation Is Necessary

1. Seek the Lord first. Spend time in prayer and the Word, seeking direction and timing before holding this conversation (James 1:19–20).

2. Be sure your desire to confront stems from right motives—spiritual restoration for your husband and love for him as your brother in Christ—not in order to "fix things" more to your liking (1 Thessalonians 5:14–15; Hebrews 12:14–15).

3. Search your own heart first—is there anything in your own life that needs to be confessed to God or your husband (Matthew 7:5)? If you have unresolved issues, you need to deal with those before confronting anyone.

4. We can't come to our husbands with a pious, holier-than-thou attitude and expect to be heard. God opposes that kind of heart (1 Peter 5:5). It will be difficult, but your approach must be filled

with grace, forgiveness, humility, and love (Ephesians 3:17; 4:31–32).

5. Consider writing out your concerns in a letter. Most men don't respond well to emotional pleas. Putting things in written form may prevent that type of confrontation.

6. Before confronting, release unrealistic expectations. Depend on the Holy Spirit to bring conviction, not your words. Resolve in your heart that this work is the Lord's.

7. Share your heart and express your needs in an honest but gracious manner—not accusing or placing blame. Let him know you're giving him time to consider what you've shared, but if he's practicing a sinful lifestyle and unwilling to repent, you'll appeal to your church leadership for help.

8. Absolutely do not remain in a situation where you or your children are in danger. Please share your situation with friends or your church family and bring in necessary authorities to provide help and protection.

9. Diligently, specifically, and regularly, intercede in prayer for God to work as you wait. Pray from a hopeful and confident position—but not one that is demanding. Give your husband time and space.

10. If your husband remains unrepentant in sin and that sin reaches a level that requires the intervention of spiritual leadership, you will need to follow the process of confrontation as outlined in Matthew 18:15–18.

Allow him to reap the consequences of his own sin. He is responsible before God for his actions. No matter how difficult it is for you to watch—don't bail him out. God can use this time of humility and brokenness to bring him to a needed place of repentance.

CHALLENGING YOUR MAN
TO ROBUST CHRISTIANITY

Often we attempt to encourage our men—but come on so strong it seems like nagging. Rather than cheering on my man, it can easily become more like ordering him around. If the men around us have lost the joy of manhood, their confidence to lead, and the desire to cherish us, it may be that we have stripped them of their courage. That's when it's time to find creative and supportive means to bring out the best in him.

Men are created as protectors. As a result of emasculation, bitterness, resentment, or other heart issues, a man can lose his desire to live out his calling. He can become passive, wimpy, or angry. But if a woman will approach her man with a sincere appeal for help and protection, she can inspire and motivate him to step up to the plate and pick up his role again.

Keep in mind that your husband's devotional life, process of growth and spirituality will look different than yours, but be honest with him about your need for him to serve as your spiritual leader. Just letting him know that you *need* him to step into that role may give him the confidence he needs to move forward. But if he makes an attempt and you shut him down with criticism or voice disappointment, he may not venture out to lead again. Encourage small steps. Try loving suggestions that appeal to his chivalrous heart.

If your husband doesn't regularly pray with you, ask him occasionally, "Could you pray with me about this? I'm really struggling with . . ." Give a specific need and issue an opportunity for him to step into the role of champion. Don't use the request for him to pray as an opportunity to bludgeon him with things he needs to change, or ask him to pray because you're struggling with him, ways he's failed, needed improvements, etc. Ask him to pray for you because of specific *needs in your life*, not his:

* I've recognized I need to grow in the area of . . . will you pray for me?
* I'm struggling finding time to fit it all in, will you pray for me to have wise time management skills?
* I'm having a hard time keeping my cool with the kids lately—it seems like everything causes me to blow up . . . will you pray for me?
* It's getting close to my time of the month and I really don't want to turn into a witch this time . . . will you pray for my emotions?

Letting him hear your heart of struggle and appealing to him for help can be a huge source of encouragement for a man who may have the false impression that you really don't *need* his help. Ask him to pray *with* you, not just promise to pray *for* you later. No matter how small his effort, let him know (repeatedly) how much it means to you to know he's praying for you.

You may have dreams of your husband leading you and your children in nightly devotions, while he has plans to camp out in front of the TV until bedtime. Don't demand for him to conform to your vision. Make praying for his spiritual hunger and growth a priority (privately), but don't put on pious airs that indicate you're more "spiritual than him." Encourage his hunger for the Word in small ways:

* Occasionally (*not* with regularity or in a way that over-whelms him) share with him an interesting verse or one that you find encouraging and ask him his thoughts.
* If he's a reader, buy him interesting books that will whet his spiritual appetite.
* If he's willing, ask him if you can share a message or

an inspiring video clip that you came across that you thought he might like (again—this is only occasionally, not in a preachy, suffocating way).

* Ask him if he would mind reading a chapter from the Bible at the end of mealtimes as a way of finishing off the meal with the family. Perhaps couch it playfully with a smile. "Trade off—I'll feed you a good meal physically, if you'll feed me and the kids a chapter of Scripture."

Anything that he's willing to do, any small steps he takes, needs to be followed with huge amounts of approval and appreciation from you. When it comes to influencing your husband to godliness, there are no pat answers or easy solutions. Many men feel intimidated by the daunting idea of being a "spiritual leader" and have no idea what that means or looks like.

Be patient.

Be kind.

Be loving as he finds his way.

A WORD TO THE
FIERCE WOMAN WHO IS SINGLE

Whether you're single because you've never been married, are widowed, or divorced, or are currently single but preparing for marriage, I hope you'll soak up the truths in this book for yourself and others. As a single woman who hopes to be married one day, it is vitally important to be preparing your heart for that relationship. I also encourage you to become a champion of the marriages around you.

You can begin preparing yourself for marriage by implementing the character traits of the Beautifully Fierce Woman in your daily relationships with others. You can be intentional in grappling with the destructive components of fierceness and begin to get victory over those common tendencies before entering marriage. Don't waste your time of singleness in selfish pursuits but use this season to glorify God in your role as a soft warrior:

* Study godly role models of singleness in history and Scripture.
* Don't limit your friendships to other singles but hang out with couples and families.
* Look for ways to serve others in your church family— the elderly, young moms, widows, and teens.
* Pass on the truths you've learned in this book to women who are struggling in their marriage.
* Don't spend your time pining for a man but spend lengthy amounts of time with the One who will never leave you or forsake you—find your joy in Him.

CHARACTERISTICS OF A BEAUTIFULLY FIERCE WOMAN

1. HER IDENTITY AND VALUE ARE ROOTED IN HER RELATIONSHIP WITH CHRIST RATHER THAN A RELATIONSHIP WITH A MAN.

2. SHE'S FILLED WITH GRATITUDE FOR GOD'S GOOD GIFTS. HER HEART IS RULED BY THE PEACE OF CONTENTMENT.

3. SHE COURAGEOUSLY FACES HER FEARS RATHER THAN RUNNING OR HIDING IN SHAME.

4. SHE'S PASSIONATE ABOUT THINGS THAT MATTER RATHER THAN LIVING FOR THE TRIVIAL.

5. SHE LOVES GOD AND OTHERS. SHE'S MORE FOCUSED ON GIVING LOVE THAN GETTING LOVE.

6. SHE'S WILLING TO BATTLE FOR A WORTHY CAUSE RATHER THAN SHRINKING IN DEFEAT.

7. SHE GRABS THE HEM OF GOD'S WILL AND DOESN'T LET GO.

8. SHE PROTECTS AND DEFENDS THE HELPLESS RATHER THAN USING HER STRENGTH TO BULLY OTHERS. SHE IS KNOWN AS A SINCERE ENCOURAGER.

CHARACTERISTICS OF A DESTRUCTIVE FIERCE WOMAN

1. SHE'S ESTABLISHED HERSELF AS HER OWN AUTHORITY. HER IDENTITY FLOWS FROM THE FAULTY PERCEPTION THAT SHE'S IN CHARGE OF HER LIFE AND HER INDEPENDENCE IS HER HIGHEST VALUE.

2. SHE'S ALWAYS PULLED BY THE LURE OF "MORE." HER DESIRES ARE NEVER SATISFIED.

3. SHE'S UNAWARE THAT INGRATITUDE, PRIDE, AND FEAR ARE THE DRIVING COMPONENTS OF HER LIFE.

4. SHE'S PASSIONATE ABOUT THINGS THAT MATTER TO HER. SHE LIVES WITH A SELF-CENTERED AGENDA.

5. SHE LONGS FOR LOVE AND AFFECTION, BUT CAN COME OUT SWINGING IF REJECTED!

6. SHE'S GOES TO BATTLE OFTEN, MISTAKING HER BELLIGERENCE FOR HEROISM.

7. SHE GRABS FOR POWER AND NO ONE AND NOTHING PREVENTS HER FROM GETTING HER WAY.

8. SHE USES HER STRENGTH TO BULLY OTHERS. SHE MAY NOT RECOGNIZE IT AS BULLYING, BUT HER CONTINUAL CRITICISMS, NEGATIVE PERSPECTIVE, AND HARSH TONES ARE LIKE ACID.

CHARACTERISTICS OF A BEAUTIFULLY FIERCE WOMAN	CHARACTERISTICS OF A DESTRUCTIVE FIERCE WOMAN
9. SHE'S HONEST BUT KIND.	9. SHE'S HARSH AND BLUNT IN HER HONESTY AND PROUD OF IT.
10. OTHERS FEEL COMFORTABLE IN SEEKING HER COUNSEL.	10. SHE IS OFTEN INVOLVED IN CONFLICTS WITH OTHERS.
11. SHE EMBRACES GOD'S WORD AS HER ULTIMATE AUTHORITY RATHER THAN BEING SWAYED BY THE VOICES OF THE CULTURE.	11. SHE MAY CLAIM GOD'S WORD AS HER ULTIMATE AUTHORITY, BUT HER STUDY IS MERELY ACADEMIC; IT DOESN'T AFFECT HOW SHE TREATS OTHERS.
12. SHE FAITHFULLY CONFRONTS BY SPEAKING TRUTH IN LOVE RATHER THAN ENABLING SIN BY KEEPING SILENT.	12. SHE USUALLY HAS NO TROUBLE CONFRONTING, BUT HER MOTIVE IS FOR PERSONAL GAIN OR COMFORT AND HER APPROACH IS DEMEANING.
13. SHE WALKS IN CONFIDENCE AND HUMILITY THAT FLOW FROM HER RECOGNITION OF CHRIST'S WORK OF GRACE IN HER LIFE.	13. SHE WALKS IN ARROGANCE AND PRIDE BUT IS BLIND TO HER LACK OF HUMILITY. SHE VIEWS MEEK BEHAVIOR AS A SIGN OF WEAKNESS. SHE SINCERELY BELIEVES HER PERSONAL CONFLICTS STEM FROM OTHERS' INEPTNESS, LACK OF SPIRITUALITY, OR INFERIOR BEHAVIOR.
14. SHE HAS THE POWER TO INFLUENCE AND INSPIRE BECAUSE SHE LIVES UNDER THE SPIRIT'S CONTROL.	14. SHE CRAVES POWER OVER OTHERS AND HAS MASTERED THE ART OF CONTROLLING THEM THROUGH SUBTLE MANIPULATION.
15. HER LIFE IS LIVED ALL OUT FOR GOD'S GLORY RATHER THAN THE SMALLNESS OF SELF.	15. ALTHOUGH SHE MAY NOT ADMIT IT, HER LIFE IS DEVOTED TO SELFISH PURSUIT. SHE'S ONLY SATISFIED WHEN SHE GETS HER OWN WAY; SHE'S UNHAPPY WITH ANYTHING LESS.

Recommended Resources

Books (in alphabetical order by author):

Gary Chapman, *5 Love Languages: The Secret to Love That Lasts*
(Northfield); provides insightful and revealing explanations of
how to understand what communicates love to your mate.

Nancy Leigh DeMoss, *Biblical Portrait of Womanhood* (Life
Action Ministries); penetrating questions interspersed with
Scripture—this is the little booklet God used to open my eyes
to the fact that maybe my husband wasn't the whole problem!

Nancy Leigh DeMoss, *Lies Women Believe: And the Truth That Sets
Them Free* (Moody); I recommend everything Nancy has in
print; but this book especially has been helpful to women
across the world in recognizing lies they've believed about God,
priorities, marriage, emotions, and more. She then sheds light
on how we can be delivered from bondage and set free to walk
in God's grace, forgiveness, and abundant life.

Linda Dillow, *Creative Counterpart* (Thomas Nelson); wise insights
with practical help in becoming not only the wife God desires
you to be, but the woman He created you to become.

Linda Dillow and Lorraine Pintus, *Intimate Issues* (Waterbrook Press); answers the twenty-one questions about sex most frequently asked by Christian wives.

Cindy Easley, *Dancing with the One You Love* (Moody); presents encouragement for living out respect in difficult situations, such as with a chronically ill husband; a husband who is often absent; when there is economic role-reversal.

Emerson Eggerichs, *Love and Respect: The Love She Most Desires; The Respect He Desperately Needs* (Thomas Nelson); provides practical and proven explanation of the needs of each marriage partner.

Mary A. Kassian and Nancy Leigh DeMoss, *True Woman 101: Divine Design* (Moody); is the only one of its kind—an eight-week study of womanhood that is a combination of weighty theology with practical wisdom. (Watch my friends and me on the companion DVD having fun gabbing all about it!)

Stormie Omartian, *The Power of a Praying Wife* (Harvest House); provides specific and practical intercession for husbands; millions of women have benefitted from this valuable resource.

John Piper, *This Momentary Marriage: A Parable of Permanence* (Crossway Books); God's vision for marriage presented in a biblically sound and devotional manner. (LeRoy and I loved reading this book aloud and discussing it together on date nights!)

John Piper, *What's the Difference?* (Crossway Books); is a valuable tool for getting a handle on gender distinctions and the biblical roles for men and women. It's concise but thoroughly packed with insightful teaching.

Gary Thomas, *Sacred Marriage* (Zondervan); the marriage book I most highly recommend; it's solidly biblical, encouraging, balanced, and practical.

Online:

The True Woman Blog: http://www.truewoman.com
This blog is filled with articles from solid writers encouraging you to live out your womanhood for God's glory. You'll find helpful posts on marriage here.

My personal blog: http://www.kimberlywagner.org
Writing blog posts allows me to disciple more women than I would ever have opportunity to actually meet. In this small corner of the blogger world, women from across the globe can experience the adventure of growing together in Christ. My purpose for this blog is to encourage women to live ALL out for God's glory.

Marriage Video: http://www.youtube.com/watch?v=x-CG47kBN0M
I encourage women to invite their husbands to view this video of our marriage story together and then discuss ways they can cultivate and protect their marital love.

LeRoy and I sharing our story on the ROH Radio Program: http://
www.reviveourhearts.com/resource-library/Programs/p/
Revive%20Our%20Hearts/series/A%2520Hurting%2520Couple
%2520Finds%2520True%2520Hope/.

Revive Our Hearts' 30-Day Husband Encouragement Challenge
Whether you've been married a few days or several decades,
whether things are going great or couldn't get worse, *Revive
Our Hearts' 30-Day Husband Encouragement Challenge* is a tool
God can use to breathe new life into your marriage. You can
order online through: http://www.reviveourheart.com/.

Appreciation

T hank you, Greg Thornton, for being the first to approach me with the idea of putting our story in book form. Your encouragement and especially the prayers you and Grace have faithfully lifted to the throne for me, my family, and this writing endeavor have been a great treasure to me personally.

LeRoy, you continue to be my biggest cheerleader on this project—thank you for heaping undeserved praise and encouragement on me all along the way. Thank you for serving me in practical ways (and reading every single word!) to bring this work to fruition. Thank you for saturating this work in prayer and for also praying continually for women who will read. Rachel, Adam, Caleb, and Lindsey—your belief in this project and support all along the way have been like a battle cry for me.

Thank you, Holly Kisly—your knowledge, skill, and expertise, has been invaluable to this rookie. You believed in this from the very beginning and I've benefitted greatly from your encouraging words. You are one Fierce Woman I admire.

Pam Pugh, I will always treasure your words of encouragement. Thank you for applying your editing skills in a thoughtful, insightful manner. Your expertise is greatly appreciated.

Thank you, dear sisterhood, for your faithful prayer support and the many truth-talks you've shared with me as you've patiently and gently pushed me along this road! Nancy DeMoss, Holly Elliff, Mary Ann Lepine, Jennifer Lyell, Carolyn McCulley, Mary Kassian, and Dannah Gresh.

I am grateful for each who read, gave input, and especially prayed for the writing of the book: Lindsey, Melissa, Jeanne, Cindy, Tambra, Viv, Laura, Carolyn, Mary Ann, Nancy, Jane, and of course my mom!

Thank you, dear Dayspring Family, for your loving support and patience as I put many things on hold through the writing of the book. Thank you for praying specifically and faithfully for me all along the way.

And finally thank you, Nancy and Revive Our Hearts, for challenging me with truth, for being God's instrument to begin opening my eyes to my destructive fierceness. Thank you for encouraging me to share our story, first in an ROH Newsletter, then on radio, and finally through producing a video that has been used for the kingdom's sake beyond what we could've imagined.

A **true wȯman** BOOK

The goal of the **True Woman** publishing line is to encourage women to:

- *Discover, embrace, and delight in God's divine design and mission for their lives*
- *Reflect the beauty and heart of Jesus Christ to their world*
- *Intentionally pass the baton of Truth on to the next generation*
- *Pray earnestly for an outpouring of God's Spirit in their families, churches, nation and world*

To learn more about the **True Woman movement** and the many resources available for individuals, small groups, and local church women's ministries, visit us online:

- *www.ReviveOurHearts.com*
- *www.TrueWoman.com*
- *www.LiesYoungWomenBelieve.com*

The **True Woman Manifesto** summarizes the core beliefs at the heart of this movement. You can sign the manifesto, find a downloadable PDF, and order additional copies at:

- *www.Truewoman.com/Manifesto*

True Woman is an outreach of:

Revive Our Hearts

Calling women to freedom, fullness, and fruitfulness in Christ

P.O. Box 2000 | Niles, MI 49120

A **true wȯman** BOOK

LIES WOMEN BELIEVE

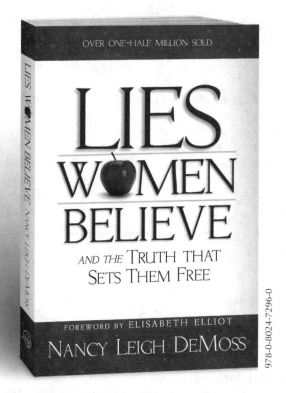

We are like Eve. We have all experienced defeats and failures, trouble and turmoil. We have all experienced a selfish heart, a shrewish spirit, anger, envy, and bitterness. And we ache to do things over, to have lives of harmony and peace. Nancy Leigh DeMoss exposes those areas of deception most commonly believed by Christian women. She sheds light on how we can be delivered from bondage and set free to walk in God's grace, forgiveness, and abundant life. The book offers the most effective weapon to counter and overcome Satan's deceptions—God's truth.

Also available as an ebook

MOODY
PUBLISHERS

www.MoodyPublishers.com

TRUE WOMAN 101:
DIVINE DESIGN

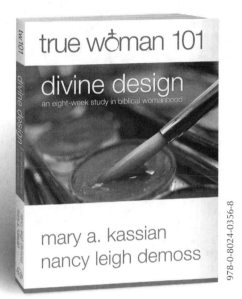

What does it mean to be a woman? The current cultural ideal for womanhood encourages women to be strident, sexual, self-centered, independent — and above all — powerful and in control. But sadly, this model of womanhood hasn't delivered the happiness and fulfillment it promised. The Bible teaches that it's not up to us to decide what womanhood is all about. God created male and female for a specific purpose. It is intentional. He wants women to discover, embrace, and delight in the beauty of His design. He is looking for True Women!